The Salesman's BIBLE

STEPHEN C. YOUNG

Published by Sales Savior Media, Inc.
Brampton, ON
Canada
L6Y 5H5

The publisher does not have any control over and does not assume any responsibility for author or third-party websites or their content.

Copyright © 2007 Stephen C. Young.

All rights reserved.
No part of this work may be reproduced or transmitted in any form or by any means, electronic or mechanical, including photocopying, recording, or by any information storage or retrieval system, without the expressed, written permission of the author.

Sales Savior is a trademark belonging to Sales Savior Media, Inc. (CANADA)
The Sales Savior Media logo design is a trademark belonging to Sales Savior Media, Inc. (CANADA)

Cover Design: Michael Lynch

Publisher's Cataloging-in-Publication Data

Young, Stephen C.
    The salesman's bible / Stephen C. Young.
        p. 292;
    ISBN-13: 978-0-9808839-0-9

1. Business—Non-fiction. 2. Sales & Marketing—Non-fiction. 3. Self-Help. I. Title

PRINTED IN THE UNITED STATES OF AMERICA

10 9 8 7 6 5 4 3 2 1

Table of Contents

Introduction 1
Chapter Overview 267

Chapter 1: Decide to Dream Again 3
   Sales People Are Not Born; They're Trained! 9

Chapter 2: The Sales Savior's 6 Secrets
             to Being the Best Salesperson 17
   The Cycle of Success 18
   Leads 19
   7 Methods for Obtaining Leads 20
   Contacts 23
   Calculating the Set-Up Rate 23
   Appointment 26
   Calculating the Hold-Up Rate 26
   Presentations & Sales 30
   Calculating Your Net Gross Percentage 31
   Determining Your Closing Average 32

Chapter 3: The Lost Art Scrolls 37
   The Ten Coincidental Personality Dispositions 38
   The Selling Personality 42
   Personality Traits of the Successful Salesperson 44
        Humor 45
        Courteous 46
        Friendliness 47
        Punctuality 50
        Assertive 51
        Charming 52
        Dependable 53

(Chapter 3 cont.)

Polite *53*
Modesty *55*
Well-Groomed & Clean-Cut *56*

Chapter 4: Hexagonal Leadership Qualities 57
    Passion 58
    Motivation 58
    Courage 59
    Faith 60
    Optimism 61
    Inspiration & Perseverance 65

Chapter 5: The Need-Greed Factor 69

Chapter 6: Salespeople are Full of BS! 75
    The I-Beam Story 78
    Being Above Average 83
    Above Average Diagram 84

Chapter 7: Little Details, Big Difference 87
    Control 88
    Consistency 98
    Momentum 99
    Momentum Diagram 100
    More Details 101

Chapter 8: Great Salespeople Build Value! 107
    What is Value? 108
    How to Build Value 111
    BBDs 112
    Value-Building Exercise 113
    Lowering the Price is Not the Answer 114

Chapter 9: Enthusiasm & Salesmanship are Greatness 123
   Keeping Pace 130
      One Month Pace Calculating Form Example.....................*131*
   Sample of Net/Gross Sales Graph 134
   What Every Distributor Needs to Know about Financing........135

Chapter 10: Asking for the Order & Closing the Sale.. 141
   The Two Basic Questions...143
   The Choice Close..143
   The Assuming the Sale Method & the Yes, Yes Method 144
   The I&W Method..149
   Third Party Closing 153

Chapter 11: Overcoming Objections..........................157
   Why do People Object? 158
   The 7-Up Approach to Closing and Answering Objections 159
      Step 1. Listen *159*
      Step 2. See the Objection the Way You Want to See It.................*164*
      Step 3. Repeat the Objection...*165*
      Step 4. Agree & Reverse *166*
      Step 5. Isolating the Objection *167*
      Step 6. Inform (Diversionary Reasoning) *169*
         "The Fifty Cent Pay-Cut Close" 172
         "The Mortgage Close" 174
         "The Reduction to the Ridiculous Close" 176
         "The Prescription Close" 177
         "Switching Close"...178
         "The Kid and Scooter Story"..179
         "Live Forever Close" 180
         "The Honeymoon Close"...180
         "Puppy Dog Close"...181
         If & Would 183
         Think Outside the Box 186
         Critical & Strategic Thinking 187
         Tailoring Closing Techniques 189
      Step 7. Ask for the Order Again!..*190*

**Chapter 12: Recruiting In-Home,
        Casual Recruiting & Ad Hiring** 191
  A Natural Progression 191
  Duplicatability 192
  The Most Valuable Possessions 194
  Think Before You Leap 198
  Salesperson or Customer? 203
  Is Up-Line Behavior Consistent With Logic & Growth 204
  The Psychology for Sabotage 205
  Upward Mobility 207
  Recruiting as a Lead Source 209
  Contacting Potential Recruits 209
  Newspaper Contact 213
  Having the Lead Program First 214
  Training 225

Chapter 13: STDs—Attrition Doesn't Lie! 229

Chapter 14: Everyone's a Salesperson 247
  The Science of Selling for Everyday Life 252

**Chapter 15: The Greatest Marketing Support
        Campaign of All Time** 255

References 275

The Salesman's Bible

Stephen C. Young
a.k.a. 'The Sales Savior'

This publication is designed to provide accurate and authoritative information in regard to the subject matter covered. It is sold with the understanding that the publisher is not engaged in rendering legal, accounting, or other professional services. If legal advice or other expert assistance is required, the services of a competent professional person should be sought.

> ~From a declaration of principles jointly adopted by a committee of the American Bar Association and a committee of publishers.

Introduction

"The perfecting of one's self is the fundamental base of all progress and all moral development" (Confucius [u.d]).

This book is a practical guide for anyone wishing to understand the fundamentals of what is perhaps the toughest of all sales endeavors: direct sales. This author's philosophy is that every human interaction is founded within a sale, just as it can be said that every tree is founded in a seed. Therefore, it is with the utmost respect and admiration that I pass along this life-changing knowledge to you.

You may have decided to learn about sales because you are considering a job opportunity in this field, or you may already be involved in sales and simply desire to learn how you can increase your closing average. Regardless of why you may be reading this material, I would like to thank you for the opportunity to share with you what I've learned through my own, time-tested experience.

I commend you for having taken the first step by picking up this material. It shows that you are a person who prizes knowledge and recognizes the value in the experience of others.

Now I challenge you to take the next step. Learn, with grace and eloquence, the tools that have empowered and accomplished an untold number of sales. Knowledge is power only if one can commit it to action.

Let's start off by defining some of the terms you will read about in this book. Each chapter begins with one or more definitions which will help you to better understand the material. For example:

- **Identity Modeling**—Mirroring the method and style of another, both physically and mentally.

Chapter 1

Decide to Dream Again

Let's begin by preparing mentally. This is a very important and often overlooked stage in the birth of a great salesperson. We take this crucial first step by identifying some of the traits of successful salespeople. I call this stage "identity modeling". Before becoming successful, each would-be salesperson must first make a decision similar to the one you are being asked to make: the decision to commit oneself to the sales profession. I am reminded of a quip from the movie *The Hunt for Red October*. "When he reached the new world, Cortez burned his ships. As a result, his men were well motivated" (DeWay & McTiernan, 1990).

Many times I have observed people who skipped this all-important step and when they stumbled, they did not stand fast in the profession. People today look at the word "decision" and do not fully grasp its meaning. As a society, we have come to use this word too loosely (Robbins, 1991, p. 38 & 39).

For example, you might know people who celebrate New Year's Day by making resolutions. They make what they call "decisions" to quit smoking, lose weight, and various other things. Perhaps you yourself have made similar decisions and then felt the burden of guilt when you failed to keep your resolutions. It turns out that for many, "resolve" and "decide" have lost much of their potency, and have come to mean "prefer". People would prefer to quit smoking, prefer to lose weight, but the commitment to the decision is simply not there (Robbins, 1991, p. 38 &39). How many times have you claimed, either publicly or privately, that you would achieve

3

something? And how many times could it be said that you failed to follow through? How many times could it have been true that you had stopped pursuing these previously stated goals? Was not the seedling of these statements a decision?

The word "decision" stems from the Latin word "decidere", which means to cut off. A true decision means committing oneself to an objective and *cutting off* any other possibilities (Robbins, 1991, p. 38 & 39). Being committed to a true decision is quite possibly a lifelong commitment. Until demonstrable success has been achieved, this promise you have made to yourself must remain your focus. Keep your eye on the prize!

> How long does a parent give a child to learn how to walk? Two days? Two weeks? Two years?
>
> There is no timeline is there? Because parents have made a true decision to teach their children to learn to walk, it is not surprising that most children do, in fact, learn to walk. Instead of setting time limitations, parents have adopted the "try until!" approach. This approach has been proven to be highly effective throughout the ages (u.a.).

This demonstrates that if you are serious about your career in sales it is incumbent upon you to adopt such a philosophy. If there is any possibility that you would ever consider giving up or giving in, I must advise you now to discontinue reading this book.

Like many "grapes of wisdom", the book will play several roles: that of a teacher, coach, motivator, and disciplinarian (Mandino, 1968, p. 51). You may be asking: How could a book accomplish all of this? It is a teacher because it will provide specific information systems and strategic action plans that, if committed to action, will most certainly bring about amazing and seemingly magical results. It is a coaching tool because you may keep reopening its pages and poring over them as you continue to perfect and integrate the book's philosophies.

This author wishes to aid you in your quest by passing on the wine of wisdom gleaned from the frontline trenches in the war between success and failure. Why wine, and not "grapes of wisdom"?

Because many grapes are crushed and refined in order to produce wine (Mandino, 1968, p. 51). Even then, the process is not complete. It is vital that the conditions are right, and much time and patience are needed. As the new wine ages, it becomes even better.

So too, have the contents of this book been refined. These strategies have been tested in the field and proven effective. Nineteen years in direct sales in an industry that has no tolerance for failure has prompted me to adopt these orphaned treasures—the knowledge was there, but I didn't see it until after I had been through much struggle. Experience has shown me that the strategic action plans in this book are both sound and timeless.

It is a motivator to all who are interested in achieving greater sales results because the information within causes excitement to well up within us. This excitement comes from the realization that although you may have failed to produce the results you have promised in the past, it may be that you have simply lacked the information needed to achieve those results.

Yes, you can expedite your own success by learning from the failures of others. And should you ever fail to achieve a goal, realize that you are truly blessed indeed. For each failure has inherent within it, a valuable lesson. Thomas Edison said, "I am not discouraged, for every wrong attempt is another step forward" (Edison, as cited in Robbins, 1992 p. 42). Nietzsche said, "What does not destroy me makes me stronger" (n.d.).

If you gain anything from this book, you have succeeded in sampling the tiniest essence from one of our discipline's "grapes of wisdom". If you are able to inculcate this wisdom and apply it, the fruits of your labor will be doubled. With each bit applied to your career and to your life, you will feel yourself attaining a higher level of enlightenment and inner peace.

This book will serve as a disciplinarian. As you continue to read and reread these pages, you will be able to expose your own weaknesses and be provided with specific strategies with which to resolve them. Break your old habits and replace them with winning action plans. It is not about how many times the world invents itself to you, but rather the number of times you can reinvent yourself to the world. Now that we recognize that this book is a guide and not a solution-providing magic wand, we must define what our goals will be while reading it.

First, what is a goal? Throughout the years, many works have been written regarding goals and goal setting. There has been much talk of how important goals are. Indeed, goals are the basic foundations of every achievement. But what comes before a goal? A dream!

"We are who and what we are because we first imagined it" (Curtis, n.d.). Not just any dream. Not one that is seen while sleeping and then quickly dismissed and forgotten. This is the kind of dream that is fixed in your mind, clearly describable to others with detail and passion.

> Through some strange and powerful principle of 'mental chemistry' which she has never divulged, Nature wraps up in the impulse of strong desire, 'that something' which recognizes no such word as 'impossible', and accepts no such reality as failure (Hill, n.d.)

How will you recognize this dream? Dreams have the potential to empower the one and motivate armies of the many. Within such a dream you can find the excitement and motivation which can inspire you to make that full commitment. Within such a dream is the energy and force to grant ordinary people great power, giving them purpose. A dream is also seen as the "[most]…jealous of all lovers" (Sanders, 1991). A dream-yoke is a heavy burden, and it requires much of you, as its labors are long. What does all this mean? Your dream will, when it becomes clear, motivate you to rise early and work late in order to meet the challenges presented to you. If a genuine benefit is to be gained, it is certain to present challenges for those who would attain it. So first, a dream! But what about the all-important goals we spoke of earlier? "A goal is quite simply a dream with a deadline" (Hill, as cited by Lamb, 1992)!

It is necessary to attach a timeline to the accomplishment of these dreams. For in nature's wisdom she has built into mankind a sixth sense. What most do not realize is that it can be used and controlled. What is this sixth sense? It is the power of perception beyond the five senses; it is a keen intuition which you can use to accomplish your goals. As you gain information, your sixth sense—your intuition—will help you to prioritize that information according to importance in order for you to structure your processes and timelines accordingly. The more often you visualize your goals, the more clear they become, and the sharper your intuition in such matters will be.

This is why many motivators and lecturers endorse daily affirmations. However, mere words do not provide the fuel of passion! The vision must be seen, and indeed, even rehearsed. By rehearsing your vision, you will come to learn what will work and what might need to be changed in order to fulfill it. The obstacles and challenges may appear, but you will learn how to conquer them. "We will find a way, or make one" (Hannibal, as cited in Robbins, 1992, p. 44).

Tom Lamb, the former President of Rexair Inc., once stated, "When it comes to goals and goal setting, the sports world is not unlike the business world." Through observing the sport of hockey, it is clear how the setting of goals will inevitably bring with it challenges and risks. In hockey, a goal is scored when you are able to direct the puck into your opponents' net. One of the opposing players will be guarding the net in order to prevent anyone from getting the puck past him, thereby attaining their goal. He is appropriately called a goalie. His job is to prevent you from reaching your goal. This can translate into the world off the ice as well. There are people who might not want you to attain your goals. Some may go so far as to use whatever skills they possess to accomplish this task (Lamb, 1992).

You have learned by now the importance of a dream. You have realized the need for a deadline by which you wish to accomplish this dream, and thus you're committed to a goal. You have decided to achieve it!

Now you must set milestones for yourself. At times you may find the burden of competition at the very least, lonely. You will undoubtedly face many challenges: your real life goalies. And you may come to realize that "sometimes you are your own goalie" (Lamb, 1992). Do not let this discourage you or make you afraid to try.

"The entrepreneur is essentially a visualizer and an actualizer. He can visualize something, and when he visualizes it, he sees exactly how to make it happen" (Schwartz, u.d.). "The only thing we have to fear is fear itself" (Roosevelt, n.d.). Fear is often the thing that thwarts the achievements of man.

When we create the glory of achievement, we have conquered the great demon of fear. Success is not merely the arrival at one's goal, but the way in which it has been achieved. I congratulate you for having the courage to dream and set goals, and the will to achieve them.

How important are these goals in the big picture? They are essential! All dreams are carried with pride in the hearts of trailblazers like yourself, and they are an integral part of the accomplishment of the five Ps. The five Ps are critical to your success in sales, now and in the future, and they stand for the following:

"Prior Planning Prevents Poor Performance" (Farlex, 2005).

The ultimate goal in reading this book is not material wealth, but knowledge, "for wisdom is better than rubies. All the things that may be desired cannot be compared to it" (Proverbs 8:11, 1901, World English Version).

The following acronyms have kept me on my course and are invaluable to the discerning salesperson. The first of which is the five Ps: "Prior Planning Prevents Poor Performance" (Farlex, 2005).

- **WIT. W**hatever **I**t **T**akes ... *to achieve it* (Robbins & McClendon, 1997 p. 129).
- **SIB. S**ee **I**t **B**ig (u.a.)! No matter what your goal or dream, always see it big!
- **PMA.** We must always strive to maintain a **P**ositive **M**ental **A**ttitude (Hill Stone, Mandino, 1960, p. 12). This is the glue that binds the others together.
- **KYP. K**eep **Y**our **P**eople. "I would rather have one percent of a hundred men, than a hundred percent of one man" (Getty as cited by Eves, 2007).
- **STTY. S**tay **T**rue **T**o **Y**ourself. If you forget who you are in the process, all is lost.
- **BIAHP. B**elieve **I**n **A H**igher **P**ower. Everything happens for a reason. There can be no sweet taste of victory without the agony of defeat.

The last fundamental acronym is **WIN**. We all want to WIN! Therefore, to keep us on track we must continue to ask ourselves, "**W**hat's **I**mportant **N**ow?" (Riley as cited by Kuypers, 2002. p.13).

> Sure I am that this day—now—we are masters of our fate; that the task which has been set before us is not above our strength; that its pangs and toils are not beyond our endurance. As long as we have faith in our own cause and an unconquerable will power, salvation will not be denied us (Churchill addressing the US Congress in 1941).

Sales People Are Not Born; They're Trained!

- **Selling**—The transference of one person's thoughts and feelings about a product or service to another person.
- **Salesperson**—One whose job it is to solicit another, through the art of assertive and persuasive negotiations, to purchase a product or service.
- **Selling Enthusiasm**—The display of exuberant charisma directed toward the vigorous pursuit of obtaining the sale.
- **The Gift of Gab**—An expression which implies that a person is able to express himself well by manipulating language in such a way that it has a psychological impact on the listener.
- **Myth**—An idea that has been believed by some, but later has been proven false (dictionary.com Unabridged V1.1, 2007).

During my career many people have thanked me for the impact that the knowledge of how to sell has had on their lives. Others have listened to my words, but could not get the sense of them. They watched as I performed a sales presentation and used what they heard to make an excuse for themselves. They would tell me that I had the "gift of gab." They would tell me that I was born a salesman! This always preceded their claim that they "didn't feel like they could do it."

I often wondered about what they were saying. Did they mean that they thought they were incapable of reading from a demo book? (A manual sometimes used to aid the salesperson.) Did they mean that they were physically incapable of extracting the product from the box? Did they mean they lacked the ability to speak?

Over the years, I have witnessed the most amazing results from those who were debilitated in some way. A dear friend who was crippled and in a wheelchair, suffering with Crohn's disease, and gulping down pills as part of his daily regimen, was able to drag himself (literally) to the doors of prospective customers. Within a short time he would emerge, having obtained the sale. He said that he would rather greet the homeowners under his own power, without his chair. This man has since lost his life to the disease, but not his legacy. His memory inspires me to this day. He, too, had the "gift of gab" or more specifically, he had gained an education in psychological communication (In loving memory of Bobby Begg).

Another young man who decided to go into sales, was born with a birth defect in his hands. He had undergone more than twenty corrective surgeries and was told that each surgery held an increased risk. His index and middle finger were crossed on both hands and when we met he could not shake my hand. Only nineteen years old, he attended a seminar I was giving and became inspired. Despite his obvious condition, he pressed on. I would often joke with him that he was sure to succeed as luck was on his side (his fingers were always crossed).

He attended the week-long training seminar and boasted that he would outsell the rest of the attendees. After I left his area to speak in the US, we were able to talk several times about his progress. He was able to sell at first, but then quickly spiraled downhill. After his first sale, he completed a staggering fifty presentations without another sale to his credit.

So in light of this, let us dispel our first myth. "Practice makes perfect!" This statement is not only untrue, it is incomplete. Practice does not make perfect. Perfect practice makes perfect.

What's the difference? If you are doing something incorrectly, and you continue doing it incorrectly over and over again, what will you have succeeded in accomplishing? You will only succeed at becoming good at what is faulty. If at first you take time to learn how to perform an act correctly, then when you practice it, you will indeed perfect it!

So what happened with our young apprentice? At first he was inspired by my teachings and motivated to succeed. This empowered him to get his first sale. But when the pressures of daily anxieties and worries had drained his enthusiasm, he was lost. He began to question whether or not what he had learned was really true. Did his teacher simply possess this "gift of gab" he had heard of?

I decided to take him under my wing for a time, so I returned to his area and asked him to accompany me on several direct sales presentations. While he believed that we would certainly obtain some measure of success he was not mentally prepared for the shocking results he would soon bear witness to.

We rode together on fifteen sales presentations, and we wrote up business on fourteen of those occasions. He went from believing that the product was very difficult to sell and that only those with the gift of gab could accomplish it, to believing that it was possible to sell to almost every prospect one encountered. Belief that it is possible is the foundation for every sale's fruition.

After only ten days in the direct sales, face-to-face, door-to-door, in-home demonstration vacuum cleaner business, he watched as I earned in excess of ten thousand dollars. I paid his hotel bills and provided for all his expenses as well as giving him a little pocket money. What made the experience even more surreal for him was when I cashed my check at the local bank and placed seven thousand dollars in his hands (for motivational purposes only). He had never before held so much cash in his hands. But more exciting than holding this money was the realization that it was *real* and *liquid*.

He knew that if we chose to, we could spend it all that very day without hesitation or worry. I explained that the true knowledge of selling is like discovering a tree in your backyard whose fruit was money! With this knowledge, anyone could liberate themselves from the prison of daily monetary worries (In loving memory of Patrick, "P.J." Hayden). As Richard Lovelace (n.d.) once said, "Stone walls do not a prison make, nor iron bars a cage."

Ask yourself this question: How many times in your life have you been stressed in some manner because of money? How many times have you had to sacrifice time with loved ones because lack of knowledge and experience caused you to have to work long hours to make ends meet? A huge number of all spousal arguments revolve around family financial issues. With estimates that fifty percent of all marriages are ending in divorce it is no surprise that financial burdens carry with them a heavy load.

> ...those who are determined to be rich fall into temptation and a snare and many senseless and hurtful desires, which plunge men into destruction and ruin. For the love of money is the root of all sorts of injurious things, and by reaching out for this love some have been lead astray from the faith and have stabbed themselves all over with many pains (1 Tim 6:9,10, 2006. *New World Translation Bible* p.1492).

Knowledge of selling may not make you rich but it is certain to make your life easier. Besides, it has never been proven that money can solve any of our problems. Many of the world's wealthiest are in sad circumstances, such as being addicted to illicit drugs or plagued by worries and depression.

So what is the value of this knowledge? Being rich in wisdom is truly most profitable! A mansion can be broken into and its contents looted, but a person who has wisdom and knowledge cannot be robbed of it. "Do not store up for yourselves treasures on earth where moth and rust destroy and where thieves break in and steal..." (Mat 6:19, *New International Version Bible*, (1973). I encourage you to consider these lessons and meditate upon them, as they will be beneficial to you for all time to come.

Should you be empowered to change your life in some positive way and find that one day it has all been stripped from you, don't be disheartened because it was with knowledge that you were able to accomplish these things and it is with this knowledge that you can rebuild.

Back to my lucky friend. After our time selling together, he was granted the greatest gift a salesperson could receive: *belief*. Without the belief that a goal is attainable, a person easily stumbles. For the force of words from friends, family and even enemies without understanding, can easily trip up anyone who doubts the path on which they walk.

Throughout my career as a teacher of direct sales, I have had the opportunity to reason with both the "I cans" and the "I can'ts." Those who said, "I will!" and those who said, "I might..." One thing I am sure of with regard to *belief* is that the "I cant's" *do not* possess it. "If you think you can do a thing or you think you can't do a thing, you're right" (Ford, 1947).

Whenever you have stated "I can't!" you have indeed placed a ceiling on what you could achieve, have you not? You must have an unshakable belief; a faith in what you are doing, in order to succeed in sales, and in life. You must believe in your product and in yourself in order to sell.

"The only thing that stands between a man and what he wants from life is often merely the will to try it and the faith to believe that it is possible" (Devos, n.d.).

Another man I regard as highly inspirational was an elderly gent I met when he first attended one of my seminars. At 79, he had invested a lifetime in the acquisition of this magical knowledge: direct selling.

We stayed in contact until he was 83, and he confided in me that what I was teaching was sorely lacking in most so-called "salespeople" today. He said that retail clerks seemed to know very little of what he called "the true art of selling" (Diwell, Les, Personal Communication. July 12, 1993).

In his lifetime, he had observed the decay of trust between the customer and the salesperson. He remembered when a prospect's handshake and word were as good as an ironclad contract. He remembered how advertising had attempted to make extinct those who had once dedicated themselves to the "*art of selling*." This empowering discipline was under attack.

Modern technology in the form of radio and tv advertisements was now attempting to replace the intimacy between the prospects with the mere exchange of information. Would the "art of selling" soon vanish (In loving memory of Les Diwell)?

"This information is not reserved for a select few, with the right credentials, or money, or background…" (Robbins, 1992, p. 37). It is available to everyone who desires it. It can empower each of us to make the necessary changes in our lives to succeed not only now, but also in the future.

Today could be the very day you awaken from your slumber and choose to never again allow your past to rob you of your future (Robbins, 1992).

Is it really true that only some are born with this "gift of gab" I spoke of? Of course not! We are no more born with the gift of gab than we are born with the gift of operating an automobile. I know of no scientific research that has found a newborn displaying this "gift of gab". Yet how then can it be said (by some) that an individual was born with the gift of gab? Obviously this statement cannot be taken literally.

We are all capable of accomplishing a simple, common task (to sell) when given the knowledge and the tools to perform it, regardless of education level or social status.

When you ask a child, "What do you want to be when you grow up?" you might be surprised by their answers. Some might say a fireman, a policeman or an astronaut. Others might say a doctor, a nurse or perhaps a cowboy. But seldom will any of them say a negotiator; a salesman. At first, young children are not privy to the force of words, but they will soon learn.

Children are generally very inquisitive and fast learners. It isn't long before they understand the force of words and in some cases the art of selling. This has been observed from before a child can even articulate words.

A newborn baby can only cry to convey its thoughts of boredom, loneliness, discomfort or hunger. In a short time, the baby is able to learn that crying can communicate to the parents what is wrong. I cry, and I am fed. With another cry, my diaper is changed. With still another cry, I am held. Some parents claim that they can differentiate between the cries. Thus, at a very young age, the force of communication is learned. Perhaps it could even be said that dependent upon the response of the parents to these cries, a child may neurologically link emotional success with his communication.

Therefore the gift of gab, although not something you are born with, can begin being learned at a very early age. Later, as the child learns to communicate, this reasoning is either dispelled or reinforced. For example, a child asks his mother for a toy. If the mother "spoils" the child, the child may learn to be comfortable asking for things. The sales theory being that when that child becomes an adult, he will be more prepared to ask for the order when selling. If, on the other hand, the child is initially denied a toy, but fails to ask again, he gains little experience in negotiating. However, if the child is denied and then is given the opportunity to explain what he wants and why it might be good to entertain the idea; this can create some form of lasting benefit, regardless of whether the idea is accepted or denied, and as long as acceptances have been granted in the past, a child may learn and reinforce this negotiation, this gift of gab. More specifically, the child is learning how to psychologically reason and communicate. "Without knowing the force of words, it is impossible to know man" (Confucius, n.d.)

Coming from a family with two sisters and a limited budget, I learned early on the force words could have. A split family afforded me the opportunity to negotiate on every shopping adventure with my mother and sisters. Being the only male, outnumbered three to one, it became necessary to learn psychological reasoning and communication. Being the baby, though, did offer some added negotiating power according to my sisters, who claim they never received as much success when attempting negotiations for wants and desires.

As children, we are aware of the force of words and the success that comes from understanding how to sell. Rarely, though, will a child realize that selling is, in fact, what he or she is doing! I have noticed this and similar behavior in people of all ages, from child to adult.

It is interesting when school children interact during recess. From time to time they will become involved in what I call "power struggles". This is another time when their sales skill is tested and refined.

A child may call another child a name, which degrades the latter in front of his peers. Rather than cowardly accepting the degradation, a child who has been trained in the force of words, (manipulation of language, and the art of selling) will respond with a competitive communication, which balances or even shifts the power to him. Thus, the art of selling can be seen in all levels of daily life. All forms of communication, in actuality, are a form of selling.

Another example with children can be observed when watching them trade things. Children trade many things such as marbles, cards, toys, comic books, etc. A child who has had more training than another (in selling) may amass a greater holding of such toys. In the world of a child, toys represent the basis for his monetary system. In this way, toys can be likened to money for adults. Children attempt to collect and amass toys, while adults attempt to collect and amass money.

A wise person will understand the power of enhanced communication and how that relates to persuasion and good negotiating skills. Further, he will understand how these relate directly to one's quality of life, good or bad.

We can also see how early the concept of ownership can be observed in children, especially when a child is being asked to share a toy that he does not wish to share. They will say things like "That's mine!"

What can we learn about this gift of gab from children? That it is learned, not genetic!

The level of sales training one has undergone by the time one reaches adulthood could be extraordinary, or it could be perfunctory and mute. However, it is very encouraging to know that these skills are learned, and not genetically passed on, as some have implied. This means that like any other skill, it can be learned at any age, refined and improved upon. Even if you have never before sold anything in your life, and you are determined to learn these skills, you can have every confidence that you will be granted the opportunity. "…Ask, and it will be given you; seek, and you will find; knock, and it will be opened to you. For every one who asks receives, and he who seeks finds, and to him who knocks it will be opened" (Luke 11:9 & 10, n.d., *The Bible, Revised Standard Version*). It is encouraging that you will have very little mental reprogramming to do as you embark on this journey of discovery.

Unfortunately there are many contradictory views on selling strategy. For this reason some have been taught poor salesmanship skills (through no fault of their own).

These poor skills create a variety of stereotypes pertaining to what a salesperson does and how a salesperson behaves. Individuals who have been taught things that disagree with what is written here should ask themselves this question: If the quality of my life, as achieved through persuasion and a series of aggressive and assertive negotiations, is what it is now, how can I plan for a future that is far greater than what I am currently experiencing? The answer is quite simple. We need only reprogram those sections of what we have learned that are not empowering us to achieve the results we truly desire.

Visualize your brain as a super computer with an almost limitless capacity for memory. If you have inserted a disk with a file that contains text with errors, it is not necessary to delete the entire disk. You simply edit the parts that need it. Similarly, if you have some proper sales experience, you probably do not have to forget all of it.

This book will allow you to find the misinformation that may have crept in, or bad habits that may have taken root over time. "I am not ashamed to confess that I am ignorant of what I do not know" (Cicero, n.d.).

Imagine how your entire life could be transformed simply by practicing skills and concepts that really work! Your sales training may be starting here with this book, or it may have started at home, at school, in the park, or even in the crib. No matter when or where you started (if you feel like you're behind), remember that it is not necessary for you to catch up on what you may be missing. Instead, learn the skills described in the coming chapters and you can lead the sales race. "Self-Conquest is the greatest of victories" (Plato, n.d.).

Are you ready to learn the most powerful information systems ever taught? Congratulations! You are about to be inducted into the elite and guarded society of professional direct sellers.

Chapter 2

The Sales Savior's 6 Secrets to Being the Best Salesperson

➢ **Target Market**—The particular measurement of those determined most desirable (potential customers) based on demographics and any other information, which concludes that a populous is predetermined to result in net sales.

➢ **"Total Quality**—This is the triple objective of any organization: to provide a quality return for shareholders, QVALITY (Quality & Value) + ACE (Above Customer Expectations) for customers, and a quality of life for the people in the organization" (u.a.).

➢ **Set-Up Rate**—The measurement of potential customers who book an appointment to view a sales presentation.

➢ **First Sale**—The demarcation of the moment the salesperson first exhibits an influence on a potential customer.

➢ **Hold-Up Percentage**—This is the measurement of the number of booked sales appointments that are accomplished.

➢ **The PWEC Principle**—States that a majority of all the appointments that do not hold-up are caused by procrastination, peer pressure, we forgot, working late, emergency or cancellation reasons. An appointment that is reset for another date and time is not considered a cancellation. An appointment where the potential customer refuses to view the presentation at any time in the future is considered a cancellation.

➢ **Net Gross Percentage**—The measurement of the number of total sales orders resulting in a successful positive (for the company) financial transaction.

➢ **Gross Sale**—The measurement of the total number of orders taken.

➢ **Cognizance Threshold**—The demarcation at which the average potential customer is likely to forget an appointment.

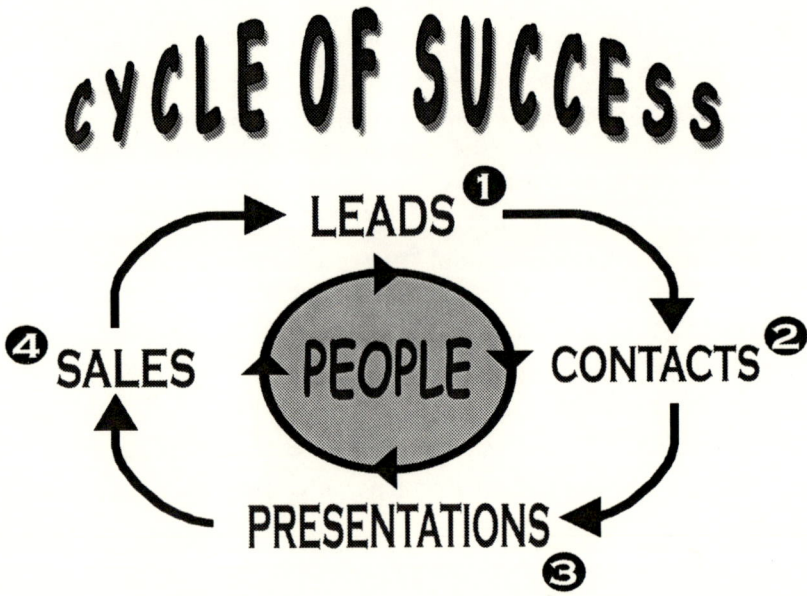

Taken from the Sales Savior's
"6 Fundamentals for Selling"

There are six basic things at the root of every sale. These six fundamentals are, in some cases, understood but rarely spoken of. Only true professionals both understand them and manipulate them to their advantage. These six fundamentals (we'll call them: "The Sales Savior's 6 Secrets for Being the Best Salesperson") govern all direct sales. They are: the Cycle of Success; Personality Types; Control; Building the Problem and Solving It; Building Value; and the Need-Greed Factor.

These things are present to one degree or another regardless of whether or not you choose to benefit from them. Let's take a few minutes to explore each one and discuss their impact. First, the *"Cycle of Success."* We have already discussed that it is important to WIN, or to ask ourselves, *"What's Important Now?"* (Riley, as cited by Kuypers, J. p.13).

The cycle of success is a guideline to help you in determining WIN and deciding where you are with respect to your direct sales goals.

The age-old question: "Which came first, the chicken or the egg?" has been pondered by many generations. Though there has been much debate, no definite answer has been given—until now. The answer? Neither. It was the lead! In the sales business, the lead is second in importance only to preparation. Some sales books even pass over preparation as an assumed consideration and reason that the lead is the first step in obtaining the sale.

Let's assume that you have *prepared* yourself both mentally and physically to sell, and we are now pondering What's Important Now.

Leads

The first position on the Cycle of Success is the *"Lead"*. In direct sales and sales through face-to-face in-home demonstrations, we must first consider how we will generate leads. Many failures have befallen educated and experienced sales professionals who underestimated the importance of leads. When examining direct sales logistics, it can be said that lead acquisition is to direct sales, what advertising is to retail sales. Let people know you exist! "When business is good it pays to advertise; when business is bad, you've got to advertise" (u.a.).

7 Methods for Obtaining Leads

If you do not have a lead—a prospect in which you can create interest in your products—then what value is there in your product or your ability to sell it? There has never been, nor will there ever be, a sale made on this earth which did not begin with a lead!

Some methods for obtaining leads may include:

◆ Door knocking (Offering a gift and performing upon invitation. This can be great because you chose the area.) or registering people for some sort of promotional draw. (Some offer a second instant win card and encourage the prospects to call in to the office immediately to claim their prize.)

◆ Asking your customer base to provide you with a list of their friends, family members and associates. Then have the customer contact these leads and book future demonstrations with them for you (better hold-up and closing averages).

◆ Collecting from a draw box at home shows or locations that your target market may frequent, such as dry cleaners, etc. For example: Win two adult tickets to a movie & a medium three topping pizza. This box might do well at a movie theater. To claim their prize they must see a no obligation presentation of your product in their home (You deliver gift card/gift certificates). They must be qualified as part of your target market (company rules).

◆ Performing 30 second surveys via the telephone (gathering intelligence to accurately target the market you want), then entering them in a drawing from which you select "winners." Call them back and insist they see a demo to redeem their prize (as part of your advertising campaign).

◆ New recruits may obtain high quality leads by contacting their (qualified) personal circle of friends and family and asking them to see a demonstration in order to gain some training and valuable experience. Smaller distributorships (consisting of a distributor and a few salespeople) may wish to offer to train their new sales representatives in the field). This increases the chance a sale will be made because the distributor can negate the new recruit's selling errors, and ask for the order. Ensuring the new recruit makes his/her first sale is critical to limiting attrition among new sales representatives.

- Acquiring leads from another company that shares your target market. For example: If your target market were homeowners with carpet (vacuum sales) you might obtain leads from a carpet installing company or a carpet cleaning company.

- Using the postal service (you can also hand deliver to select neighborhoods) to send out scratch and win cards (similar to lottery tickets) to your target market. Winners will have to call you to claim their prizes and then must see a demo at the time of delivery (explained of course by the person fielding the incoming calls and the legally required tiny print on the card).

With regard to your target market: remember, the middle-class buys 80% of all high-dollar direct sale items. The lower-class will maintain a higher closing average because they're not targeted as often, but the finance company will turn down a great number of their credit applications. The upper-class are often harder to get an appointment with, but maintain a decent closing ratio.

After you have established a method for obtaining leads, it is absolutely crucial to examine the quality of these leads. The question is: "Are you reaching your target market?"

What is your target market, and of what importance is this information with regards to leads? Your target market is the portion of potential customers who possess the financial resources to purchase your product and share a propensity for doing so.

Consider the following illustration: A real estate agent decides to look for potential customers (leads), at the local unemployment office. He is successful in obtaining many leads and contacting them. He even manages to take several orders and returns home that evening full of confidence and renewed enthusiasm for the real estate business. The next day the finance manager (mortgage co.) approaches him and explains that each of his potential customers (already mental customers) has been turned down for credit, and thus the sales cannot be processed and no check will be forthcoming. Upon hearing this, the salesman's renewed enthusiasm and sense of accomplishment are replaced with a grimmer reality and the bitter aftertaste of disappointment and failure.

Obviously the mistake he made was not in choosing his profession, nor in his salesmanship. He failed to consider the importance of contacting his target market. Simply stated, he failed to realize that the *quality* of the lead is subsequently more valuable than the quantity.

Some sales organizations have engaged in poor methods for obtaining leads simply because they regarded any success as a standard from which to grow. For example: the realtor company recommended to its sales staff that the local unemployment office might be a place where leads could be obtained.

The realtor company's salespeople get busy and obtain over one thousand leads over a period of one year. They are excited by the potential sales. All the leads are contacted, and as many orders as possible are negotiated. The realtor's salespeople manage to sell two houses. The two houses were sold to government-employed unemployment office staff workers.

In spite of the meager volume of net sales, the realtor's sales staff had taken over five hundred orders, which impressed the realtor's management because the realtor's sales people had recorded the highest gross closing average in the company's history.

There is much concern in accounting, however, when the director states that the company is in financial difficulty. Many man-hours have been exhausted, not including paperwork, facsimiles, photocopies, etc. The sales department decides that by increasing the total number of leads, the total number of completed (net sales) will also increase. They decide to include a dozen other unemployment offices in their market.

This illustration shows how some companies have been led astray by a few successful selling attempts in spite of having failed to reach their target audience. This kind of reasoning can trap a company in a vicious cycle where they think more leads make more completed sales, but really, more (poor quality) leads only makes for more expenditures, and they spiral into debt. In this case the financial ends do not justify the means. Thus it is necessary to remember this catch phrase with regards to leads, "Quantity yes, but quality first!"

Contacts

The second position on the Cycle of Success is the *Contact*. When a method or methods for obtaining leads has been demonstrated to be successful, then those leads must be contacted. This can be done directly (in person) or indirectly (through another form of communication, such as by phone, or electronically). It is important that this stage be completed with a minimal, but forecasted and acceptable loss of leads. In other words, it is not realistic to believe that every lead contacted will continue on to the next stage.

Calculating the Set-Up Rate

This loss can be calculated and given a specific value using the following formula:

$$SUR\% = (\#LCPO/\#LCNO)100$$

SUR=Set-Up Rate
LCPO= # of Leads Contacted with a Positive Outcome
LCNO= # of Leads Contacted with a Negative Outcome

Take the total sum of *leads contacted with a positive outcome* and divide this number by the total sum of *leads contacted with a negative outcome* and then multiply the result by one hundred. The remaining number is the percentage of positive outcomes. Subtract this number from one hundred percent and you will be left with the percentage of negative outcomes.

By using this formula when contacting leads, you will be able to determine the most successful methods for contacting your leads. You will also have a way for tracking *total quality* (improvements made).

If a change in your contact style increases the percentage of positive outcomes, then you may choose to adopt this new style permanently (trial and error). **Please Note:** *The method used for obtaining leads may corrupt the contact stage's success ratio.*

It is also important when making contacts by phone or electronically to consider the time of day. If you are contacting potential customers/leads in other time zones, this is particularly vital.

Consider, for example, Charlie. Charlie sells satellite dishes. He believes that he could do well by selling his product to persons in rural areas where cable television is not available. He learns that there is a great demand for this type of product in the Philippines, but Charlie lives in San Antonio, TX. He devises a method for obtaining leads through his cousin who lives in the Philippines. At first, everything is going well and Charlie has his cousin send the leads to him via email. He decides that the time is right for contacting these leads.

That afternoon around three o'clock, Charlie begins enthusiastically calling the leads. He is surprised when the Filipinos answering are rude and insulting. He completely abandons his idea to sell there, deciding the people are not very receptive. What Charlie didn't realize was that the problem was not with his contact style, but with the fact that he hadn't checked the time difference between Texas and the Philippines. He was actually attempting to contact them at four o'clock in the morning! It is little wonder that they all seemed rude and insulting. Of course this is an extreme case, but it illustrates a potential stumbling block and something that should be considered when contacting leads.

Let's look at another example. Mary was looking to sell cosmetics to working women. She took this job to make extra money and to keep busy while her husband was at work from 7am to 3pm.

After establishing a method for obtaining quality leads (working women) she began contacting them. She found that she had great difficulty reaching them. She tried around nine in the morning. She tried around eleven in the morning. She even tried around one in the afternoon. Finally, she tried just before her husband returned home at three in the afternoon. Yet her percentage of positive outcomes did not increase, nor did the number of contacts she was able to make.

Mary began to get discouraged. She met a successful salesperson at her company named Sue and decided to ask for help. Sue asked Mary what the problem was and Mary explained the trouble she was having with contacting leads. Sue was quickly able to diagnose that the reason Mary was experiencing this difficulty was because the working women she was trying to contact were at work during the hours Mary was calling. Sue told Mary that she might have better luck if she tried contacting her leads in the evening, after typical business hours.

Mary tried one last phone session, but this time at six o'clock in the evening. Her number of contacts increased by over six hundred percent, and the number of appointments she was able to obtain also increased significantly. Remember how important it is to consider all aspects when attempting to make contacts.

Finally, the view by the salesperson of what the contact should consist of and why, can have a dramatic impact on the results. If the salesperson begins this phase with any less enthusiasm or strategic planning than they would show while performing a demonstration, the consequences could be dire. The contact in many ways is what I call the *first sale*. It is selling the potential customer (the lead) on why they should take time to allow you to interest them in your product. Thus your communication should consider the four remaining secrets of the Sales Savior, which will help you be the best salesperson possible. (These will be discussed later in detail.) If you are using the telephone to make contact, there is a simple tip which can have dramatic influence on your results: Always smile!

> "The thing that goest farthest towards making life worth while, that costs the least, and does the most, is just a pleasant smile…It's full of worth and goodness too, with manly kindness blent. It's worth a million dollars and it doesn't cost a cent" (Nesbit, n.d.).

This may sound absurd because people cannot see you over the telephone. However, I have noticed that the potential customer has an innate ability to recognize and sense a genuine smile and the non-threatening tonality which accompanies it.

In recent years I have found that the most effective method for producing quality results in this area is to delegate the contact stage to your customers if the leads originated with them. Plan 'B' is the old fashion method (which applies to all leads not originating with a customer). Do it yourself. To help make this easier, examples of telephone scripts and how they should be arranged will be discussed in detail in a later chapter.

Appointments

When a contact approach has been successful at piquing the interest of the potential customer, a time must be agreed upon for the sales presentation, or what I call the *appointment*.

If the potential customer does not have time for the presentation immediately, then it is acceptable to arrange an appointment. The most crucial factor in appointment making is timing. Because most individuals do not regularly plan their day-to-day activities more than forty-eight hours in advance, and their capacity for remembering activities planned any further in the future than that is diminished, it is unrealistic to believe that every appointment will result in a sales presentation performed when it was originally scheduled to be performed. This begs the question: What factors directly influence whether or not we will perform a scheduled demonstration?

Calculating the Hold-Up Rate

The number of lost presentations can be assigned a value using the following formula.

$$X=(P/AS)100$$

X=Hold-Up Percentage
P=Presentations performed
AS=Appointments Set

The sum of sales presentations completely performed divided by the sum of appointments set, then multiplied by one hundred equals the *Hold-Up* percentage. If you subtract this figure from one hundred you will arrive at the figure determined by the "**PWEC**" principle. **PWEC** is an acronym for **P**rocrastinate, **P**eer Pressure, **W**e forgot, **W**orking late, **E**mergency, and **C**ancellation principle. The law of PWEC, states that a majority of all appointments not resulting in sales presentations will be a direct result of one of the factors in the following paragraphs.

Procrastination, or putting things off, is generally cultivated from childhood. For example, a mother asks her young son to do the dishes after dinner. He replies, "In a minute, Mom!" or, "As soon as this television program is over."

Procrastination is also encouraged in our everyday expressions to each other, such as in these examples when a person is departing from a conversation at work. A person might say: "Don't work too hard." Or: "Take it easy." These phrases both support and provide recognition of procrastination. Many people have become a slave to procrastination and find themselves consistently late for meetings and work. Even in scholastic settings, students can be observed cramming for exams. What is cramming? Cramming is the realization of procrastination followed by an attempt to catch up at the last minute. In fact, people in all walks of life can often be seen scrambling to get things done at the last minute.

In contrast, successful businessmen rarely procrastinate. Perhaps this is because the knowledge of your business promotes a healthy passion for it. I have never met a person who wasn't in a hurry to succeed. Therefore you might say that knowledge is the key to breaking the procrastination habit.

If the prospects *knew* how much fun they were going to have on the presentation and that they would be making a purchase that would really benefit them in the future, would they still put it off? I am sure you can see the paradox. Rather than focusing on trying to cure people of this habit, we must simply recognize its impact on our sales business.

Peer Pressure can also affect your hold-up percentage. After speaking with an enthusiastic and charismatic sales representative who has been properly trained, it is natural for the potential customer to become excited about the appointment. "Nothing is so contagious as enthusiasm; it moves stones, it charms brutes. Enthusiasm is the genius of sincerity and truth accomplishes no victories without it" (Lytton, B., n.d.).

Often the potential customer's excitement translates into a cause for conversation and the desire to share his excitement with friends, relatives, neighbors, and even work associates. However, this excitement can become a cause for jealousy. For some reason our peers engage in a psychological game of snakes and ladders. Some of our peers will elevate our excitement by sharing in it; these are the ladders! Others will attempt to disparage us, and these the snakes! These *interrogators* ask questions about the potential product or service you might be interested in, not to gain an understanding of why you might be interested, but to find fault with it or even to merely dampen your excitement.

Why? As childish as the behavior may sound, it is often because they are jealous that you may have something that sounds more interesting and desirable than what they have. "Jealousy is an awkward homage which inferiority renders to merit" (De Puisieux, n.d.). This may sound like a juvenile activity for adults to engage in, but really, adults are simply children who grew up. Believe me when I tell you that childish behavior is not reserved only for children.

The "We forgot" factor of the PWEC principle brings us back to what we read earlier. The average person's propensity for recollecting appointments booked more than forty-eight hours in advance is at best perfunctory. In all probability it *will not* be remembered.

Thus, if the appointment were booked for a date beyond what I call the *cognizance threshold*, it would be imperative on the part of the salesperson to re-contact the potential customer within the parameters of the forty-eight hour window to confirm the appointment.

Confirmation should *not* sound like this: "Mrs. Johnson, do you still want me to come over?" Instead, have an associate call and say something like: "This is (associate's name) from (company name), Mrs. Johnson. I just wanted to let you know that (name of salesman) is planning on being at your place at (name time of appointment) but we have an urgent message for him, could you have him call the office when he gets there? Thank you and we hope both you and your husband enjoy the presentation."

It is true that the redundancy of this procedure may in fact create an adjusted hold-up percentage, because the duration of time between the initial contact and the secondary contact have allowed for a multitude of risk factors to truncate the excitement of the proposed appointment, and may have induced listlessness and apathy toward it. However, even if the prospect's excitement has diminished slightly, it is still worth it to perform the demonstration. After all, the show is about to begin, and they're likely to get all the excitement they can handle once you arrive.

A Note for Distributors: Another interesting observation involves the salesperson's attitude toward the appointment at the time of confirmation (if this stage is even necessary). If the Distributor mistakenly delegates the confirmation protocol to a sales representative who doesn't really want to run the appointment, you should expect a compromised hold-up percentage.

The PWEC principle also encompasses unforeseen occurrences such as the demand for the potential customer to work late. Working late is the example given, however, fatigue, illness, poor time management, and lethargy are all arguable justifications for a poor individual appointment hold-up.

From time to time (although rare), emergencies can also affect the hold-up percentage. A potential customer could have been involved in a car accident on the way home, for example. Or perhaps your potential customer has to take an injured child to the hospital for treatment. It is unrealistic to expect them to be available for the appointment under such circumstances.

Please note that if you have found yourself validating your unusually low hold-up percentage with what seems to be one emergency after another, there is most likely cause for concern with the quality of the leads or the manner in which you are contacting/confirming them.

Cancellations are a forecasted and acceptable loss when determining hold-up percentage. Professional salespersons trained in the art of script writing and salesmanship techniques will often encounter cancellations. In fact, the more proficient you become at contacting potential clients and booking appointments, the greater the potential for increased cancellations will become (sheer quantity will increase all PWEC factors). This is because well-constructed contact scripts have been communicatively and psychologically tested, and offer the potential customer a significantly reduced range of possible and probable negative replies.

In other words, these scripts have been designed to offer the potential customer (lead) a limited number of predictable and predisposed responses. So, after pondering the fact that the salesperson has outwitted him using sales techniques, the potential customer may in fact realize that the level of residual interest in the new product or service does not have the puissance to sufficiently cultivate a strong enough sense of curiosity. The customer rebels against what he feels is a form of entrapment by purposely evading the salesperson, or in fact canceling the appointment altogether.

Another possible causality for cancellations is that the potential customer does not possess enough information about how the potential product or service can benefit them and therefore they do not wish to take time to view it. (This is seldom the case but worth a quick mention. Nine times out of ten the opposite is true! Remember curiosity, not too much information, killed the cat.) In some cases, the salesperson making contact provided the potential customer with enough information for the potential customer to deduce that he has no need for the product or service to be discussed, and therefore no time should be wasted viewing it. This is common with new salespeople who are overly enthusiastic and suffer from verbal diarrhea.

Take the pricing information, for example. You don't want to tell the prospects the price until you can build the value that justifies it. If asked, "How much is it?"

It is best to respond that your company has products that range in price depending on people's needs and that the only way to know the price would be to assess their needs. This approach is honest and shows that you care about the prospects, and do not want to remark without first gathering enough information.

When making contact, the presentation stage will become corrupted if curiosity is not created without giving away any real information, which might negatively influence the potential customer, or allow the potential customer to justify why they should not purchase. For example: If they already know the price of the product, they may continue to mentally justify why they ought not purchase while viewing the presentation, rather than becoming fully immersed in it. Or if you've already told them about all of the feature benefits your product offers, your presentation may be boring due to redundancy. It is important to note that we are not trying to sell the product over the phone.

Presentations & Sales

The final stage in the Cycle of Success is a byproduct of the percentage of appointments which were accomplished, namely sales. Notice I said byproduct. Most salespersons view the sale as the ultimate achievement and put little merit in the process itself. However, this kind of thinking lends itself to disheartening eventualities (particularly in the beginning of a person's sales career, when they are more prone to self-doubt and worried about rejection), especially if your ultimate goal (the sale) is thwarted in some manner. Remember that the sale is obtained throughout the entire process and the presentation; not merely at the conclusion of it.

What does this mean? The sale is the successful transference of the thoughts, feelings, and motivations about a specific product or service to another. This is accomplished through motivational education combined with the other five secrets of selling, namely: personality types, control, building the problem and solving it, building value, and the need/greed factor.

Because the sale is made during the presentation and not upon its conclusion, it may be said that a salesperson may have accomplished a sale and yet for some reason failed to consummate it. How is this possible?

Suppose in the beginning of the Cycle of Success a poor quality lead was able to infiltrate the process. Instead of reaching your target market, you were reaching persons in considerably low-income brackets who (*really*) could not afford your product. An extreme example could be selling private jets to small children. It is possible to perform a sales presentation which accomplishes the task of transferring the salesperson's thoughts, feelings and motivating factors to the children. They may be genuinely excited, knowledgeable and motivated to sign a purchase order with the express intent to purchase. However, because they have little or no income they are unable to complete the transaction. Thus a sale has been made, but the order is not able to reach maturity and manifest itself in the form of monetary value or revenue.

Some have argued that this is not a sale, and that sales are only those endeavors which are able to reach maturity and result in revenue gains. With this philosophy, it is understandable why the sales process has become clouded in mystique. Some have segregated the accomplishment of taking an order and witnessing its maturity into tangible revenue gains by labeling the former as a gross sale and the latter a net sale. Yet for those whose compensation relies solely on commissions, gross sales seem of little consequence. Gross sales should not be ignored, however, because they show that the method of sale in itself was not a flawed one, and could be improved upon—along with the gathering of more quality leads—to acquire more net sales in the long run.

Calculating Your Net Gross Percentage

It is possible to assign a value to both the percentage of sales presentations resulting in a gross sale (closing average) and the difference between those resulting in a net sale. This is extremely important to distributors since an imbalance here results in the closure of a business over time.

$$NGP=GS/NS(100)$$

NGP=**N**et **G**ross **P**ercentage
GS=**G**ross **S**ales
NS=**N**et **S**ales

I once ran a direct vacuum sales office (where the vacuums retailed for $2800.00 each) in an economically depressed area. I was able to generate 80 sales a month (scrutinizing every lead). After a closer examination revealed that only 15 had been approved and paid by the finance company, a serious dilemma arose. As a distributor, I was working very hard to cope with our business demands. My sales representatives were also expending a lot of effort. Though on the outside we were positive, neither of us was very happy on the inside (monetary woes & fatigue). Soon the sales representatives began to believe that even if they did their jobs correctly, they could not make enough money to provide for their families, so they quit. I ended up closing the office and relocating it at a loss of more than $25,000.00 not including time invested and expected revenues. I lost an additional $25,000.00 in unpaid loans to my sales representatives as my wife and I were eager to assist them financially until we could figure out how to overt this crisis.

A distributor without people is reduced to a salesman with a great personal commission and little chance of producing any significant volume. "We will not be defeated from the outside, but rather from the inside" (Spencer, R., January 19, 2007 Personal Communication at HyCite Corp.).

Determining Your Closing Average

To determine your closing average, simply divide the number of gross sales made by the number of sales presentations completed, and then multiply this figure by one hundred. This is your closing percentage, also known as your closing average.

CA=GSM/SP(100)

CA=**C**losing **A**verage
GSM=**G**ross **S**ales **M**ade
SP=**S**ales **P**resentations

This can be calculated immediately after each sales presentation but is more accurate when the number of sales presentations is increased tenfold. For example, if a person completed ten sales presentations and obtained five gross sales in a period of one week, he might conclude that his closing average was fifty percent. Most would regard this as a considerably above average closing percentage If he waits until he's completed a further ninety presentations (tenfold), having one hundred completed presentations under his belt, the salesperson might find that the closing average has improved, been maintained, or diminished. If the closing average is extremely high, it is likely to diminish in the future. An exception would occur if the definition of what consists of a gross sale has been altered. For example: If we started qualifying every prospect that said they would purchase in the future as a gross sale.

Why may the closing average diminish over a greater number of presentations and how should we view this? Many salespersons define their ability to succeed by their closing average. Thus compared to someone whose closing is sluggish, those said to maintain a higher closing average are generally regarded as being superior in sales ability and more valuable to a company. This latter part is often a misconception. A salesperson usually begins selling (actually showing) a product that she believes in, and that she believes will be met with receptiveness by the target market (often starting with friends and family). She is very enthusiastic, masking herself in confidence and convinced that her endeavors will meet with certain success. This overwhelming sense of excitement, enthusiasm and confidence often consumes her as well as the persons to whom she is presenting. Thus the sale is made! "Nothing great was ever achieved without enthusiasm" (Emerson, n.d.).

After a period of time has elapsed, and the salesperson has cooled off, she finds herself questioning how she was able to generate sales in the beginning, and she may even begin demoralizing herself by believing that her initial sales were accomplished largely by luck, or some other circumstance, which cannot be directly attributed to her. "Luck is when preparation, meets opportunity" (Fribourg, F. 2002, *Personal Communication*).

Another probable cause of a diminished capacity to create sales may be present when the quality of leads is poor and a reduction of trust between the leads and the salesperson is revealed. The following example from a direct vacuum cleaner sales company illustrates these points.

New salespersons are asked to begin showing the product to their friends, family and associates. On most occasions, armed with inadequate training, these highly enthusiastic and motivated individuals embark on a new career in sales. In the beginning, most of them are able to generate one or more sales. This is largely due to three reasons. First, they have a high level of enthusiasm, which is easily transferred to the prospects. Second, they have an established trust already existing with the prospect. Third, the prospects have a special/personal interest in helping the sales person succeed. This is often the case when parents purchase from their children.

For these very reasons, many direct sales organizations obtain a large percentage of their target market leads from their newly enlisted sales people (customers as described later) and their lead trees. In fact many are dependant upon them!

Thus as the quality of the leads begins to erode and the salesperson begins to present to individuals with whom they have little or no prior relationship, and these individuals have no special interest in helping the sales person achieve success, the capacity for an increased closing percentage diminishes. At this point, true salesmanship and skill are required. Some distributors have called this diminished closing observation, "hitting the rookie wall." "For knowledge, too, is itself a power" (Bacon, F., n.d).

Because rookie salespeople usually do not receive adequate training (short initial training period), they hit that wall and immediately begin demoralizing and degrading themselves. A small percentage of these newly enlisted salespersons enjoy the luxury of previous sales experience or the ability to learn and adapt quickly, which allows them to continue creating an average closing percentage. This is why a high percentage (seventy percent and more) of individuals who begin with a high closing average will watch it level off and find a balance indicative of the genuine figure. It is similar to a man jumping onto a scale. The indicator may, at first glance, rise above the actual weight of the man. However, given a few seconds of consistently applied pressure, the properly functioning gauge will level off and find a balance indicative of his true weight.

The larger number of presentations used when calculating the closing average, the more accurate the closing percentage figure will be.

"All wish to be learned, but no one is willing to pay the price" (Juvenal, n.d., ¶17). This is especially true of those seeking to know their closing average, desiring immediate self-gratification over truth.

Exactly how the sale is accomplished will be described by the other five secrets of selling, and in greater detail throughout this book. I hope from your reading, you have come to the conclusion that sales is not a career for the lazy and lethargic, or for those lacking the hunger for the wisdom that experience wishes to impart. "Lives of great men remind us. We can live our lives sublime, and departing, leave behind us, footprints on the sands of time" (Longfellow, H. W., n.d., ¶5).

Is it really possible to sell eighty percent of your target market using the knowledge of direct selling? Some say not, but for a few select direct sales people, it is. The secret was revealed in the ancient "Lost Art Scrolls", and their translation of "The Ten Coincidental Personality Dispositions".

Chapter 3

The Lost Art Scrolls

- **Ten Coincidental Personality Dispositions**—A descriptive term used to illustrate ten potential customer personality predispositions.

- **Closing Average**—The average number of times a salesperson is successful at obtaining the order from a given number of sales presentations.

- **Assignable Causes**—This is a term used to describe the reason for the loss of a sale based upon wrong behaviors or communications.

- **Non-Assignable Causes**—This is a term used to describe the reason for the loss of a sale based on uncontrollable environmental or behavioral predispositions.

- **OAC**—On Approved Credit

- **Second Sale**—A term used to describe the act of successfully selling yourself prior to the actual sales presentation.

The Ten Coincidental Personality Dispositions

According to four ancient scrolls found frozen in the ice during a routine excavation in Antarctica (translated from an ancient Hebrew dialect), the second fundamental for selling is revealed when we understand personality types. In these scrolls was a passage about these "personality types" detailing the alchemy of direct sales techniques known only by this vanished people's chief priests.

Let's examine what these scrolls—now dubbed "The Lost Art Scrolls"—said about the personality types of your potential customers. There are ten different personality types, called the Ten Coincidental Personality Dispositions.

Consider the illustration on the next page and you will begin to see how these coincidental personality dispositions impact your sales career. Of a randomly chosen group consisting of ten potential customers, twenty percent *are not* predisposed to mature into a net sale. On the other side of the group, there are twenty percent who *are* predisposed to mature into a net sale. This leaves a remaining sixty percent of the group. Of the remaining sixty percent (six potential customers) three tend to lean toward readily maturing into a net sale, while the other three tend to lean toward the twenty percent who will not mature into a net sale.

The difference between this last group (sixty percent) and the first two groups is that when adept sales skills are applied to this group, they are likely able to profoundly and dramatically exert influence, which can persuade the potential prospects to develop into a net sale.

Under the theory of "The Ten Coincidental Personality Dispositions", it is possible for a properly trained salesperson to obtain a closing average of up to eighty percent, i.e., the 60% of the last group plus the 20% of those already predisposed to mature into a net sale.

The remaining twenty percent are those who are best described as unsellable. However, one should note that by scrutinizing and inspecting the quality of the leads, one may in theory be able to segregate and discard some of this cantankerous twenty percent prior to presentations. This means that one could possibly obtain an even higher closing average than eighty percent. This juvenile twenty percent, are usually characterized as stubborn, arrogant, foolish, rebellious, in a state of denial, or those not prone to reason.

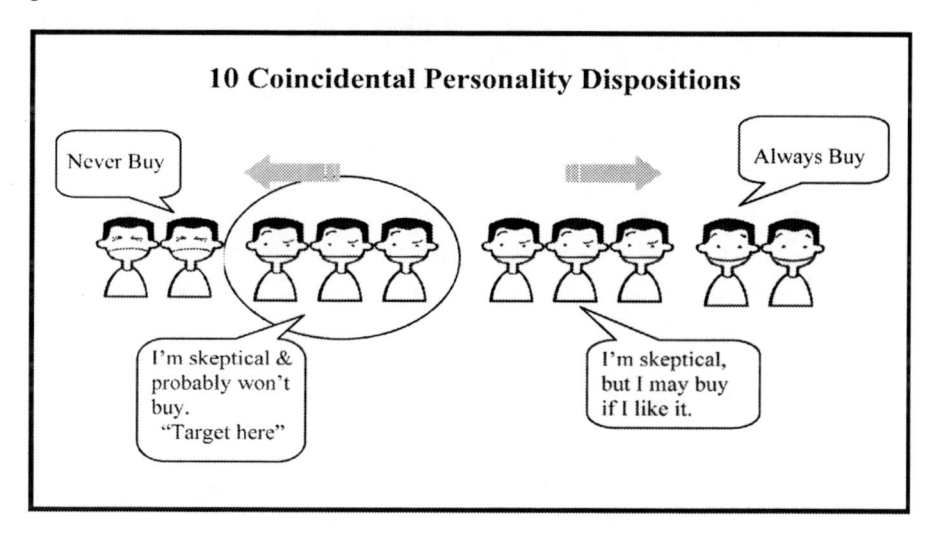

10 Coincidental Personality Dispositions

Never Buy

Always Buy

I'm skeptical & probably won't buy.
"Target here"

I'm skeptical, but I may buy if I like it.

While these last 20% might often be perceived as stubborn or arrogant, this does not mean that everyone who declines to buy fits into this characterization. However, when designed and performed correctly, a genuine sales presentation for those potential customers who are prone to reason and logic should almost always result in a gross sale.

This can be likened to a magic trick. When practiced and performed correctly, a magician is able to predictably fool the audience with an illusion almost every time. On the other hand, a sloppy apprenticing magician may easily and inadvertently expose the illusion as nothing more than slight of hand.

A high percentage of gross sales should result in a net sale (ninety percent or more). In many scenarios, "The Ten Coincidental Personality Dispositions" theory is discredited because the results of tests performed do not support it. However, these are usually the results of those who have failed to perform the tests using salespersons who actually possess the skills to perform 'genuine' sales presentations.

Instead, salespeople used in the test lack the proper training and experience, hence the discrepancies in test results.

Another scenario is when persons used in the test are actually taught poor sales methods. These individuals claim to have been instructed in sales and support the belief that they are true sales professionals because they have been able to obtain a closing average above twenty percent (Using "The Ten Coincidental Personality Dispositions" as standard).

They are baffled by the revelation that all of the new techniques they attempt cause temporary increases in their closing average, but seldom result in any lasting increases.

The ancient scrolls direct us to look closely at the six essentia at the core of any successful salesperson. If these have become tainted at any time during the learning process, they will negatively impact their potential for closing once they are eventually revealed. If a piece of fruit has a rotten core, it won't be long until the entire fruit is spoiled.

If detected early on, portions of the fruit may be safe and enjoyable, but before eating we would most likely cut the spoiled parts away and throw them in the trash.

We would no longer consider the portion that we threw away, nor would we dig it back out of the trash and eat it. Similarly, we should discard old sales habits that have been shown to thwart our sales efforts.

When speaking of differing direct sales perspectives, the author of the "Lost Art Scrolls" counsels us: Many people who have consulted with me on direct sales have claimed to integrate standard techniques into what they call "their own [selling] style." Suppose a doctor was going to perform surgery on you, and prior to administering the anesthesia, he confided in you that they would not be using the textbook surgery method that he learned in medical school, but instead he would be using "his own style." He knew that it had been successful a couple of times in the past and it might actually work. Is this the physician you would want performing the surgery (u.a.)?

People have asserted that no two personalities are the same and therefore similar results cannot be achieved. Thus a salesperson's "style" evolves. If companies began hiring people with wildly individualistic work methods, how efficiently would those companies run? Most people advertise their educational backgrounds on resumes for just this reason: to show that they have received a standardized education and learned similar work methods. If having unique personalities means that we cannot share similar views on how to accomplish a task, the entire world could cease to function. It is true that we are all different, but we are all also capable of performing tasks in a similar way. In this way, similar results may be achieved.

The best method for accomplishing a task is to follow the practices that have already been successful in the past. Of course, people not being identical, some variance will undoubtedly occur. These variations can be a direct result from some wrong behavior or communication, also known as assignable causes.

Some non-consistent variations, referred to as "common" or "non-assignable causes", can be directly attributed to the twenty percent of The Ten Coincidental Personality Dispositions: stress, fatigue, body chemistry, and cultural, religious or ethnic background similarities or dissimilarities between the salesperson and the potential customer. These are also called random variations.

The scrolls admonish: A good habit for any successful salesperson is to assert first that every presentation is sellable. Then, after each sales presentation where a gross sale has not been the result, determine whether the loss of the sale should be attributed to assignable causes, or non-assignable causes.

If you make the determination that the reason for not achieving a gross sale is because of a random variation, a "pattern of objections" will not be observed.

By writing down the objection given on every sales presentation (not resulting in a gross sale), a professional salesperson can watch for patterns to develop in the prospects' objections (their reasons given for not buying).

If a similar objection for not buying is given on three or more consecutive presentations, and the leads have not been corrupted, than the variations are assignable causes and careful consideration should be given to the process of the sales presentation. If it is determined that the variation is due to non-assignable causes, then the process is considered uncontaminated and the result recorded. No residual action is required.

(Chalk it up to experience!)

The Selling Personality

Now we should discuss what types of personality traits make up a great salesperson (a great salesperson being the kind that you and I would like to buy products from again and again). A reproduction of the ancient drawings contained in the Lost Art Scrolls (as depicted in the illustration above) shows there are many layers of personality traits stemming from the core.

Around the core, represented by your mind, body and spirit, are the five sides of the enthusiasm pyramid. It appears as a triangle in the illustration because of the view created when a three dimensional object (a salesperson here, shown as a sphere) is dissected into two halves. Surrounding the core are five sides of enthusiasm. A sphere was chosen here to represent the salesperson because humans are similarly three-dimensional. However, unlike inanimate objects, we consist of many personality traits and characteristics. The traits closest to the core are those with the most influence on our outward behavior as well as our unconscious behaviors. Thus, enthusiasm is always demonstrated to be at the very heart of all successful salespersons.

Outside of the enthusiasm pyramid are three personality traits. These are patience, honesty, and morality. The dictionary defines patience as "quiet, steady perseverance; even tempered care; diligence..." (Patience, n.d., *Dictionary.com Unabridged*). Honesty is defined as being "truthfulness, sincerity, or frankness" (Honesty, n.d., *Dictionary.com Unabridged.*). Morality is being "...concerned with the principles or rules of right conduct or the distinction between right and wrong; ethical..." (Moral, n.d., *Dictionary.com Unabridged*). As illustrated, these personality traits are key and along with enthusiasm, are vital to being the best salesperson you can be.

The following personality traits make up another layer around the sphere. These include: humorous, courteous, friendly, punctual, assertive, charming, dependable, and polite. Listed below is each trait and definition.

- **Humorous**—"Characterized by humor; funny; comical" (Humorous, n.d., *Dictionary.com Unabridged*).
- **Courteous**—"Having or showing good manners" (Courteous, n.d., *Dictionary.com Unabridged*).
- **Friendly**—"Favorably disposed; inclined to approve, help, or support" (Friendly, n.d., *Dictionary.com Unabridged*).
- **Punctual**—"Strictly observant of an appointed or regular time; not late; prompt" (Punctual, n.d., *Dictionary.com Unabridged*).
- **Assertive**—"Confidently aggressive or self-assured; positive" (Assertive, n.d., *Dictionary.com Unabridged*).
- **Charming**—"A particular quality that attracts; a delightful characteristic, pleasing..." (Charming, n.d., *Dictionary.com Unabridged*).
- **Dependable**—"Consistent in performance or behavior; trustworthy." (Dependable, n.d., *Dictionary.com Unabridged*).
- **Polite**—"Showing good manners toward others, as in behavior, speech..." (Polite, n.d., *Dictionary.com Unabridged*).

How can a discussion of these personality traits aid you in becoming a more successful salesperson? By evaluating our own personality traits, we may be able to find areas that could use some added attention.

Let's review some of the ancient illustrations found in the mysterious Lost Art Scrolls, and take a few minutes to do some self-examination. Aren't there some areas of your personality that could use some attention? By becoming self-aware, we are taking the first step toward enlightenment.

Unfortunately, in the early 1900s the Lost Art Scrolls mysteriously vanished en route to the Smithsonian National Museum of Natural History in Washington, D.C. All records of their existence have also since mysteriously vanished, but their wisdom remains.

No one knows for sure who authored the secret Lost Art Scrolls, but one thing is certain: throughout the ages, whoever has practiced their medicine has unlocked the gates to financial freedom and, some say, a new sales-Eden.

The following discussion regarding the personality traits of the successful salesman is this author's recollection of the message the Lost Art Scrolls conveyed.

Personality Traits of the Successful Salesperson

A sphere is "a solid object with a surface on which all points are an equal distance from the centre." (*Kernerman English Multilingual Dictionary*, n.d.)

Sometimes others have a keener sense of humor than our own. What we find extremely humorous may not seem very funny to our potential customers. Because we must remain polite and courteous, remember to keep your material clean. When you have obtained the right type of (humorous) material for your sales presentation, it will evoke laughter on most occasions. When you hear that sweet sound, equate it with the ringing of a cash register because you have "made one small step" in the sales process, but "a giant leap" in your relationship with the prospects (Armstrong, 1969).

I have observed moments when a salesperson changes emotional and facial expressions dramatically (within a relatively short timeframe) and inserts some humor into her material that the potential customers don't seem to immediately understand, and consequently appear perplexed. In other cases, I have seen prospects try to maintain poker faces, showing no signs of emotion. In both of these scenarios, if I were doing the presentation, I would simply say, "Tough crowd!" Usually, at that point, the prospects' smiles would break out and laughter would ensue.

Many times the potential customer is afraid to show any emotion with regards to the sales presentation for fear that this display may fuel the confidence and assertiveness of the salesperson and her expectation of an order. In other scenarios the prospects believe that they will have greater bartering power if the salesperson believes they are not truly interested or emotionally engrossed in the product(s) or the presentation.

Keep in mind, however, that the twenty percent of The Ten Coincidental Personality Dispositions characterized as un-sellable may also have poker faces. If your best material has no effect at all, you may wish to check your potential customers for a pulse. Just kidding!

Humor

"To promote laughter without joining in it greatly heightens the effect" (Balzac, n.d.).

"The person who cannot laugh is not only fit for treason and deceptions, their whole life is already a treason and a deception" (Carlyle, n.d.).

Very few salespeople have been quickly dismissed when first having succeeded in creating laughter amongst potential customers. What if you do not possess a comedic disposition, or have been described as having a poor sense of humor? Like any other kind of skill, you can work on it. For example you may wish to attend some comedic clubs to obtain some humorous material that you can use during your sales presentations. Perhaps you could find some material on the internet or at your local library. You may want to try some of the material out on a friend before integrating it into your sales presentation.

Courteous

Being courteous is something that is not only expected in today's marketplace; it is demanded! In all your dealings as a salesperson, and a member of society, courteousness is a quality that you should definitely be characterized as possessing.

"Life is not so short but there is always time enough for courtesy" (Emerson [n.d.] See "R" section). "The small courtesies sweeten life; the greater ennoble it" (Bovee, n.d.). Take caution, though, to not become unbalanced with courtesy. Do not, for the sake of courteousness, refer to your potential customers as Mr. or Mrs. so and so. Unless you are a child, this behavior runs contrary to friendliness and charm. Being on a first name basis is always preferable prior to, during, and after the sales presentation. Our given names are not only unique, but a cause for great affinity. Most people genuinely like their names and enjoy hearing them spoken aloud. Friends certainly do not call on us using our surnames, but strangers, it seems, always do. To remove yourself from the category of stranger and place yourself firmly in the category of friend, using a potential customer's first name is key. After all, who would you rather buy a product from, a friend or a stranger?

"Father calls me William, sister calls me Will, Mother calls me Willie, but the fellows call me Bill!" (Field, n.d.) Many salespeople I have met have felt strongly that it is a sign of respect to call people by their surnames, a habit they learned from childhood, but they have not deduced how it has negatively impacted their adult life. Perhaps in more formal settings, such as in the military or formal work environments, using people's surnames is still appropriate. However, working as a direct salesperson, frequently spending time in someone's home is not that type of environment. So be courteous, but as in all things, be balanced.

Friendliness

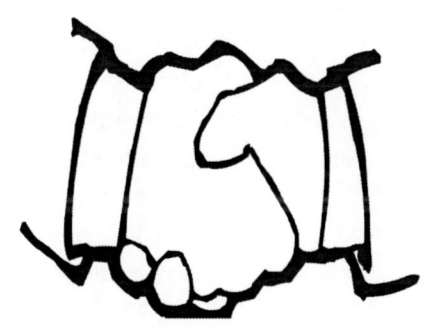

Friendliness is also very important, because as salespersons we are unfamiliar with many of our potential customers prior to the sales presentation. We should take time to consider how we might quickly make friends with our potential customers. To best do this, we should use what Mother Nature gave us. What do I mean by this? Most people believe that salespeople are primarily great "talkers." This is true. However the best salespeople are also excellent observers and listeners. Mother Nature has supplied us with eyes and ears as well as a mouth. You've probably heard the mnemonic, "Listen twice, speak once." How can this help us make friends quickly? By observing the potential customers, their apparel, and their environment, a salesperson can find potential points of interest which the would-be customer may enjoy talking about. It is recommended that the salesperson find something to offer the potential customer a genuine compliment on.

It is also incumbent upon the salesperson to elicit a subject of interest for the potential customer to talk about. Most people love to talk. Just think of the enormous amounts of money spent on phone bills, internet chatting and text messaging around the world!

My experience in direct sales has afforded me many opportunities to make friends and influence customers. When I was in the field, I managed to become a specialist in several areas. There is a saying, "Jack of all trades is a master of none" (u.a.). This would seem to indicate that a person cannot become a specialist in many subjects, but let's take a closer look at what I mean.

If you assert that, as a salesperson, you are a master of the selling arts, then it is easier to let go of the other things you know. Do I mean that you should forget everything else besides selling? No. What I mean is that you should know what you know, know it well, and respect others for what knowledge they have. To make friends, compliment the potential customer on something that you have observed about him, and then ask him for a piece of advice on how you might accomplish something similar.

By specializing in listening and observing, you automatically specialize in selling, and you can then let everything else rest.

"Many receive advice, but only the wise profit by it" (Syrus, n.d.)." For example, on one occasion, I approached the door of a potential customer, anticipating the appointment and bubbling with enthusiasm. On my way up the driveway I noticed a well-manicured lawn with beautiful flowers. I also spotted, through the open garage door, a tricycle, a hula-hoop, a newer model minivan, and a set of golf clubs. From this I was able to deduce several things:

The well-manicured lawn and flowers indicated that someone must have been spending time caring for it and was clearly interested in the physical appearance of the house. This meant that the people who lived here were likely to be neat and tidy, which seemed of importance to a vacuum salesman.

The tricycle and hula-hoop in the garage indicated to me that these people were probably a working family with young children. Children are prone to spills and other messes—also very good conditions for a vacuum salesman.

At this point, I had already observed the potential for two compliments and two sources of undoubtedly great pride.

The golf clubs indicated that someone in the house was likely to be a golf enthusiast. Here was another hot topic to work with and get some advice on.

What about the newer model minivan? That indicated that someone in the home was likely to have a full-time job and be creditworthy. This is an important consideration for a vacuum salesman, especially one who accepts monthly installments as an acceptable method of payment.

When I met the potential customers, I immediately offered my name (first & last) explaining what company I represented and why I was there, also asking their names in the process. While I was "setting the stage," (which we'll discuss in greater detail later) I began making friends, which I call the "second sale". I asked who was responsible for such a beautiful and well-maintained lawn and garden. To that, Mary (the wife) replied, "I am. But Bill (her husband) helps me sometimes."

"Well it really looks gorgeous! What was that red looking flower I saw?" Mary asked which one in particular I was referring to, and we walked to the front room with windows fully overlooking the front grounds. I pointed out the one I was curious about, and she began explaining not only what kind of flower it was, but under what conditions it grows best, the time of year to plant such a flower; what soil conditions are necessary, and her secret for increased growth and brilliance of color (for ten minutes I just listened and nodded). A simple compliment and immediately she could let down her guard and begin talking about a favorite subject.

My participation was actively listening with genuine interest, and I knew that the cash register was ringing and that I had made another big leap toward obtaining the sale and I hadn't even got out the product yet. By showing an interest in a subject that Mary loved, she and I had become friends. "The only way to have a friend is to be one" (Emerson, n.d.).

Regardless of whether you feel you have a good understanding of a potential customer's hobby or other favorite subject, it is always permissible to request advice on how you might improve your understanding.

In contrast, if I had gone into their home and said, "Your lawn looks… not bad, but mine is really spectacular!" the effect would not be nearly as positive. In fact, quite the opposite, don't you agree? Be sure to compliment and ask for advice rather than saying anything negative, which would turn the potential customers off and likely lose you the sale.

Once I felt I was on friendly terms with Mary, I felt empowered. When I arrived, I was out-numbered two to one. Now, Mary and I outnumbered Bill. It was now time to turn my attention to Bill. I noticed some golf trophies on the mantle and quickly deduced that Bill might be the golfer. I asked who had won all the trophies, as I inspected them admiringly.

Bill said coyly, "I am."

"Are you a professional?" I asked.

"No, but I like to play on weekends. I won that one at this year's tournament for the blind," he replied.

"Wow, you must be really good to win a trophy! I've played a few times, but never accomplished anything like this. What kind of score are you averaging?" I asked.

"My score is usually in the low seventies," he confided.

"I don't know anybody with a score under ninety. I once managed a ninety-five," I said (for those unfamiliar with golf, a lower score is better).

Bill smiled and asked where I liked to play. I mentioned a couple of places I had been and told him I had real trouble with the driver. I felt comfortable with the irons, but managed a horrible slice whenever I used the driver. In the blink of an eye, I had one of Bill's drivers in my hands and he was watching my technique and offering suggestions on methods I could use to correct the problem.

After a few minutes of talking, I said, "I almost forgot why I came here. I am supposed to show you a presentation on my product. Perhaps we should get that over with so we can talk some more later."

Making friends can be as simple as good observation, followed by a compliment and a request for some advice. The subject may not always be golf or a well-manicured lawn, but anything from big screen televisions, family photos, or vehicles can also be excellent topics for discussion. You must simply find something they are proud of that you can offer a sincere compliment on. And make sure to not act like you are more knowledgeable than your potential customers. This will usually not provide the proper foundation to support your friendship-building endeavor.

Later, once you are doing your product presentation, it is not only permissible but also certainly encouraged that you appear very knowledgeable about your products or services. Remember, you are a specialist.

The key to friendliness lies in being friendly and kind to others. The bible admonishes, "Therefore all things whatsoever ye would that men should do to you, do ye even so to them…" (Mat 7:12, *KJV Bible*, 2007). Notice it does not say, "What men do to you, you must likewise do to them." It says all things *you want* men to do to you… A simple distinction, but a big one! Befriend all your potential customers and you will find that in your life, regardless how much you sell, you will be rich with friends.

Punctuality

Be punctual! I have never met a person who enjoys waiting for anything or anyone. Being punctual for appointments demonstrates that you value the potential customer's time. It shows appreciation for the opportunity which you have been granted to display your goods or services. To give you some everyday examples of the fact that people genuinely do not like waiting, consider that most people enjoy the events in their lives more than the time leading up to them. Therefore, many people find themselves speeding everywhere they go. People are always in a hurry.

As the speed of information has increased, humans have attempted to keep pace. We roll through stops signs, and accelerate at the very first inkling of a traffic light turning yellow. The grocery stores have added a fast lane to cut down on waiting times and expressways have been added to highways to cut down on waiting caused by traffic congestion. Automated banking machines are everywhere and checks are being replaced by bank cards, keeping us from having to wait for money. Clinics have sprung up all over to cut down the wait for medical treatment, and some auto insurance companies offer a free rental car while your car is being fixed so you don't have to wait. Entire companies have been built to eliminate waiting.

If you wish to take into account traffic or unforeseen occurrences, then you may want to book your appointments between times, telling the customer you will arrive between six and seven, rather than specifying a particular time. Six would be your aim, but seven o'clock would still be tolerable. This ensures you won't be considered discourteous for being late.

"Know the true value of time; snatch, seize and enjoy every moment of it. No idleness, no laziness, no procrastination: never put off till tomorrow what you can do today" (Chesterfield, n.d. ¶10).

Assertive

Assertiveness means to state something positively or demonstrate the existence of something. Therefore, when practicing your craft—selling—it is vital to speak with confidence. You must be able to demonstrate both the necessity for your product or service, and that by using your brand in particular, the client can better benefit.

In the past, salespeople were taught aggressive tactics. These were able to create some added sales, but only at the expense of the individual salesperson's reputation and the creation of negative stereotypes for all salespeople. Many legal battles have occurred and the public has sought protection from such "sales predators." Many governments are now passing legislation which allows the customer greater freedoms when wishing to cancel orders. Times now allotted for returning purchases can range anywhere from two days up to one year, or in cases of misrepresentation, indefinitely.

Because of the overly aggressive salesperson, many purchasers felt pressured to buy products instead of being sold on them. It has been said that pressure is what turns coal into diamonds. But remember, pressure is also what broke the camel's back.

It has been demonstrated that non-offensive techniques, such as reverse closing, reduce power struggles between the salesperson and the potential customer and provide a better overall sales experience for both the customer and the salesperson. We do not want aggressive salespeople; we need assertive ones. We need salespeople who are capable of convincing us that we want to purchase an item rather than those who would make us feel forced to do so. In any case, aggressive selling has actually thwarted the efforts of the best salespeople causing irreparable damage to our profession's reputation, all to get a short-term, immediate gain.

Aggressive selling has been shown to substantially degrade the acquisition of leads. There is a saying that "good news travels fast, and bad news travels faster" (u.a.). This aptly describes how the destructive power of aggressive selling spreads. The key to this problem is to replace the aggressive behaviors with assertiveness. Sales and lead acquisition will mutually increase as a result of this adjustment.

Because the public can see the difference between an aggressive salesperson and an assertive salesperson, and vastly prefer the latter, it is necessary for salespeople to learn and practice assertive techniques over aggressive ones in order to stay competitive and financially solvent.

Charming

Charm is another great asset of the successful salesperson. "Charm… it's a sort of bloom on a woman. If you have it, you don't need to have anything else; and if you don't have it, it doesn't much matter what else you have" (Barrie, n.d. ¶27).

Being charming is being able to enchant the prospects in such a way that the entire sales presentation takes on what seems to be a magical aura. It is a characteristic of the Art of Selling. It is performing the sales presentation to the absolute delight of the potential customer. It also has lingering after affects. Like leaving a great taste on the palate after a delicious meal, charm leaves your prospects wanting more even after you have finished. It can be said that many a sale was gained by this attribute alone. "You know what charm is: a way of getting the answer 'yes' without having asked any clear question" (Camus, n.d.).

Dependable

Instilling in the potential customer the belief that you are dependable will also aid your endeavors to sell. If a customer is afraid that they may not be able to rely on you in the future for after-sale service, they may decide to purchase elsewhere. Letting the potential customers feel secure is very important when obtaining the sale. Therefore, you may wish to introduce into your presentation examples of how you were there to aid customers who have purchased from you in the past. In this way you can let the prospects know that they can rely on you based on your previous track record. Remember not to sound alarming. Make any after-sale service sound like it was a result of something simple and easily corrected. "Let us have faith that right makes might, and in that faith let us, to the end, dare to do our duty as we understand it" (Lincoln, n.d.).

Polite

Politeness is, for obvious reasons, important to a salesperson. "There is never a second chance at making a good first impression" (u.a.). This is so true!

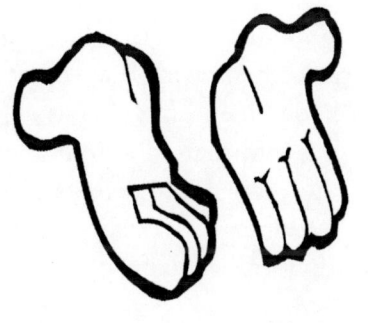

Generally speaking, potential customers will make an assertion as to whether or not they like you within the first fifteen minutes of meeting you. This may seem shallow to you because it is obviously not possible for them to really know you in fifteen minutes. So it could be said that they are really deciding whether or not they like the personality you have chosen to reflect, as they have perceived it within the fifteen minutes.

It is not possible for you to reprogram your entire personality in order to sell, and moreover, it is not necessary. You may choose to imitate the behavior and speech patterns of any person or group of persons on whom you have chosen to model your sales abilities. If, for example, you are not skilled in judging what your potential customer considers polite, simply model your behavior on someone you feel acts and speaks in a very polite manner. As a result, you will eventually find yourself acting politely. You will even find yourself acting politely when you are not selling because you have sown a habit (Mandino, 1968, p.57)

Politeness is the act of showing regard for others (Politeness, (n.d.). *WordNet® 3.0. Dictionary.com*). I also believe that when we refer to politeness, we are including honesty, for I cannot imagine a liar described as having regard for others.

This brings about an important question. Can a salesperson really be honest in today's market? Is the withholding of knowledge consistent with a lie? If you have to lie, you haven't fully learned the art of selling. The true masters of selling entice others with the truth! They do not misrepresent products or services in order to make them sound or appear better. They draw attention to the value of the product or service by illustrating how those products or services fulfill the potential customer's wants and needs. (Even if these wants and needs have been primarily drawn attention to by the salesperson.)

It is permissible and encouraged to say, "I don't know" in response to questions that you do not have the answers to. However, it is best to assure the potential customer that you will find out, and then do so. This will build trust and integrity. Contrary to those who believe that by admitting ignorance you are exhibiting signs of weakness, or incompetence, you are actually showing that you are strong and not afraid to admit that you don't know everything. But also, you are showing that you are willing to find out this information on their behalf.

You may note that in the surface ring illustrated on p. 42, there are nine remaining personality traits. These are kindness, caring, cordial, modest, eloquent, genuine, pleasant, well-groomed, and clean-cut.

- **Kind**—"Of a good or benevolent nature or disposition, as a person" (Kind, n.d. *Dictionary.com Unabridged*).
- **Caring**—"To have an inclination, liking, fondness, or affection" (Caring, n.d. *Dictionary.com Unabridged*).
- **Cordial**—"Courteous and gracious; friendly; warm" (Cordial, n.d. *Dictionary.com Unabridged*).
- **Modest**—"Having or showing a moderate or humble estimate of one's merits, importance, etc.; free from vanity, egotism, boastfulness, or great pretensions" (Modest, n.d. *Dictionary.com Unabridged*).
- **Eloquent**—"Characterized by persuasive, powerful discourse..." (Eloquent, n.d. *The American Heritage® Dictionary of the English Language, Fourth Edition*).
- **Genuine**—"Free from pretense, affectation, or hypocrisy; sincere..." (Genuine, n.d. *Dictionary.com Unabridged*).
- **Pleasant**—"Pleasing in manner, behavior, or appearance" (Pleasant, n.d. *The American Heritage® Dictionary of the English Language, Fourth Edition*.
- **Well-groomed**—"Having the hair, skin, etc., well cared for; well-dressed, clean, and neat: a well-groomed young man" (Well-groomed, n.d. *Dictionary.com Unabridged*).
- **Clean-cut**—"Neat and wholesome: a polite, clean-cut young man. (Clean-cut, n.d. *Dictionary.com Unabridged*).

Modesty

If you consider the remaining traits, I think you will agree that these characteristics are all excellent for anyone to emulate. Modesty can be especially important when we have learned to possess all the skills outlined in this book. All too often a salesperson who is well trained realizes the amazing financial rewards which accompany all those trained in the craft, and they have become puffed up with pride and haughtiness. This vanity deteriorates the other good personality traits and acts like a mental deprogramming device.

Well-Groomed & Clean-Cut

Appearing well-groomed and clean-cut are very important during the eggshell period, whether we like it or not, because the prospects will judge us. If you're wearing a t-shirt that says, "I eat at Hazel's", ripped jeans and holey sneakers, you have probably already done enough damage to the sale that any further explanation or sales skills are moot (Lamb, 2000).

"People buy from pretty people" (Lamb, 2000). That does not mean that we all need plastic surgery, but "it doesn't cost much to shave, or make sure your hair's done right, or shine your shoes, or clip your fingernails" (Cunningham, 1989). Obviously cleanliness is of great importance as well. "Men in general judge more from appearances than from reality. All men have eyes, but few have the gift of penetration" (Machiavelli, n.d. ¶7).

That is the conclusion of the wisdom of the Lost Art Scrolls regarding the personality traits of the successful salesman, but what they have to say about leadership may have an even greater impact on your success. That, I'll save for another chapter.

Chapter 4

Hexagonal Leadership Qualities

In the illustration below, you can see the hexagonal leadership qualities spoken of in the Lost Art Scrolls. Imploding into the leader are the characteristics of a visualizer and an actualizer. Leaders must be able to create within their mind's eye a crystallized picture of the goals they wish to achieve.

True Leaders Emanate Sales Power

To demonstrate your commitment you must physically and mentally rehearse your dream scenario until it is actualized. You have to savor your dreams! Relish the emotions of your accomplishment and you can associate intense pleasure with its actualization, thereby drawing close to you the necessary tools you will need to accomplish it (Robbins, 1991, p. 119). This will stir an enormous amount of excitement and enthusiasm within you.

If you do not feel the bubbling sensation of excitement and enthusiasm, then either you have not fully committed yourself to the dream or you have not been able to internally crystallize the vision of its accomplishment. You have to believe!

Of course there is one other scenario…

Passion

You have not chosen a dream for which you harbor a genuine passion. "Passion is universal humanity. Without it, religion, history, romance, and art would be useless" (Balzac, n.d.).

How will you appreciate the magnitude of what you learn if you have no purpose? With passion, the explosion of qualities which cause others to admire, imitate, draw close to, be inspired by, and follow you will be effortless.

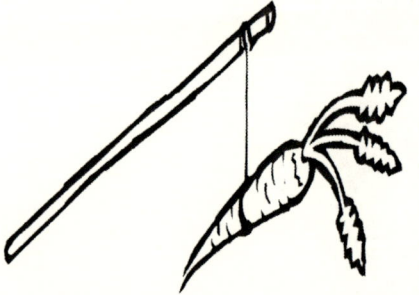

Motivation

You must possess the ability to motivate others. Motivate them to purchase your product or service now. Motivate your salespeople to work and grow in the art of selling. "The final test of a leader is that he leaves behind him in other men the conviction and will to carry on" (Lippmann, n.d.).

When it comes to distributors, and how you can motivate others, keep in mind what Napoleon Hill said: "It is literally true that you can succeed best and quickest by helping others to succeed" (Hill, n.d). When you have helped enough others to get what they want, the balancing laws of nature assure us you will not be denied!

Courage

You must possess courage. There is not a successful salesperson on earth who has not faced his share of rejection and yet carried on in spite of it. "When moral courage feels that it is in the right, there is no personal daring of which it is incapable" (Hunt n.d. ¶19).

Will you, when faced with mounting rejection, slough it off and shine? When doubts have weighed heavily on your mind and threaten to rob you of your dreams, will you beat them back? Courage will!

Courage grants us the power to approach one more potential customer when not a single thing has gone right. Courage is one more presentation; one more lead; one more recruit; one more business card; one more phone call; one more client; one more attempt. Without doubt, the very moment that your courage flows, a reversal of fortune can allow you to claim the reward of a sale at the end of a long day.

It takes courage just to face the achievement of your dreams. Many people secretly fear the fulfillment of their life's pursuit. Perhaps this is because they do not know what purpose they would have after accomplishing their life's ambition. "The crowning fortune of a man is to be born to some pursuit which finds him employment and happiness, whether it be to make baskets, or broadswords, or canals, or statues, or songs" (Emerson, n.d.).

Some fear the fulfillment of their dreams because they do not really feel that they deserve the benefits of them. For many years I did everything I could to motivate and help my salespeople, even to the point of advancing them tens of thousands of dollars. One of my partners used to accuse me of "selling the farm" (Stone, D., Nov 22, 2004, *Personal Communication*).

This business permitted me the opportunity to earn a handsome living (so easily). I confided to my wife that I didn't think I deserved to be granted this awesome key to financial independence. I realized that in many cases I wanted the success of my would-be apprentices with more conviction than their own passion could manage.

The key to this business is to be wise enough to acquire the education you need and willing enough to use it; a prerequisite for joining this band of gypsy-like megalomaniacs and entrepreneurs helplessly addicted to the lure of easy money. I challenge you to "talk the talk", and "walk the walk." For it is written that it is much more difficult to walk the path than to know it!

Arthur Miller said in his book *Death of a Salesman*: "He's a man way out there in the blue, riding on a smile and a shoeshine. And when they start not smiling back—that's an earthquake…A salesman has got to dream, boy. It comes with the territory" (Miller, 1948).

Faith

It requires faith to be a great salesperson and leader. "Now faith is being sure of what we hope for and certain of what we do not see." (Hebrews 11:1, 1973, *New International Version Bible*)

Faith is the carrot for perseverance, the invisible reward at every milestone. Faith is your unwavering belief that you can and will succeed, despite any persecutions, stumbling stones, or roadblocks.

Faith is something that requires many successes to cultivate, while it seems that a lack of faith can have a reverse domino effect regarding your sales. For example, I once experienced an uncomfortable slump in sales. This happened partially because my lead source had become corrupted, and partially due to my location at the time, but most importantly because of my attitude toward the business. I began to have a negative outlook and I questioned my previously held convictions.

Like the Stockholm syndrome that POWs and hostages engage in, I, too, began to identify with my captors, my customers. Perhaps the product was too expensive. Perhaps times had changed and a new era of "poor sales" had been ushered in while I wasn't looking. I began to dread my next would-be failed sales call. You can see how this type of thinking can have a profound effect on your future sales outcomes. Our mental state is vital when it comes to selling, and we must be certain to keep thinking positively. The simple business of selling can easily become as structurally unsound as a house of cards if negative attitudes prevail.

So if I lose my faith, where shall I look for it? There are two places you can find your "sales faith". First, rebuild by mentally reliving the successful sales calls you have made in the past. See yourself selling to different people over and over again. Do this until your confidence is built up again and then get back into the fight as quickly as possible! The second place to look for your "sales faith" is wherever there are successful people doing what you do; even if that means riding with another sales representative. I have learned as much from the thousands of people I've trained as they have from me! Go out with people who are doing well. At least you might learn some new tricks, you may realize that you are excellent at what you do and had no reason to doubt yourself in the first place.

How do you know if you've regained your faith? When you no longer feel the need to look for it, then you have found it!

Optimism

"An optimist sees an opportunity in every calamity; a pessimist sees a calamity in every opportunity" (u.a.).

A great salesperson is at all times perceived as the optimist. Their positive outlook on life is a silver lining on the cloud of doubt. It's the fire that spurs others to reach for the cup of life; the land of opportunity where the seeds of all dreams are first planted. A true optimist seeks out opportunities:

> A multimillionaire was once interviewed on a national television program where he was asked to recall his story. He said that he had been employed at a gas station when he was younger.
>
> He was an optimist and an entrepreneur. He dreamed of one day owning his own service station. He began to work very hard towards the fulfillment of his dream, saving as much money as he could.
>
> He soon realized that his dream might not be fulfilled because it would take him too long to save all the capital he needed. He decided to go to Las Vegas and gamble with the money he had saved to that point.

He purchased a round trip ticket in the event that if he lost everything, he would still be able to get home.

He got a room in a hotel and divided his money equally over three days. On the first day he had begun to gamble he experienced some ups and downs, but by night's end had lost everything he had set aside for the day.

The next day he began gambling again and lady luck still had not shown her face. Once more he had lost everything! He hoped that things would change on his third day, but decided that no matter what happened, he would follow through with his plan. His dream was worth it. Once again his luck was not good and he lost all his remaining money.

He still had a ticket home, which he had already paid for and he wondered if he had done the right thing. Unfortunately, on the way out of the casino, Mother Nature called. He went to the men's room to use the facilities but discovered that in order to get into the stall it required you to deposit a quarter, which he did not have. He swallowed his pride and asked a gentleman who was leaving the restroom if he could spare a quarter so he could use the facilities.

The man did indeed give him a quarter. As he went to deposit the quarter, the door of the stall opened as another man exited. He put the quarter back in his pocket and relieved himself.

As he was leaving the casino he saw a slot machine, which only took quarters. So he took one last chance on his luck. Believe it or not, he finally won! He cashed in the quarters for dollars and soon he was back up at the tables.

He gambled all that day and by the time it came time for him to catch his plane he had won back all the money he had lost and even gained quite a substantial amount.

He decided to bump his ticket up to first class so he could enjoy the flight home. He hadn't enough capital to fully realize his dream yet, but he was happy and optimistic.

While sitting in first class he met a young investment broker who was very excited about some investment opportunities, and who wished he had enough money with which to invest. It wasn't long before the young broker's enthusiasm spread and he decided to invest his winnings with him.

Within a short time the investments yielded a fantastic profit and the man became a multimillionaire. I am not sure whether or not he did see the fulfillment of his dream, but he was asked during the interview whether or not he had ever thought about going back and finding the man that gave him the quarter, and he replied "No. But I have searched the world over for the man that opened up the door for me." (Hannenberger, July 15, 1999, *Personal Communication*)

Many people believe that it is hard to maintain a positive outlook on life in such trying times. However:

Life is just like the tide. Whatever goes out, that's what will come wash right back into your face. It's like that ole car battery. It has a positive and a negative. Sure you're gonna have negative things happen to you. I'm not saying you're not going to stub your toe. But before that car can go, you have to combine the positives and the negatives, and all life is exactly the same way. Besides, eighty percent of the people we complain to don't give a damn, and the other twenty percent are glad that you got that problem, because it's not theirs. Don't pay any attention to these people. Make a plan and work your plan! (Dodd, 1991)

Misfortune seems to follow the pessimist like a storm cloud. This analogy isn't that far from the truth. You see, we get what we focus on in life. If you are positive, you most likely see the world as a better place, an opportunity, and the chance to grow and fulfill your dreams. You see these dreams clearly in your mind's eye and you believe they will be realized without a doubt. Your focus is on what you want. Your brain is able to easily interpret these focuses as necessary and maximize its resources in the pursuit of these things. Life is your journey not your arrival.

In contrast, the pessimist sees the world as a place where you are robbed of your dreams. It is a place where every occurrence is another attack on oneself; where steppingstones become stumbling blocks! "I can" becomes "I can't." They complain to everyone they meet about the weather, their job, their family, their finances, and even religion and politics. They mentally rehearse every negative thing that happened to them that day and then share it with those they love the most. They pass down the "…river of life…" "…caught up in the current…" of everyday happenings (Robbins, 1991. p. 41).

What they don't realize is that their brain, their mind, is always in pursuit of something more. Although they may have given up on one level, Mother Nature has programmed the brain to keep on striving for something greater. That is why, even in our sleep, we dream.

When we are bored, our brains discover new things for us to do. Most people, after a stressful day on the job, find themselves trying to slow their brains down. If it is true that the brain is constantly working to draw close to us the tools needed to accomplish our wants and desires, then we should interpret the brain's focuses as its means for doing just that.

Therefore the pessimist focusing on negatives is, unfortunately, actually asking his brain to acquire the tools necessary to create even greater and more sensational problems.

Some others become engrossed in their worries. It has been said regarding worry: Worrying is the art of rehearsing negative experiences, which may or may not ever be realized. It was said once that "eighty percent of the things we worry about, never happen" (u.a.). Perhaps this is the way the brain entertains itself while searching for the next negative occurrence. In this way it acts like a negative mental screen-saver.

The bible says:

> On this account I say to you: Stop being anxious about your souls as to what you will eat or what you will drink, or

about your bodies as to what you will wear. Does not the soul mean more than food, and the body than clothing? Observe intently the birds of heaven, because they do not sow seed or reap or gather into storehouses; still your heavenly father feeds them. Are you not worth more than they are? Who of you by being anxious can add one cubit to his life span?

Also, on the matter of clothing, why are you anxious? Take a lesson from the lilies of the field, how they are growing; they do not toil, nor do they spin; but I say to you that not even Solomon in all his glory was arrayed as one of these. If now, God thus clothes the vegetation of the field, which is here today and tomorrow is thrown into the oven, will he not much rather clothe you, you with little faith? So never be anxious and say, 'What are we to eat?' or, 'What are we to put on?' For all these things the nations are eagerly pursuing. For your heavenly father knows you need all these things. Keep on then seeking first the kingdom and his righteousness, and all these [other] things will be added to you. So never be anxious about the next day, for the next day will have its own anxieties. Sufficient for each day is its own badness. (Mat 6:25-34, 2007, *New World Translation Bible*)

What are we to conclude of this? Always be an optimist. The winds of success are unpredictable, but if you remain optimistic, it is certain that in due time, they will blow on you.

Inspiration & Perseverance

Your demonstration of character and behaviors can inspire others. Inspiration and perspiration, after all, are the true keys to the gates of success. There is one more quality, however, which every leader possesses: perseverance. Those wishing to become master salespeople must adopt the "try until" approach that we spoke of earlier. You must never, never, never, not ever, think of giving up or giving in.

A great salesman named Tom Lamb once sent me a letter containing this story and words of encouragement, along with a small lapel pin with a gold frog on it. It read:

Dear Sales Savior,

In our business, the winners are those who plan to win and those who are prepared to win. You see, our business (Sales) is not unlike many sporting events. There will be times when the ball is thrown over your head or the ball doesn't quite reach the basket.

In baseball, many of the World Series have been won by teams that had to come from behind to win. Similarly, the team that had to mount a comeback has won many a Super Bowl. Likewise in basketball and boxing; sometimes you win the game with that last desperate free throw; sometimes you have to pick yourself up when you're flat on the mat and get back in the ring to win with that final knock-out punch! You see, Sales Savior, our business doesn't always give us exactly what we want. If we are going to enjoy the rainbow, we must sometimes stand in the rain.

Consider the story of the two frogs that found themselves in a bucket of buttermilk outside a farmer's door. At first they both tried to escape, but to no avail. One of the frogs would not give up. He just kept right on kicking and splashing. The other was not so optimistic. He gave up.

The next morning the farmer came out and found that there was a dead frog in the buttermilk. This was the one that gave up. What of the other? He just kept on kicking and splashing until he had churned for himself a pad of butter from which he could jump.

The moral of the story is to never, never, never think of giving up. Just keep kicking and splashing and one day you will have a pad from which to jump.

Wear this frog to remind you to never give up. Now, if you ever feel that the story has become childish and foolish, just mail it back to me. I wish you much success in business and in life.

Sincerely
Tom Lamb, 1991
President, Rexair Inc.

I wore this little gold frog pin with much pride throughout my sales career and used it to inspire and motivate others. Tom has since mailed out many of these frogs to salespeople under my direction, and never has he asked a single thing in return. A great salesman, motivator, and leader! I have frequently looked back upon this letter as a source of great inspiration and perseverance, and that is why I am sharing it with you.

"Victory belongs to the most persevering" (Bonaparte, n.d.).

Chapter 5

The Need-Greed Factor

The third ingredient in "The Sales Savior's Six Secrets for being the Best Salesperson" is called the *"Need-Greed Factor"* (NGF). The NGF asserts that every sale is a product of one of these twin powers. Think about every product you have ever purchased in your lifetime. Do you agree that it can be said that you either felt that you needed the product or service, or you were enticed to own the product or service (luxury/greed)? It is important for every salesperson to recognize that the NGF is the basis of every sale, and therefore a focal point.

First you must categorize your product by how you will be presenting it. Will you be primarily selling the product to satisfy the potential customer's need, or the potential customer's greed?

It is true that many products will satisfy a percentage of both need and greed, but the root of the sale will be based primarily in one of the two powers. What is the difference between selling need items as opposed to selling greed items? Many times it is the target market that changes, such as the difference between those who might purchase a minivan and those who would purchase an exotic sports car. Both vehicles satisfy the need for transportation. However, the minivan is relatively inexpensive and holds many more passengers compared to the exotic sports car. Thus, a minivan is much more likely to be categorized as a "need" product where as the exotic sports car, while it fulfills the need for transportation, is much more rooted in the greed category. It's primarily being purchased to satisfy the ego, not the need for transportation.

Toilet paper, groceries, refrigerators, ranges, homes, telephone service, television, wrist watches, vehicles, education, water, electricity and many more are today considered need items. People feel like they do not have a basic quality of life without them. But even these products range from basic models which appeal to the need to high-end models which appeal to the greedier side of the need category.

If you are selling a product or service which is primarily rooted in the need category, you will most likely have a larger target market and a greater certainty that you can accomplish the sale. This is not to discourage those who have chosen to sell luxury or greed items. If the item you're selling is rooted in the greed category, it is to your benefit to appeal to other needs of your potential prospects, such as their need to feel important or compete with peers.

Today, more than ever, personal appearance and the view of others toward us, has caused society to become deeply engrossed in products which we feel denote a higher standard of living. Many people attempt to establish their self-image using these kinds of external markers.

If you endeavor to create greater sales volumes, it is incumbent upon you to establish the category your product or service is most deeply rooted in and to shift your sale presentation to best enhance and/or compensate for the lack of the other. Today's marketplace not only wants its needs fulfilled, but a growing number of people are now demanding products and services to fulfill both desires. Can it be said that one of the twin powers in the NGF outweighs the other? Yes!

If a salesperson could only choose one of the powers of the NGF to establish, she would be derelict to choose the greed factor. It is certain that 75% of the world's sales are rooted largely in the need factor and only 25% are rooted primarily in the greed. Establishing a need for your product or service is of the utmost importance. I have taught throughout the years that establishing the need is far greater than any other purpose of your sales presentation and should be priority. Keep in mind that the need may be intangible, financial, or emotional. It may not be what you first assert it is.

I use the following story to illustrate:

A young man went in to see the doctor. He complained that every part of his body was hurting. He was in terrible pain. The doctor began his examination as usual. He asked the young man if it hurt when he touched his own knee. The young man cringed, and cried out as he touched his own knee. The doctor asked if it hurt when he touched his own hip. Again the young man cried out as he touched his own hip. The doctor was perplexed.

"Does it hurt when you touch your elbow?" The young man cried out once again as he demonstrated to the doctor.

The doctor thought about it carefully and then smiled. The young man wondered what was behind the doctor's smile, and all the while he was in terrible pain. The doctor ordered some x-rays and after confirming his earlier suspicions, he explained to the young man that he was suffering from a broken finger.

Obtaining a sale is similar to the doctor's diagnostic ability. The salesperson diagnoses the potential customer's need and then shows how their product or service satisfies it. Thus, a sale is made. This is why it is so important to get your prospects talking. If the doctor had done all the talking and failed to listen to his patient, he may not have made the correct diagnosis.

Black & Decker, a successful company, manufactures several lines of drills, which are sold in stores all over. It was claimed that one year they had accomplished the impossible with regards to sales. They had generated over a million dollars' worth of drill sales.

This accomplishment was even more amazing considering that statistics had shown that their target market had no want or need for drills or drill bits. Nor did their target market consider a drill or drill bits to be deeply rooted in the greed factor of the NGF. How then, was this amazing accomplishment achieved?

Perhaps you own a drill. Nobody really wants a drill. What we want are holes or a faster way of pushing screws. This is how the need for a drill was revealed.

A drill salesperson would want to incorporate into their presentation the way in which a drill can create various sized holes and the benefits of having those holes. An added benefit would be to demonstrate how easily screws could be driven and how the drill acted as a time saving device. The creation of the need factor in this case was indisputable.

I once heard a joke regarding the sales profession, which also illustrated the NGF. It went like this:

> There once was a young man with a speech impediment who sought employment with a toothbrush manufacturer.
>
> He claimed he had no experience in sales but was very eager and ambitious. The director of marketing decided to give the young man an opportunity. He gave him a box of toothbrushes (not very many) and explained that in the past they had marketed them at grocery stores, dentist offices, and pharmacies.
>
> The young man knew that selling the toothbrushes would not be easy for him because of his speech impediment, but he was determined nonetheless. In a couple of hours the young man was back at the manufacturers requesting more toothbrushes.
>
> The director of marketing was pleasantly surprised and consigned the young man an entire case. By day's end the young man had returned once again. He explained, "The... the... these tooth brush... brushes are sell... sell... selling li-like hotcakes!"
>
> The director of marketing was very impressed and confided in the young man that he had broken the previously held sales record for most volume in a day. The director asked the young man if he would mind if he accompanied him while he sold for a day, so he could see for himself how the young man was able to create such volume.

The young man agreed and the next day they both went down to the local grocery store where the young man had set up a booth from which to work.

On the table he had a large bowl of chips, which he offered free to passersby. He also had another bowl with a complimentary dip. The director watched as a man took a chip, dipped it, and began eating.

Instantly the man's face quirked and he said, "This dip taste like crap!" The young salesman smiled confidently while displaying his products and said, "It *is* crap! Would you like to buy a toothbrush?" (u.a.)

This is just a joke, but it illustrates the importance of recognizing the NGF and its affect on your sales presentations. What are we really selling? This is the question that the NGF asks. If your product is clothing, are you simply selling fabric? Fabric sewn together is not likely to be worth what you might be asked to sell it for. However, instead of selling fabric sewn together, you could choose to sell a feeling. How great the person wearing this particular article would feel while wearing it. The need is not necessarily the same as the need for any other piece of clothing, but the need to create the feeling of self-confidence, respect, and pride while wearing this particular piece of clothing.

If you are selling an air purification appliance, you might notice that the plastic, metal, and filter are not worth what you are asking, regarding the individual cost of the parts, or if you are asserting that the potential customer needs yet another appliance. However, if you assert that you are actually selling clean, fresh, breathable air, the sale instantly becomes easier to obtain. After all, how can you put a price on clean air?

When the need is established, the sale becomes easy to obtain. If you are already in sales, when was the last time you asked yourself, "What am I really selling? What is the true nature of my product? Is my sales presentation consistent with its root in the NGF? How can I better establish the need for my product? What can I do now to be the very best salesperson? What can I say to answer almost any objection and still get the sale? How can I get my prospects to buy at my price?"

These questions and many more will be answered in the following chapters as we continue with "The Sales Savior's Six Secrets for being the Best Salesperson".

Chapter 6

Salespeople are Full of BS!

- **BS**—This acronym stands for **B**uild the problem & **S**olve the problem.
- **Commitment Questions**—These are questions whose answers have been predetermined to intensify the potential customers' commitment to purchase.

Great salespeople throughout the ages have long known a basic principal behind the successful sales presentation is the BS Process. Build the problem and Solve the problem! In order to benefit from the NGF, a successful salesperson will incorporate a series of illustrations within the sales presentation which successfully build the fear of a problem and the consequences of it within the potential customer. In other words, we establish the need.

The sales presentation will then illustrate how the introduced product or service will solve that problem. If the cost of the product or service being introduced seems to the potential customer to be at least fifty percent less than the cost of the damage caused by permitting the problem to exist, then the potential customer is most likely to purchase the product or service. How is building the problem accomplished?

Let's use waterless, greaseless cookware as the example of the product being introduced. The salesperson would have a section of the presentation solely dedicated to building the problem.

"Can I see some of your cookware? As far as *pots and pans* are concerned, these are great".

Notice the way the salesperson refers to the prospect's cookware as "pots & pans." Already the prospect's (currently used) product is being depreciated.

"Did you know that for years they made pots and pans like yours out of aluminum and cast iron? Aluminum is a great conductor of heat but it leaches into your food during the cooking process. They have even linked aluminum to Alzheimer's disease. If you wrap meat up in aluminum foil and place it in the refrigerator overnight, the next day you will discover pits in the aluminum where it has seeped into the meat; in effect, poisoning it. **Does that sound healthy or unhealthy to you?**

"What's great about aluminum is that it is very light. Did you know that aluminum is also a very porous metal? Let me explain what that means. When you heat up the metal, the pores in the metal expand. As the pot cools down, the pores constrict, grabbing on to bits of food, and cleaning agents from the cleaning process. Then we put the cookware away in an un-refrigerated cupboard. The microscopic bits of food begin to rot and create bacteria. The next time you use the pot when you heat it up, the pores expand and release these bits of microscopic bacteria and rotted food into your meal! **Does that sound healthy or unhealthy?**

"Have you ever scrubbed this pot with a scratch pad or steel wool? Did you notice how the dishwater turned gray? That was the aluminum coming off in the water. **Is that really the kind of pot you want to prepare your family's meals in?** Cast iron is even more porous than aluminum, and it also rusts. Do you think this would be a good alternative to aluminum?

"What about the new cookware you see at grocery stores and department stores today? It is light and coated with a thin layer of silver-looking paint called Teflon. Teflon helps foods to not stick to the cookware. Thus, to combat the negative effects of metals like aluminum and cast iron, companies are now coating them with Teflon. They cook evenly and don't stick. There is only one side effect to Teflon. Many people make the mistake of using metal utensils when preparing food and it scratches the Teflon. In a short time larger pieces of Teflon begin to flake off from the pan's surface. What most people do not realize is that manufacturers who sell Teflon-coated cookware state on the pan's label that in the event the Teflon should become scratched, the pan should be thrown out immediately. Teflon is poisonous to humans if consumed! Most people buy the pan and throw away the wrapper without even reading it, not realizing that it is anything more than advertising. Do you think that these companies should be permitted to sell such dangerous products to the public? **Do you think it is wise to prepare your family's meals in this kind of cookware?**

"Let's add this tablespoon of baking soda to a piece of your cookware. Now we'll add a half-cup of water and boil it. Let's do the same with this new waterless greaseless cookware made from 18/10 surgical grade stainless steel. (A few minutes pass.) Let's taste a sample from our new cookware and one from your old pots and pans. They should taste the same, right?"

You will now find your customer sputtering with the unpleasant taste of the soda water mixed with the toxins from their pan, "Peww. Uagggg! That tastes disgusting!"

"Now try the sample from our **premium cookware**."

"That's better. Why does it taste so terrible from my pan?"

"Because of the way the pores trap bits of food and chemicals from the cleaning process. **Are you sure you want to keep cooking with that?**"

As you can see from the above segment of a waterless, greaseless cookware presentation, building the problem is essential to obtaining the sale and verifying for the potential customer the *need* for something different to cook with. The script quoted above is a prime example of the BS Process. The next step in the BS Process is to solve the problem.

"Our new waterless, greaseless cookware harnesses the positive contribution of aluminum while rendering its negative side effects harmless. We have taken an aluminum base, which transfers heat very quickly and evenly, and encapsulated it in 18/10 surgical stainless steel. The nice thing about stainless steel is that, as you can see, it's esthetically pleasing and it will never rust! Do you know why they call it surgical stainless steel? It's because they are made of the same material as surgical tools; doctors need to use tools that are made of non-porous materials when operating so as to keep them completely sterile and not transmit any bacteria to the patient.

"Likewise, this new cookware has no pores in which food or chemicals can become trapped. It also doesn't break down when you clean it, so you have the healthiest method for preparing your family's meals. **Isn't that what's really important?**

"Because it transfers heat so evenly and quickly, you will no longer have to use intense heat while you're cooking. That means there will be less chance of you over-cooking your food. **Have you ever burned something you were cooking?**

"You will even save a lot of energy (thereby saving money and the environment) by cooking on lower temperatures. In fact, you can benefit from cooking with steam, which means you will also use less water. Cooking vegetables in a lot of water causes the vitamins and minerals in your foods to be lost in the cooking process.

"With this new waterless, greaseless cookware, you will be able to maintain many of the natural vitamins and minerals because the vegetables will actually be cooked in their own natural juices. This way, your family will benefit from the good, wholesome meals you prepare. This will help them to be better prepared to fight off different sicknesses. Not to mention how much better the food tastes when it is prepared in our new premium cookware."

In this segment of the sales presentation, the problem is solved with the salesperson's product, thus completing this portion of the BS Process. Note the careful crafting of the salesperson's statements, showing how the problem was built in the setting up of the first part of the demo and solved in the conclusion of the presentation.

Also note the questions in bold. These are called **Commitment Questions**. They are very important and will be discussed in greater detail in chapter 7. They serve to hold the BS Process together and give it additional power.

So does the BS Process really have a profound effect on the outcome of a sales presentation? Let me give you an illustration which I have found helpful over the years in the classes in which I teach direct salespeople why the BS Process is so important.

The I-Beam Story

Have you ever seen one of those steel I-beams used in constructing high-rise buildings?

On a sunny day, if I offered to pay you one thousand dollars to walk across a hundred foot length of I-beam while it was on the ground, would you do it?

When I asked this of my students, almost everyone in the class agreed that they would. I then asked if they would walk across it if it were suspended twenty feet off the ground. Only this time I would pay ten thousand dollars to anyone who would cross it unaided.

Eighty percent of my class agreed that they would still do it. The other twenty percent claimed to be afraid of heights.

I continued. Would they walk across the beam if it were ten stories off the ground for a hundred thousand dollars?? Only a few more students dropped out of the running. This group seemed very brave.

I then asked if they would be willing to walk across the beam if it were fifty stories off the ground. Only now, the weather was no longer sunny, but begun raining a freezing rain that coated the beam with a very slippery layer of ice, and the wind had picked up to thirty kilometers per hour. This time I offered to pay a cool million dollars to anyone who would cross the beam.

What do you think the group said this time? At this point even the brave had succumbed to fear and reason, and they refused to commit what they considered an act of suicide. When asked about this sudden unwillingness, they all agreed that the million dollars was worthless if they did not survive.

I then asked them to consider another story. A young, pregnant mother gave birth to her first child. She was initially frightened when she went into labor because she had never had a child before. But all went well and she soon wept with joy at the sight of her new baby boy. She named him Patrick and when they cuddled together for the first time, she thought about how precious he looked as the innocence in his eyes captured her heart. His big eyes just stared at her and she realized that he was dependent on her for everything. At that moment she felt a love deeper than any she had ever known.

A nurse came and said that she needed to take the child and clean him up. She left with the baby, and did not return. Later, the police came to the mother's hospital room and informed her that the nurse had suffered from a psychological break from reality and had kidnapped Patrick.

Panic gripped the new mother. Police located the nurse on the top of a developing high-rise. S.W.A.T. had already been deployed and asked the woman what her demands were. They had found her perching atop a steel I-beam, holding the baby by one foot upside-down. In her other hand, she held a razor-sharp samurai sword. The psychotic nurse asked that the mother be brought to the opposite end of the I-beam.

The police could not take a shot at the nurse because of the terrible weather. It was freezing rain, and the winds had picked up to thirty kilometers per hour.

The mother quickly agreed and was hoisted to the beam. When she arrived the nurse had a crazed look in her eyes. She said if the mother would walk across the beam she could prove her love and have the child back unharmed. If she didn't, she would cut the baby in half.

What did the mother do?

To this, my class unanimously agreed that the mother would cross the beam. Wouldn't you for your child?

This fictional illustration demonstrates the seriousness and the impact of the BS Process on your sales endeavors. Under the same conditions, you would refuse to cross the beam for a million dollars. Yet when it comes to a mother crossing the beam for her child, you know she would do it, even though you agree that she is probably not any more likely to successfully negotiate the beam.

This means that **people will do anything, if the reason is big enough**!

What is the BS Process all about? Simply stated, it is giving people a **big enough reason** to buy your product or service. Do I mean actual kidnapping and extortion as in the illustration? Of course not! I simply mean building a big enough problem (crisis) with your sales presentation to motivate the potential customer not only to act, but to act now. If you want to acquire the sale you must first give the potential customer a reason.

Once you have successfully created the problem, you must then illustrate to the potential customer how your product or service can solve their problems, their wants and their needs.

For most of us, recognizing the wants and needs of others is not really that difficult because we have received some training in this arena. For example, consider a child who has come home late from school and knows that her parents will be worried and angry. The child knows that she is late partially because she stayed for ten minutes after class helping some of her classmates with their homework, and partially because she got carried away in a game of ball with friends on her way home.

She looks at her watch and realizes that she is more than two hours late. She thinks about how angry her parents are certain to be and how might they react?

When she arrives home, her parents are waiting just as she suspected. They angrily ask, "Where have you been?" To this, the child replies that she was asked to stay late and help some of the other children. She never mentions the ball game, reasoning that this fact would only bring about negative repercussions. The parents tell their child that they were worried sick, but sympathize with her and even praise her for her unselfish and kind acts towards others (If they only knew, huh?).

The point is that even as children, we often exercise enough foresight to understand what people want to hear, and what they need to hear. This is a very important distinction to a salesperson.

"…know what your prospects want to hear, and need to hear" (*Tommy Boy*, 1995).

Satisfy these desires while introducing your product or services and you are certain to generate many happy customers. By following the basic standards of the BS Process, it is often predictable how the potential customer will react and respond. The successful salesperson will be able to have an answer for everything. Do they really know everything? No. But what they do know is how to plan ahead.

Successful salespeople know that in order to obtain the sale they must first build the problem and when they do this, the potential customer's desire springs forth. Then the salesperson must demonstrate how the new product or service fulfills these new desires.

Legendary salespeople create the script they will use prior to the sales presentation and then use it. This script—which appears to be non-scripted dialogue—is *special* in comparison to standard language because it has been predetermined to create the greatest possible psychological, emotional, and physical impact on the potential customer. Every question has been well thought out. Most of the questions asked are phrased in such a way that the number of logical and probable answers has been limited. Even the probable answers to these questions have been predetermined to aid in the obtaining of the sale.

This state of readiness translates into greater confidence and assertiveness during the sales presentation because the salesperson does not have to calculate and predict every possible answer or objection that might arise, such as when open-ended questions are asked. For example, consider the following contact script segments and see if you can figure out why the first examples are more successful.

"Hello, is this Mr. Jackson? Hi, Mr. Jackson. This is Todd calling from your local satellite provider. I was given your name from your sister Connie. Did Connie tell you I'd be calling? Great! Then you know I'm calling to set up an appointment with both you and your spouse so I can come over and tell you about some special offers we have for you. <u>Is it best to see you tomorrow, or the following day? Would you prefer a daytime appointment or an evening appointment? Okay, would between five and six o'clock be good, or would between eight and nine be better?</u> Okay great. So I'll see you tomorrow night between eight and nine o'clock, all right? Great, thanks a lot for your help, and I'll see you tomorrow."

The underlined segments show choices for the potential customer to choose from. Notice there is no option for refusal. Listen and see what it might sound like from a salesperson that doesn't fully understand the art of selling.

"Hello, is this Mr. Jackson? Hi, Mr. Jackson this is Todd calling from your local satellite provider. I was given your name from your sister Connie. Did Connie tell you I'd be calling? Great! Then you know I'm calling to set up an appointment with both you and your spouse so I can come over and tell you about some special offers we have for you. <u>So what do you think? Would you be interested?</u>

You see in this second scenario that the salesperson has asked a question in an attempt to set up a presentation but phrased the question in an open-ended way making it impossible to predict what the potential customer's response might be. Therefore, it can be said that a salesperson is only as good as the person who wrote the sales script (also known as the pitch), and the person using it!

Just as a great actor can have their career stifled by a poorly written screenplay, a great salesman with a poorly written sales pitch will also flounder. Of course, just remembering all the words is not enough, and those claiming to be adapting the script to their own personalities have not discovered that the true sale is made in selling the pitch.

Selling really is a lot like acting. The difference between good and bad acting/selling is the degree to which the audience believes it to be real, i.e., your audience needs to believe that the pitch is not a rehearsed script, but in fact your genuine language and personality.

Some customers may argue that they have observed salespeople who do not use a pitch when selling; that they appear to sell naturally. This is a product of the following three scenarios:

- ➤ **One**—these salespeople understand some or all of "The Sales Savior's Six Secrets for being the Best Salesperson" although they may not know them to be actual and verifiable principles.
- ➤ **Two**—the salespeople may simply be using whatever they can spontaneously improvise at the time based on knowledge of selling tactics, and finally…
- ➤ **Three**—salespeople really do not understand the force and power of what they are attempting to use. With regard to the latter, any child can pick up a hammer but I wouldn't pay him to build my house.

Being Above Average

Consider another sports example. Many people around the world play baseball. Some young children are even on teams representing their schools, communities and various geographical locations. They would all consider themselves to be baseball players, would they not? Yet a *professional* baseball player is compensated for playing the game at specific times and also for practicing between games. This is the difference between those salespeople who improvise and attempt to sell and those who use some or all of the basic salesmanship principles; the professional, skilled salespeople are properly compensated (via their sales) for their work. The more skilled they are, the greater their compensation.

While mediocre sales skills might get the job done, they only produce a mediocre salary. Those who have developed their sales skills have an above average closing ratio and receive above average salaries! The difference between the two is sizable.

What is average? At the top of every organization you find the very best people, and at the bottom, the very worst (see p. 84). If you are said to be average, that means you are in the middle, or lukewarm. "I know your works, that you are neither cold nor hot. I could wish you were cold or hot. So then, because you are lukewarm, and neither cold nor hot, I will vomit you out of My mouth" (Rev 3:15 & 16, *New King James Version Bible*, 1982).

It could be said then, if you are average, you are the worst of the very best people in a company, or you are the best, of the very worst people in a company. I am quite sure you would not wish to be considered a candidate for either of these two titles, would you? (Sanders, 1991)

Above Average Diagram

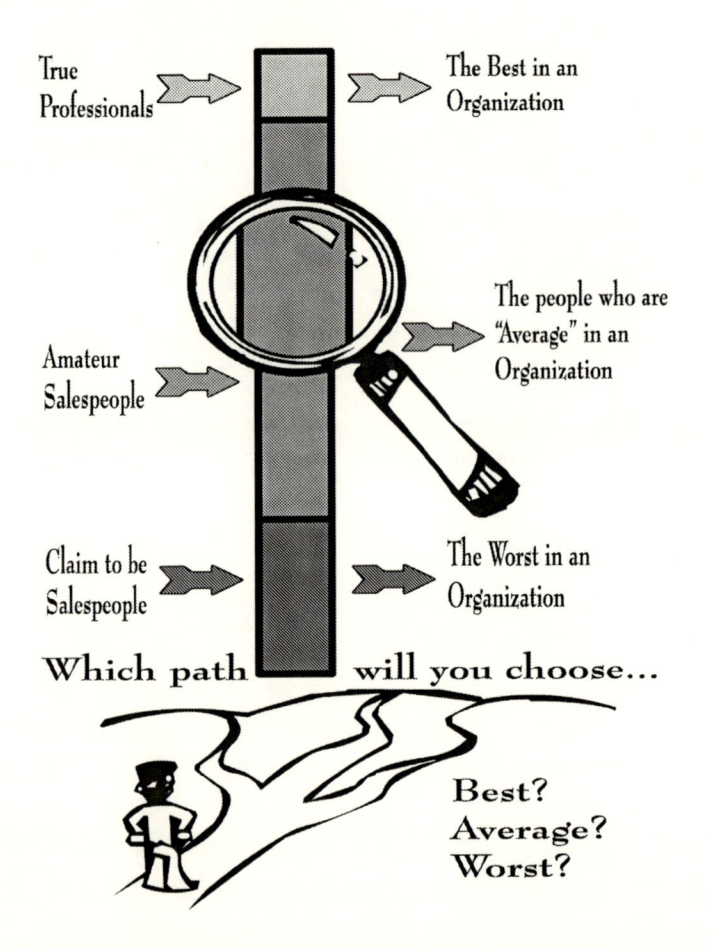

True Professionals → The Best in an Organization

Amateur Salespeople → The people who are "Average" in an Organization

Claim to be Salespeople → The Worst in an Organization

Which path will you choose...

Best?
Average?
Worst?

"It is not the crook in modern business that we fear, but the honest man who does not know what he is doing" (Young, n.d.).

I have always reached for the goal of being above average, and it has paid off in ways I could not have dreamed. When you are above average at work and in life, you hold the keys that open many a door. Try it for yourself (being above average) and let me know what doors are opened for you.

Another important thing to remember when considering the BS Process and your sales pitch is your control and syntax. Control will be discussed in detail in the upcoming chapter.

Syntax is the order and sequence in which the pitch is made. Making adjustments in the syntax of the pitch can completely alter its effect and meaning. Take the following sentence: Stewart sunk his teeth into the bear. Adjusting the syntax to change the order of subject and object, we get: The bear sunk his teeth into Stewart. Believe me when I tell you that that is a very different experience (Robbins, 1991, p. 113)! Changes in syntax can change the entire meaning.

Once the pitch has been established, it is imperative that those learning it follow it as closely as possible. What you say and how you say it really do matter.

Are there any subtle details that can make or break your chances for success? If so, what are they? How can you make more money and grow your business faster by learning about them?

Chapter 7

Little Details, Big Difference

- **Control**—"To exercise authoritative or dominating influence over; direct" (Control, 2007. *The American Heritage® Dictionary of the English Language*, Fourth Edition).
- **Momentum**—The term used to describe an invisible force which causes something in motion to continue in that motion with less effort than was required to initiate the motion.
- **Street Smarts**—The ability to read or interpret people's behavior and communication.
- **Rhythm**—The regular rise and fall in the flow of sound and speech.
- **Warm Market**—A salesperson's immediate circle of associates including friends and family.

There are a few small details that can make a big difference on a sales presentation. At first they may seem insignificant, but later they might be the only explanation for the loss of a sale.

There are two important things to practice and understand in all areas of business and life. First, it takes a big person to deal with little things and not themselves become small. And second, the true measure of a person is not determined from the ground up, but from the heart up. (Fribourg, 2007, *Personal Communication*)

Let's take a closer look at some of these details.

Control

What impact does control have on our sales endeavors? How can we exercise control in our sales presentations? The answer to these important questions is why control is one of "The Sales Savior's Six Secrets for being the Best Salesperson".

During the sales presentation, the salesperson and the potential customers participate in a joint communication process. A very successful distributor (high-level sales representative) I know used to say, "There are two sales forces at work in every home. Either you will sell the potential customer on the reasons why they should purchase your product, or they will sell you on the reasons why they shouldn't" (Bechalani, October 12, 1992, *Personal Communication*). In other words, whoever possessed the greatest amount of control over the situation would win. I believe this is true of most communication.

An example of control can be observed in children when they are engaged in communicative power struggles. One child may say something insulting to put down the other. If the other is able to retaliate with her communication in such a way that the control/power over the situation is regained, it is referred to as a "comeback."

"He that is firm in will mold the world to himself" (Goethe, u.d.).

In sales, it is very important to control the communication so that one always keeps the ability to readily have a comeback. This control must be exercised from the very beginning of the sales presentation with a goal of closing the sale and asking for the order. Let me explain why. If the salesperson goes through the sales presentation allowing the potential customers to maintain control throughout, but near the end of the presentation attempts to shift the control back to himself in order to close the sale, the shift in control may be negatively perceived by the potential customers and the sale can be lost.

Likewise, if a salesperson begins performing a sales presentation allowing the potential customer to control and dominate the communication, and then a third party is introduced to aid in the closing, the potential customer is likely to perceive the shift in control by the third party as an act of pressure, once again rejecting the reasoning behind the [third party's] closing techniques.

Why is this? The potential customers may believe that the salesperson's initial, non-dominating personality is his true personality and therefore reason that the second, in-control personality is actually a façade, merely used to apply pressure in order to force them to purchase.

At this point the potential customers may begin communicating defensively, a natural reaction to the shift in control, and the sale is likely lost. Another natural reaction to a shift in control is when the prospects fear the consequences of their loss of control and attempt to regain it by *offensively* communicating why they will not be purchasing; a sort of pre-emptive strike.

Both offensive and defensive communications are an indication that the prospects are no longer willing to listen. In sales, losing control of the situation is a lot like losing your balance. Expect to fall.

How can we use control effectively in our sales presentations? One of the best methods I have seen for maintaining control during a sales presentation is with Commitment Questions.

Commitment Questions accomplish several things. They help keep the potential customer's attention during the sales presentation, especially when their names are incorporated. They also help the prospective customers reason and draw conclusions about what they have learned. Commitment Questions test the integrity of the potential customer's ability to listen and comprehend the communication of the salesperson. They are an evaluating tool which the salesperson can use to gauge their teaching skills effectiveness.

However, Commitment Questions alone are not enough. A successful salesperson will bravely and boldly face any challenge during the sales presentation which attempts to shift the control from the salesperson to the potential customer. This would include such times as when the potential customer challenges known facts or logical statements. This may occur for several reasons. One is to challenge the salesperson's salesmanship and integrity (She wants to know whether you're really a great salesperson or an imposter). People claiming to be "genuine" salespeople but who were later known to not possess good sales techniques may have fooled them in the past [See p. 84], basically wasting their time and money.

Another reason potential customers might openly challenge commonly known facts and logical statements is because they do not understand or believe the facts or statements. In this scenario, more information and reason is required *before* the natural continuation of the sales presentation can resume. Many salespeople do not realize that by putting off regaining control in these instances may cause irreparable damage to the successful outcome of the sales presentation.

I have witnessed salespeople who were directly challenged by their potential customers, and instead of dealing with the problem, their response was to deny and ignore the attempt. This response fuels the potential customer's belief that you are not fully competent about your subject, which in turn is reason enough for them to suspend all listening and reasoning efforts, as they are now viewed as a waste of time. The control is immediately shifted to the potential customer because the perception of the salesperson's [good] credibility has been disproved.

The final reason why potential customers will challenge a salesperson on known facts and logical statements is due to a desire for attention, or to be generally argumentative. The latter is used to produce a negative relationship between the salesperson and the potential customer so that this can later be used as the basis for the suspension of listening and reasoning or even the dismissal of the salesperson.

Many people enjoy attention and being the center of it. During the sales presentation (even though the prospects are our focus) some potential customers feel that the salesperson is getting too much attention from their spouse, children, and/or friends, and thus seek to disrupt the sales presentation. This is sometimes done with bold challenges and at other times with what the attention seeker perceives as humor.

Nonetheless, it is an open challenge to the salesperson's **previously agreed upon** right to perform, and have that performance received by the audience. As stated earlier, all such challenges must be dealt with immediately! Any denial or repudiation on the part of the salesperson will have severe and negative effects on the possible sale.

So how can you deal with such challenges? A salesperson who recognizes the reasons for the challenge should first try to determine which of the categories the challenger belongs to and why they are making the challenge in the first place (this will require practice because in the actual situation, you will only have seconds to respond).

If the challenge is being made in order to denounce the integrity of the salesperson or because the challenger genuinely does not understand or believe the facts or statements made by the salesperson, the salesperson should assertively demonstrate how and why these logical facts or statements have been concluded, and do this to the satisfaction of the challenger.

If the challenge is being made to usurp the attention being shown the salesperson, the salesperson should cease the continuation of the sales presentation and patiently allow the potential customer to be at the center of everyone's attention. This can be done by asking the potential customer for more insight on their ideas or details regarding their humor.

During this time, the salesperson may sit down or take a position which appears to be more as a member of the audience than the center of attention. When all of the attention is focused on the attention seeker, they will usually wish to return to their participation as an audience member because being the main focus of attention may be less comfortable than they had first assumed. This is because it is much more satisfying for them to temporarily steal the attention rather than have it solely focused on them.

Instead of getting annoyed by this, view it optimistically as the most sincere form of flattery, imitation! Be patient when exercising this response because some attention seekers possess several minutes' worth of material before they will choose to surrender the attention back to you. However, if you handle this diplomatically, the prospects are unlikely to attempt another such challenge and the remaining sales presentation can be performed smoothly. In some cases the prospects feel a sense of obligation to purchase because they are embarrassed by their earlier challenging behavior.

For those attention seekers who want to create friction and completely spoil the sales environment, a different approach should be considered. If it becomes apparent that the only cause for the behavior is to create a scene, I admonish you not to succumb to their invitation to engage in a power struggle. Rather, turn away wrath with a genuine smile and compassion. Take solace in the belief that this potential customer is, or has been under some stress or trauma which may have affected his social skills at that moment, and he is inappropriately taking out his unrelated frustrations on you.

If this happens, perhaps try to rebook the sales presentation for another time, or in the case of severe personality conflicts, perhaps another salesperson would be better able to obtain the sale. This may be necessary in such cases as extreme racial or other prejudices or conflicts that are beyond your control.

Therefore, remember that the key to maintaining control is a combination of Commitment Questions and boldly facing any customer challenges (with a few rare exceptions).

Let's examine how a Commitment Question is used in the sales presentation to demonstrate informative communication. This example is taken from a Building-the-Problem segment of a water-trap vacuum cleaner presentation. The Commitment Questions are shown in bold:

> All vacuums have five things in common. They have an intake (where the air comes in), a motor (to make it run), a bag or filter (some place to collect the dust and dirt), an exhaust (some place for the air to come out), and a dusty, musty odor. **Have you ever smelt that odor before? Would you say that it is pleasant or unpleasant?** What that odor is, I am going to come back to.
>
> But what causes all the damage in the vacuums is the bag! The bag is what we call a porous filter. Pores are quite simply tiny holes. The paper and fiber of the bag is full of millions of these tiny holes, these pores, which let the air come out, but keep the dust and dirt inside. **If the bag didn't have these holes, it would explode wouldn't it? Let's say that this is a pore magnified.** (*Salesman illustrating with his hands.*) There are two kinds of dust and dirt. Large particles, that are larger than the holes and small particles, smaller than the holes.
>
> Let's just talk about the large particles for a minute. They come along, and since they are bigger than the holes, they block the holes in your vacuum bag, clogging them.
>
> Now let's say that you had five hundred holes in your vacuum sweeper bag, and as you began cleaning you blocked or clogged two hundred and fifty, of the

five hundred holes. **What would you have done to the efficiency of your vacuum?** Let's say that you continue to vacuum and now you have blocked four hundred of the five hundred holes. **What will you have done to the efficiency now?** So what you're telling me is that the more you use your vacuum, the less you actually clean?

Now, every time you hear something about your vacuum that you don't like I want you to mentally call a strike, like in the game of baseball. **Considering the fact that your vacuum clogs up with each use, and the more you use it the less it works, wouldn't you say that that is the first strike against it?** If I were a vacuum salesman and I tried to sell you a vacuum that was designed in such a way that the more you used it the less efficient it was, would you be willing to buy it from me? Is that the kind of machine that you would want in your home?

Now let's talk about the small particles. They enter your vacuum bag and because they are smaller than the holes, they blow right through. They follow the air, which now goes to cool down the motor. **If the motor gets hot and dirty, do you think it will last longer, or shorter?** This is what we call planned obsolescence. Vacuums today are built to break down. **If your vacuum were designed so that it would break down prematurely, wouldn't you consider that to be strike two?** If I were a vacuum salesman who tried to sell you a machine that the more you used the less it worked, and that was built to break down, is this the machine you would want in your home?

(*Salesman flicks bag with his finger and plugs the intake with his hand. With the other hand he turns on the vacuum.*)

This is what comes out of your vacuum when it is clogged. (*Nothing comes out.*)

This is what comes out of your vacuum when it's not clogged. (*Vacuum salesman removes his hand from the intake and a cloud of dust billows into the air.*)

Wow! **Did you know this was happening?** Is that cleaning to you? Is it cleaning if you suck up the dirt and dust and then blow it all over your home for you to breathe and re-clean? If you had a maid come into your home with a bucket of dirt and a scoop, and she began throwing dust and dirt everywhere, what would you do with the maid?

(Potential customer says, "Throw her out!)

If you wouldn't let a person throw dust and dirt all over your home, does it make any more sense to have a machine that does the same thing to you? So if you'd throw the maid out, what should you do with this?

(Salesman points to customer's old vacuum. Potential customer says: "Throw it out!")

Making your house dirtier than when you started cleaning, now that's a big strike three. **After three strikes in baseball, what do we do with the player?**

(Potential customer says, "He's out!")

What should you do with this machine?

(Potential customer says, "Throw it out.")

Do you remember that unpleasant odor we talked about earlier? Objectionable odors stem from the breeding and multiplying of germs and bacteria. Germs and bacteria need three favorable conditions in which to breed and multiply best. These are a warm area, a dark area, and a filthy place. **Inside your vacuum bag would you say it's warm? Is it dark? Is it filthy?** So what you're telling me is that you don't own a great cleaning system, but instead you have a great incubator. You clean your home, sucking in everything from kitty litter to moldy potato chips, then you put the vacuum away in a warm, dark closet where it begins to incubate germs and bacteria. A few days later, when you turn your vacuum on again, you're sucking in the clean air from your home, forcing it through a bag filled with germs and disease, and then blowing that air back out into your home. **Does this sound healthy or unhealthy?**

How do we know that it's germs and disease? Because we can smell it! **When meat goes bad in the refrigerator, we don't have to eat it to know it has begun to decay?** We can smell it! **What about a rotten egg, or sour milk?**

(*Potential customer says, "You can smell it!"*)

It's the same with your vacuum. Some people have claimed that the air coming out of their vacuum smells good because they use Carpet Fresh powder or a few drops of scented oil on the bag. **Does that eliminate the odor from the germs and bacteria, or merely mask them?**

(*Potential customer says, "Just masks them."*)

Do you think this sounds healthy or unhealthy?

What if you were to cook a thanksgiving dinner which was complete with wine, candles, turkey, gravy, mashed potatoes, stuffing, and corn, and then decided to do some vacuuming before your guests arrived. And when you begin, you notice that your vacuum bag has been removed, and you don't have another to replace it. You decide to go ahead with the cleaning in spite of not having a bag and you can see dust and filth blowing out of the vacuum and contaminating not only the air, but also the food and the beverages you have prepared. The wine glasses now have an inch of sludge on the top. The once golden-brown turkey is now covered in dirt and the mashed potatoes are speckled with filth. Suddenly, your guests arrive. **Do you think they will want to eat the food, drink the wine, or even breathe the air?**

What is the difference between using a vacuum like yours, which blows dust and dirt into the air and everywhere, and using a vacuum with no bag at all? Your family is being forced to eat, drink, and breathe the filth from the streets! **Does that sound healthy or unhealthy? Is that the machine you really want to continue to use for the rest of your life?**

Is the health and welfare of your indoor environment important to you? How soon would you want to take care of a problem like this?

If you knew that they were selling machines that are designed so that the more you used them the less they worked, and that were built to break down, and that would blow dust and dirt everywhere, and that would poison the food, beverages, and air you breathe, would you keep one in your home?

Have you ever noticed that when you change the bag it always seems to feel more like a pillow or a loaf of bread, rather than a pail of sand? If you look inside your vacuum you'll see 80% fluffy, soft material and only 20% sand and grit. Do you know why?

You might say that with a vacuum the exhaust is what determines the intake. The faster the air can come out of the vacuum is as fast as the air can come into the vacuum; and of course the slower the air can escape your vacuum then that is how slowly the air can come in.

Now when you first start vacuuming with a new bag and clean filters, all the holes in the filters are open, so therefore the air can escape quickly. That means that the air can come in quickly and that is what you want. This way it can suck in the heavier pieces of sand and grit. After just a few minutes those holes begin to clog up. Now the air can only escape slowly. Therefore the air can only come in slowly. Instead of picking up the heavier sand and grit, it settles for the lighter, fluffier material; your carpet fibers.

Did you buy your vacuum to remove the sand and grit and protect your carpet, or did you buy your vacuum to remove your carpet and make more room for the dirt?

(*Potential customer says: "To get rid of the dirt!"*)

If we look inside your vacuum, what are you getting rid of the most, the dirt or your carpet?

Knowing these five facts about vacuums, would you say that owning one is a good decision or a bad decision? Promise me that if there was something better to clean your home with you would use it. (Vidovich, 1991)

This is just a small segment of problem building in a vacuum salesperson's presentation. As shown by this segment, problem building incorporates good, informative storytelling with conviction and reasoning, and is packed with one Commitment Question after another.

I saw potential customers who were both shocked and amazed at the poor quality of their vacuums. In all honesty, after reading the segment and reasoning on it yourself, aren't there some doubts in your mind about your own vacuum? Notice the informative phrases are always concluded with Commitment Questions which complement and conclude each thought as well as strengthen the salesperson's convictions?

When the potential customer gives the predicted answers, the salesperson knows it is permissible to move on to another point. If the Commitment Questions are answered incorrectly, it is surely a sign that the prospects did not understand or did not believe some portion of the communication. In this event, the salesperson should attempt to re-explain the section that is unclear. You may wish to use different stories and analogies which the potential customer can better relate to.

The best examples of Commitment Questions I have heard come from children. A sweet, innocent face looks up to her father and asks if he will buy her a toy. The father replies, "Yes, honey. We'll get you a toy later if you're good." The little girl follows up with, "You promise, don't you Daddy?" This is an example of a Commitment Question! Let's look at the difference between a good Commitment Question and a poor one.

Example A) Good Commitment Question

The animal proteins in meat are not good for the human body. It appears that the human body was not originally designed for the consumption of other animals. The consumption of animal proteins significantly lowers the effectiveness of the immune system, and raises serious health concerns. **Does eating the flesh of other animals sound healthy or unhealthy?**

Example B) Bad Commitment Question

The animal proteins in meat are not good for the human body. It appears that the human body was not originally designed for the consumption of other animals. The consumption of animal proteins significantly lowers the effectiveness of the immune system, and raises serious health concerns. **How do you feel about that?**

In example A, the possible answers are limited to either "healthy" or "unhealthy." Based on the factual information supplied immediately prior to the Commitment Question, it is probable that the potential customer will reply, "Unhealthy."

In example B, however, the possible answers are endless. Understand that Commitment Questions are not just questions at the conclusion of an informative story, but rather a persuasive tool used to influence the customer's reasoning process and create controlled reactions. The art of selling is morphed from society's perception that obtaining a sale is luck to it being a skill grounded in predicting psychological and behavioral patterns and adeptly interpreting those patterns.

Imagine that getting a sale is like trying to catch an oily pig. Yes, you can run straight after him, but he may randomly run in any direction, and even if you manage to catch him he is likely to slip away. A lot of times this is what it feels like for the struggling salesperson.

So what can we do to make things better? First set up a route or routes for the pig to escape, that lead to a more controlled environment conducive for catching him (In other words, a place where he will have very little room to escape from-a trap if you like). This is what Commitment Questions do in your demonstration. You anticipate that the customer will wish to escape from the purchase, especially when your demo is… let's say "under construction". The Commitment Questions negate possible escape routes and lead to a place (mentally) where the sale is easily obtained. Ah ha! You've got that slippery sucker now!

Please Note: *Regardless of what your product or service is, these basic principles may be adapted to your needs when you are able to understand how and why they are successful.*

Consistency

"I pray to be like the ocean, with soft currents, maybe waves at times. More and more, I want the consistency rather than the highs and the lows" (Barrymore, n.d.).

It is very important that a salesperson try their best to be consistent in their actions. This includes acquiring leads, contacting clients, performing sales presentations, and recruiting. Remember the fable of the tortoise and the hare. The reason consistency is so important is because results are so directly related to it. No salesperson wants peaks and valleys in their income.

Consistency is not always recommended in the beginning when you may find yourself constantly reengineering. However, as you become more certain of your sales routines, it is a very important factor. Consistently applying yourself and maintaining an earnest desire to achieve your goals significantly increases the likelihood of their fulfillment. It is better to be a shining star, even a dull one, than the brightest spark from a candle in the wind.

Many at first burst into the sales world with enthusiasm and zeal, but seemingly just as quickly dissipate and disappear.

When you are comfortable with the best sales techniques for you, and find you have personalized them you will always have to fight against the tyranny of complacency, while juggling the strong desire for consistency.

Momentum

"Getting momentum going is the most difficult part of the job, and often taking the first step is enough to prompt you to make the best of your day" (McKain, n.d.).

"Success requires first expending ten units of effort to produce one unit of results. Your momentum will then produce ten units of results with each unit of effort" (Givens, u.d.).

Momentum can be described as an invisible pair of wings which lift a salesperson seemingly out of what is capable and imaginable. Momentum is the restorer of balance. Sometimes we might get into a bit of a slump. But life seems to have a way of restoring balance. Once we get going again, momentum pushes us along, seemingly creating sales even at those times when we ought not to achieve them, based solely on our sales performance.

In my classes, I illustrate momentum with a diagram (p. 100) depicting a salesperson questioning how and even if he can negotiate the mountain to reach his goal. In the second part, he carries the weight and burden of a heavy workload while trudging up the mountain. At this stage, those who lack the proper personality traits mentioned in the previous chapters usually give up.

There is one sad thing not shown in the illustration: the number of people who gave up just before they reached the pinnacle; giving up just before their momentum was about to carry them to their dreams. It is difficult to know where on the mountain you are. This depends on the enormity of your aspirations and the length of time you have been working to achieve them.

It is sometimes difficult to feel the presence of momentum because most of us would prefer to believe that a continuing streak of sales be attributed to our own personal skill level rather than admit the aid of some invisible force. However, it is much easier to interpret and feel the void of momentum. When nothing much is happening, you don't have it!

A wise salesperson and frustrated farmer once taught me that salespeople are always doing one of three things. "They're either growing, or trying, or they're dying" (Sanders, 1991).

Ask yourself what you are doing.

Momentum Diagram

A) At first you are trying to figure out how to sell.

B) While you are discovering how to sell, the workload seems heavy.

C) By maintaining control & consistency you are rewarded with momentum!

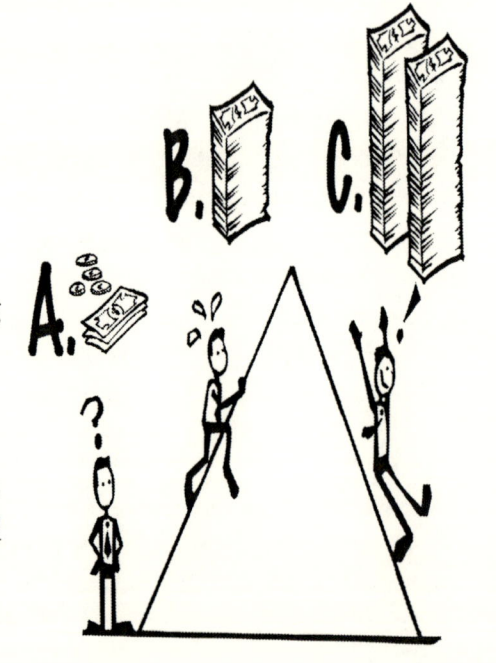

More Details

At first, when diagnosing your sales presentation to determine your closing average, most people tend to concentrate on their achievements. This is because they need sales to reaffirm their self-confidence. Later, as the accomplished salesperson matures in the art of selling, moreover in the science of it, she will tend to examine more closely not what generated her sales in the past, but what may have been missing that could have cost her a sale. Otherwise, many accomplished salespeople would find contentment at a particular closing percentage that provides a standard of living which they feel comfortable with.

One thing I have observed in the very best salespeople is that they are always stretching. They are always growing, and seeking out new and possibly preferred methods for generating sales and answering objections. The accomplished salesperson knows not only how to behave and communicate, but more importantly what the ultimate affect of any action or communication will be on the average potential customer. This affect is what governs a salesperson's actions.

Some may claim that salespeople are just good talkers and that they snowball their way through life. This view of sales people is as shallow as it is ignorant. True, some who claim to be salespeople know little of the craft. However, as I stated earlier, imitation is the greatest form of flattery! The ability to read people, sometimes known as street smarts, is the paintbrush in a salesperson's Picasso-like hands.

Another important detail to keep in mind is your facial expressions. A common mistake some salespeople have made is when their facial expressions don't reflect their communications. This causes confusion in the potential clients because they are not sure what you want them to think or feel. For example, if you were talking about a deadly disease in order to sell a vaccine, you should not be smiling and laughing. This may seem obvious, but similar situations have occurred, causing the potential customer to not take the salesperson seriously?

Rhythm is also very important to a salesperson's presentation. A great sales presentation has a rhythm. The rising and falling of the salesperson's voice feels like a song, lyrically enchanting the potential customers. At times it is intense, and at other times it is as gentle as a father whispering a lullaby to his newborn. A conductor could appear to be directing it, while a sales presentation was in progress. A very small detail, but it is one that cannot be illustrated in words. You feel it when you are present during a great sales presentation, yet you may have difficulty putting your finger on it. It is easier to illustrate the lack of rhythm when observing a sales presentation that is choppy or seems to have lost its flow.

The rhythm and tonality used in a sales presentation is unique to the sales presentation and is something that many apprenticing salespeople have difficulty with. This is because their concentration often rests with the conjugation of the actual words used by a salesperson.

Many believe if they simply learn to mimic another salesperson's words, they will automatically be as accomplished. Of course, if this were true, companies could simply train parrots to sell, and the sales force would be obsolete. I submit that whoever coined the phrase "these products sell themselves" understood that the greatest sale is one in which the customer believes he has not actually been sold a product, but rather has deduced that it is the ultimate fulfillment of his needs independent of the salesperson. This kind of selling would simply not be possible without the recognition and respect for rhythm and tonality! Again, I assert that a great sales presentation plays like a beautiful song written and performed from the heart.

Another small but important detail is your ability to perform three-dimensional sales presentations. Many salespeople can only see two sides: the seller and the potential customer. What is often overlooked is the all-important space in between. When we are selling, we should try to animate our sales presentation and our potential customers if we wish to make the strongest impact. For example, at times when demonstrating concern for your prospect, you may lower your voice and draw near to the prospects. Other times you may become more animated using your hands to communicate, and thus desire to create space between yourself and the prospects. In this way, we can take advantage of the third dimension, which makes everything we do more interesting.

What about physical and mental barriers? When you first meet a person or group of people it is natural to feel those little butterflies in your stomach. A salesperson who doesn't get nervous is unnatural. No matter how much experience you have, there is always that little bit of tickle in your gut. That is why it is so important for the salesperson to break the ice by talking and getting to know the potential customer prior to beginning the sales presentation.

On the potential customer's end, breaking the ice is especially important because it puts the potential customer at ease. I used to always mention that though I was selling a product, I was not there to wrestle them for their pocketbook. I did this with a smile and a soothing tone, and the potential customers would sometimes visibly sigh with relief. It can be just as nerve-wracking to be a potential customer as it is to be the salesperson. Once you have removed any mental barriers, you will need to work on any physical ones which might cause distractions.

The last small, but monumental detail has to do with referral leads. If you are on a sales presentation and you have asked for referrals, don't be afraid to ask specifically for your target market, such as homeowners, gainfully employed full-time, creditworthy, *et cetera*. You will always fail to get that which you don't ask for. After you have jotted down information about each referral—names, where they live, marital status, whether they have children or pets, telephone number, workplace and type, whether or not they are homeowners or renters, and what relation they are to the persons referring them—you will want to prioritize them. This is accomplished by asking the potential customer a series of questions.

Consider the following example:

"Now that we have these names down on paper, let me ask you a question, Crystal and Perry. If you were me, and you were trying to sell the (name your product), who would you go see first, and why?

"Who would you go see next and why?"

Repeat this step until all the leads have been "qualified." The next step requires a similar question. It is one that is used to determine any potential bad apples.

"Crystal and Perry, if you were me and you were trying to sell the (name your product), who would you not go see, and why?"

At this point, you may hear about credit problems, relationship problems, employment problems and various others. This is not meant to be discouraging, however. It is in perfect harmony with what we know about leads: "Quantity yes, but quality first!"

I have observed terrific results when salespeople have taken the entire process one step further by asking their customer/audience member to initiate the contact of the referrals. In today's marketplace, a general distrust for advertising mediums is on the rise. This includes the direct salesperson. This is generally the number one reason for the emergence of successful network marketing companies. Recruiting individuals to sell in a "warm" marketplace can dispel this strengthening distrust.

By encouraging your customers to contact their warm market leads on your behalf, you can overcome any reservations you might have previously held regarding telephone work, and at the same time subvert the potential for leads to dismiss the viewing of your sales presentation. You may then choose to have your customer call you in order to let you know which of the leads has agreed to view your presentation. This is best performed when you are offering the initial customer a premium gift of a value that exceeds the effort they will have to exert in order to help you arrange the appointments. By doing this, the customer can ask his warm-market leads to do him a favor. Consider the following script.

"Hello, is Tammy there? Hi, Tammy! It's your brother Stephen. How are ya? Great! I was just calling to ask you for a favor. Marionette and I just watched a demonstration of a really neat product called the (name product). Have you ever heard of it? Well, we were really impressed with the (name product) and we are currently in the process of getting one. While the guy was showing us the product, we were given an opportunity to get a thousand dollars' worth of free gifts if we could get four of our friends to take a peek at the product.

"We received a beautiful gift just for watching the presentation, so we're expecting the other gifts to be of the same high quality. I was wondering if you would do me a favor and see a presentation at your place? You are under no obligation to buy or pay for anything either, just take a look. We would really appreciate it, and you would get a beautiful gift just for watching. Could we count on you to help us out? Great! Thanks, Tammy.

"Do me a favor and call us after you see the presentation and tell us what you think, okay? The guy/gal's name is (salesperson's name) and I'm going to let them know that you've agreed to see the show, so they can call you and make an appointment, okay? Thanks, Tammy. I'll talk to ya later. Bye."

In this script, the customer is actually initiating the contact with his warm-market leads on behalf of the salesperson. As you can see, a premium gift is required to compensate the viewer for his time.

Premium gifts can be purchased at wholesale outlets such as B&F Systems or Maxam, located in Dallas, Texas. There you can find fantastic gift premiums at amazing prices. These often have their retail price stamped on the packaging and thus aid in the building of value. It is critical to this process that the gift be tangible and of considerable value.

My experience has shown that a brightly illustrated coupon for a vacation or pizza is as valuable as any non-monetary piece of paper. If you desire to acquire premium appointments, an increased hold-up percentage, and an increased closing ratio, a *premium* demo gift is a small price to pay. It may cost as much as ten dollars, but the benefits far outweigh the cost in this scenario. Far too many who have failed to accomplish their dreams can been likened to an absent-minded janitor in a gymnasium full of money. Instead of picking up the bills on the floor he concentrates on the coins, fearful he might miss out somehow. It is the first realization that must be concluded by every entrepreneur: you have to be willing to risk money to make money!

Of course, it isn't the most pleasant feeling when we are asked to risk financial resources. Consequently, all contributing factors must be thoroughly weighed in order for these risks to be educated risks based on probabilities. I have also observed, generally speaking, that the smaller the risk, the smaller the reward.

Another approach suggests that the salesperson go even further by empowering and motivating the customer to not only contact their warm-market leads, but also to book the appointment spontaneously before the sales person has even left their home. This certainly does narrow the field of possible negative influences on the customer. It also empowers the salesperson because they can still be successful in generating appointments even if they were for any reason unable to generate the sale. This diffuses the negative emotions of rejection by focusing the salesperson's attention on the future rather than the past or present.

The last pitfall I want to warn you about in this section is what I call word-whiskers. Many people have a tendency to use certain words repeatedly when they have become nervous. Some ask their potential customers questions and repeat all their answers. Some use "Uh" as a crutch while they remember what they want to say next.

Physical quirks can also be construed as nervousness, e.g., rolling your eyes repeatedly, fidgeting, biting your nails, or raising your eyebrows. Not only are these not conducive to generating the sale, but the potential customer may also misinterpret them.

All of these little details make a big difference! Think of a billiard ball, and while shooting the cue ball you may only be off by a small degree, the divergence increases with time, completely compromising the accuracy of the shot. This is how it is in sales. Small details, when compounded over the duration of the presentation, can compromise the ability to generate the sale. Remember that close only counts in horseshoes and hand grenades. Accuracy in sales can be improved, but only if we are willing to agree that generating sales is not a game of chance but a game of choice.

Chapter 8

Great Salespeople Build Value!

- **Buying Temperature**—A term used to describe the degree to which the potential customers are disposed to buying.
- **Value**—The potential customer's perceived idea of what the product is worth, i.e., the cost of the product prior to the customer's knowledge of the actual price of the product (see illustration on p. 118).
- **Burden of Ignorance**—This is a term used describe the result of a shift in power/control during communication when one party is made to feel embarrassed or stupid for having purchased a product or service with poor value, out of ignorance.
- **Buyer's Remorse**—A feeling experienced by the customer post sale that usually results in the cancellation of the sale.
- **"Know" Threshold**—A measurement used when calculating the buying temperature and amount of value built in a sales presentation. If the sale is made and

the salesperson leaves the prospect's home the buying temperature will drop. If it drops below the "Know" threshold it can cause buyer's remorse (illustrated on p. 118).

- ➢ **Purchase Demarcation**—The measurement of buying temperature at which the sale is made, as illustrated on p. 118.

What is Value?

What is value, and what direct influence does it have over our sales careers? People today rarely use the word value. When they do use it, it is usually to describe a fantastic bargain they found while shopping or to describe a quality product for a reasonable price. If you were asked, "What is value?" how would you define it? Value is the potential customer's perceived idea of what the product is worth, i.e., the cost prior to their knowledge of the actual price. Is the price the value? No, it is not. Frequently, the reason a sale is lost is simply because the price doesn't match the value according to the customer.

For example, consider John who was interested in purchasing a new computer. He did some research on the internet and found that the typical asking price for what he wanted was around fifteen hundred dollars. John decided to wait until the next year to buy the computer. He reasoned that by then, even better computers would be available.

For fun, John attended a technology workshop where new products were being introduced into the market. John found a computer which met all his needs and even came with several extra functions that would make his job much easier. There was no price on the computer, but John reasoned that with its increased capabilities, the computer would cost around two thousand dollars, maybe more. John, curious, asked the representative how much the computer cost. He explained that it was only seven hundred and fifty dollars. Before the salesperson could finish, John plopped down his credit card and said, "I'll take it!"

When we look at this scenario, what was the value of the new computer John looked at? Was it:

A) $1500.00   B) $2000.00   C) $750.00

What was the price of the new computer? Was it:

A) $750.00   B) $1500.00   C) $2000.00

If you said that the value was two thousand dollars and the price was seven hundred fifty dollars, you were right! Understanding what value is and how it works helps us to better understand why sales are lost. Value is the potential customer's perceived idea of what the product is worth. In other words, value is what the customer believes a product will cost prior to their knowing the actual price of the product. The reason John changed his mind about waiting a year to buy a computer and instead bought one on the spot was because the value, to John, was more than double the actual asking price. He reasoned that he might never get another opportunity for such a tremendous deal.

Let's look at another scenario. Janice went to the car lot with the specific intention of buying a car. She needed one so that she could get to college on time this year. Janice was interested in a compact-sized car that would be good on gas and easy on her purse strings. She had saved up twenty-two thousand dollars and was excited about purchasing a new car.

When she arrived at the car lot, a sales representative came out to greet her. He wasn't very experienced in selling and hadn't taken the time to get to know very many benefits and features of the cars he was selling. He asked her what she wanted and Janice said, "Nothing really. I'm just looking." The sales representative told Janice he would be at his desk if she needed anything.

After a short time of looking at a compact car that had no sticker price listed, the sales representative returned to Janice and told her what a great deal he could get for her. Janice figured that the car must be worth around twelve thousand dollars. She wasn't really very excited about the car.

The sales representative told Janice that he would go speak with his manager so he could get her the best possible deal. Janice agreed and while she waited, she wondered if this car was really worth as much as twelve thousand dollars. She thought it might be even less. Soon, the sales representative returned and said,

"Janice, you're not going to believe what my boss said he'll do for you. You can get the car for only twenty-two thousand dollars." Janice was shocked and quickly decided that she did not want the car. Even though she had enough money to buy it, she decided it cost far more than she felt it was worth.

She went down the street to another car lot where the sales representative took a keen and genuine interest in Janice right from the start. She asked Janice what kind of car she was looking for, and if she had a car now. Janice explained her situation and the saleswoman said she had just the car for Janice. They picked from an assortment of colors until Janice admitted she had always wanted a red one. The two of them sat in the car while the saleswoman listed all the features and benefits of, not only the car, but also the dealership and their service department. The car was a convertible, which really excited Janice, the seats had lumbar support and the car even had heated mirrors. There was a special place for Janice's sunglasses and there were several drink holders. The car also came with a very attractive sound system. The saleswoman complimented Janice on how nice she looked in the car. Janice felt really good just sitting in it.

When Janice got out of the car she had a disappointed look on her face. She reasoned that a car as nice as this one would be out of her price range, especially since the last car she looked at seemed so expensive. She said that she was tired and needed to go home and think about it.

The saleswoman said she might be able to speak to her manager and get a great deal on the car for Janice, because it had previously been a leased vehicle. The mileage was less than two thousand kilometers and it looked brand new. Janice agreed to wait for the saleswoman, but wasn't very optimistic. When the saleswoman returned, she said,

"You're not going to believe it. My boss says you can have it for only fifteen thousand dollars!"

Janice's face now displayed her decision, loud and clear. Her smile stretched from ear to ear.

"I'll take it!" she said excitedly, and hugged the saleswoman.

Notice that in Janice's first encounter she had enough money to purchase the car. Not only that, but she intended to purchase a car. Yet she declined because she did not think that the value of the car matched the price they were asking and concluded that the car was too expensive. Her perception of value was very low because the sales representative had failed to build up the value of the first car by pointing out all the great benefits and features.

In Janice's second encounter, she was preconditioned to reject the saleswoman's sales techniques because of her previous experience. But look how the saleswoman was able to sell Janice the car despite Janice's unlikelihood of purchasing that night. The saleswoman built the value higher than what she already knew the actual price would be. While Janice was busy thinking carefully about the purchase, the saleswoman knew that if Janice was teetering on the idea, she would surely be able to tip the scales in her favor if she were to come back with an asking price that was considerably lower than the value in Janice's head. Janice's emotional state was completely reversed! She began with cynicism and negative feelings about the whole process, but when she finally decided to buy the car, Janice was ecstatic! She went from not appreciating salespeople at all to hugging one in her happiness. What made all the difference in both John and Janice's situations? Value!

How to Build Value

Building value is one of the easiest and most powerful weapons in the salesperson's arsenal. To build value, the salesperson must evaluate the product. What about this product makes it appealing? Many times manufacturers will provide all the legwork. On the packaging of many products today, you find key selling points; points from which the salesperson can build value. Take for example the illustration shown on p. 113.

The advertising here, shown for Comfy Boy recliners, illustrates how manufacturers of some products can make it easier for the salesperson to build value. Sometimes there is very little provided by the manufacturer and the salesperson must evaluate the product and then formulate a number of value-building points which will strategically aid the salesperson in stirring conviction, motivation, excitement, and a sense of urgency within the potential customer. On page 113, you will see an example of how this can be done using a product void of manufacturer's advertising aids.

BBDs

One of the forefathers of every sale is the recognition by the salesperson that every potential customer wants, and even feels they need, a bigger, better deal (BBD). It doesn't matter what the product or service. It doesn't matter the size, color, or duration of relationship between the salesperson and the potential customer. Everybody wants a BBD!

Consider this illustration: Tamara walks up to Bonita and says, "That is a beautiful dress you are wearing, where did you get it?"

"You'll never believe what I paid for this dress. Just try to guess," replies Bonita.

"I don't know, but I bet around fifty dollars."

"Nope! I bought this at a sidewalk sale last year for only ten dollars!"

In this scenario, note that Bonita feels a sense of pride and accomplishment, as well as complimented, when she explains how little she paid for the dress. Why does she feel that way? Because Bonita feels that she has purchased a product whose value was in fact greater than the price. Most people, like Tamara, will believe she paid considerably more then she actually did.

What is the root of a BBD? Is it getting a product for a small amount of money? Is it buying poor quality products? Not necessarily. Some claim that the reason their products are more expensive than others is because their products have a higher quality; better raw materials were used in manufacturing and the workmanship is better. However, do not be fooled by this. A great feeling upon an achieved sale is what every great salesperson is ultimately after. Both the customer and the salesperson should experience that great feeling. The salesperson, for having obtained the sale, and the customer, for receiving the product desired at what he considers to be a great price. In other words, everybody wants the biggest bang for his buck!

Look at the illustration on the following page and you'll notice how the value-building notations have been assessed, commonly seen on manufacturer's labels.

- ☑ Handcrafted in the USA.
- ☑ Soft, durable leather material.
- ☑ Heated seat and back cushion.
- ☑ Treated with Stain Guard.
- ☑ Double-stuffed back and seat cushions for added comfort.
- ☑ Non-marking cherry wood legs.
- ☑ Perfect for relaxing & watching television.
- ☑ 25 Year Warrantee.
- ☑ 2500 retail outlets.
- ☑ Producing quality furniture since 1891.

Comfy Boy Recliners

NEW

Since 1891

Value-Building Exercise

Let's examine this globe with an eye toward value building. Notice it does not have any advertising notations. What can we say to build value? Remember, you can use physical attributes and even the absence of attributes to build value. Try to incorporate as many of the five senses as possible when building value. Observe the following interaction.

Salesperson: "Notice that it does not have a foul odor, like other plastic products. Go ahead and smell it."

Potential Customer: "That's true."

Salesperson: "Now listen as I throw it to you. What did you hear?"

Potential Customer: "Nothing."

Salesperson: "That is because of its unique wind resistant design."

Lack of odor and noise are just two examples of value building based on the absence of tangible physical qualities. Of course, it is always recommended to incorporate the obvious value-building attributes when attempting a value build. These include: size, weight, color, texture, durability, and referencing value. Portability, mapping accuracy, and the ability to easily store this globe also make it an asset for every home.

As you can see, building value is essentially using your creativity to make a list of the obvious characteristics of a product. See if you can build value on some the products around you. Practice this procedure until it becomes natural and you'll be a value-driven sales professional.

Another worthy value-building exercise is to practice building value on your friends, family, and associates whenever you're talking to others. This is a surefire way to watch your relationships blossom.

Lowering the Price is Not the Answer

Let's consider why simply getting a lower price is not the key to value. A home security salesperson knocked on all the doors on a particular street. After many rejections, one lady who lived in the neighborhood agreed to watch the sales presentation The salesperson followed all "The Sales Savior's Six Secrets for being the Best Salesperson" and pointed out all the fantastic benefits the householder could receive by installing one of their home security packages. The lady was very impressed and enthusiastic about the idea. She imagined that the cost of such a system would be around two thousand dollars, but the salesperson explained that it would only be twelve hundred and that she could pay for it over one year's time with no interest. The lady purchased the new security system and the sale was made. She was very, very happy about her purchase; especially the part about having paid only twelve hundred dollars.

Meanwhile, down the street, an associate of the salesperson employed by the same security company managed to obtain a presentation. The man invited the salesperson in. This particular salesperson had had three years' worth of sales experience but he had never learned the empowering effects of building value. He robotically and methodically sounded off his pitch. He did not believe that everyone wanted a BBD. Instead, he believed that a no-nonsense approach would be just as effective. So instead of starting with the company's suggested retail price and coming down, he immediately showed the potential customer the "bottom line." The potential customer had been mildly interested during the presentation, but when it was concluded and the salesperson showed the man the price of twelve hundred dollars, he decided not to purchase the security system.

The salesperson asked why the potential customer would not purchase. The man replied that he thought the price was too high. The salesperson asked the man if he would change his mind if the price could be lowered. The potential customer said he was unsure, but that he would consider it. Because the salesman had used his no-nonsense approach and already revealed the bottom line price, he had very little bargaining leverage. He was to be paid a commission of four hundred dollars for every sale, so he used his commission to barter. The salesperson lowered the price to nine hundred dollars and the potential customer reluctantly agreed to purchase the security system.

The salesman was excited for having made the sale, plus one hundred dollars in commission. While it was less than he normally received, he reasoned that one hundred dollars was better than nothing. He did notice that the customer was not as excited as most customers are when they purchase, but he did not consider this to be of any great importance.

The security company who employed these two sales reps later mailed out a survey requesting that their customers evaluate the sales process and comment on their experience. The first woman claimed that she was extremely satisfied and thoroughly enjoyed the sales process. She even recommended that the company consider giving her salesperson a promotion and pay raise. The second customer was not so impressed with his sales experience and wanted to know if he could cancel his order. He claimed that he didn't feel that the product was worth the nine hundred dollars he was charged.

When we consider these two scenarios, it is clear what a profound affect value building has on the sales process. Notice the first customer paid three hundred dollars more for the same security system, yet she is considerably more satisfied! Was it because her product was better? No. They both received identical products. Obviously it was not because she paid less. So why is she so much more pleased with her sales experience? The answer is: because her salesperson understood the principals behind value building and a customer's need for a BBD. She believed the value (her perceived cost) was two thousand dollars, and when the salesperson reduced the asking price to twelve hundred dollars, the lady felt as if she were getting a savings of eight hundred dollars. This is the reason she reacted with such pleasure. She felt that she received a quality product for almost fifty percent off because the actual price was so much less than her perceived cost. That was the BBD she wanted and needed.

The salesperson was also very happy because he had earned his full commission of four hundred dollars.

The second customer probably believed the value/perceived cost to be around nine hundred to one thousand dollars. When the salesman revealed the asking price of twelve hundred dollars the customer immediately refused. He also felt insulted that the salesperson would attempt to overcharge him for the security system. When the salesman lowered the price to nine hundred dollars, which in the salesperson's mind was a great favor, the man still considered the purchase for a bit before agreeing. He did not feel that he was getting a BBD. Instead he thought that he was paying the regular price, hence his reluctant attitude. The salesman was excited but the customer wasn't. This is a win-lose scenario. All great sales, however, should be (and are) win-win scenarios. Both the salesperson and the customer must win! What this illustrates is that price reduction is not a form of value building, but rather the excuse for a lack thereof!

Value is the potential customer's perceived idea of what the price/cost is prior to knowing the actual price. Therefore, value is not based on actual fact, but rather on the potential customer's idea that the price will be a certain amount. To apprenticing salespeople this fact is of great comfort and excitement because it asserts that the salesperson maintains the ability to influence the emotional state of the potential customer by augmenting the value.

Not only did the absence of value building eventually cost the second salesman the sale, but it also significantly diminished his possible commission, all while leaving a bad taste in the customer's mouth. Certainly this is an example of what not to do. This brings me to an astonishing revelation.

Throughout the years, I have witnessed many salespeople wondering why sales are elusive to some and yet flow freely to others. The answer is value building. I have heard others complain that once their sales have been accomplished, their customers have asked to cancel the order. This is "buyer's remorse."

Sales are accomplished due to the combination of two equally important and verifiable powers held by the customer: emotion and logic. Logic tells the prospective customer why they should (or should not) purchase an item, and emotion is the reason behind their level of urgency for purchasing. A potential customer will often purchase a product or service on the spot if he heats up emotionally—with positive emotion, of course—and becomes enthusiastic and excited about a product or service. This is the father of impulse buying!

However, with the progression of time, the customer's emotional attachment to the product may cool off. This is often when the customer expresses a desire to cancel the order. Simply stated, the customer cannot remember why he purchased the product and feels almost as if he had been under some form of hypnosis when he bought it.

On the opposite end of the spectrum, if the customer purchases solely based on logic, the product is likely to be prioritized as the first to be canceled should any other needs surface, especially if those needs are emotionally charged due to outside influences such as family, friends, work associates, and competing sales organizations.

Consider the following example: Donna purchased a beautiful new set of encyclopedias for her family thinking that they would really help the kids with their schoolwork. The salesperson requested a list of friends, relatives and associates who might also be potential customers. He asked Donna to call them and see if any of them would be willing to see the sales presentation. Donna was excited about her new encyclopedias and figured that most of her friends would also be interested in such a terrific deal.

When Donna called her sister, she was not expecting the response she received. Her sister asked her how much the encyclopedias were and began criticizing her for her purchase. Her sister claimed that she could buy the same encyclopedias from a store she knew of for half as much. Donna felt misled and promptly called the salesman to cancel her order. Can you see how outside influences can be the cause of buyer's remorse?

Perhaps if the salesperson had taken more time to better educate Donna as to what benefits and features made the product more valuable than the competition, then Donna might have felt empowered enough to shift the weight of ignorance back onto her sister instead of trying to shoulder it for herself.

Sometimes it is the competing salesperson who attempts to discredit or impose a burden of ignorance upon a customer in order to liberate the customer's financial resources and purchase his product instead.

Finally, buyer's remorse can frequently be attributed to a lack of properly established value. Observe the thermometer illustrated below. Imagine that in the same way water has a precise temperature at which it boils, (100 degrees Celsius) the potential customers have a precise temperature at which they will always agree to purchase. We'll call that "buying temperature." When the potential customers are in the dark lower area, they will not agree to any purchases. When they are in the middle area, they will agree to a purchase but have some reservations which may be voiced in the form of genuine objections. When they are in the top lighter area they will always purchase.

Think of the salesperson and the sales presentation as the heating element or flame. As the flame is applied to the value the buying temperature increases. When the flame is removed the temperature does not grow cold immediately, but cools off gradually. If during this "cooling off" period, the buying temperature dips below the Know Threshold, the customers will likely experience buyer's remorse. It is recommended that you build a value greater than the purchase demarcation point anticipating that the buying temperature is likely to cool off a bit when you leave.

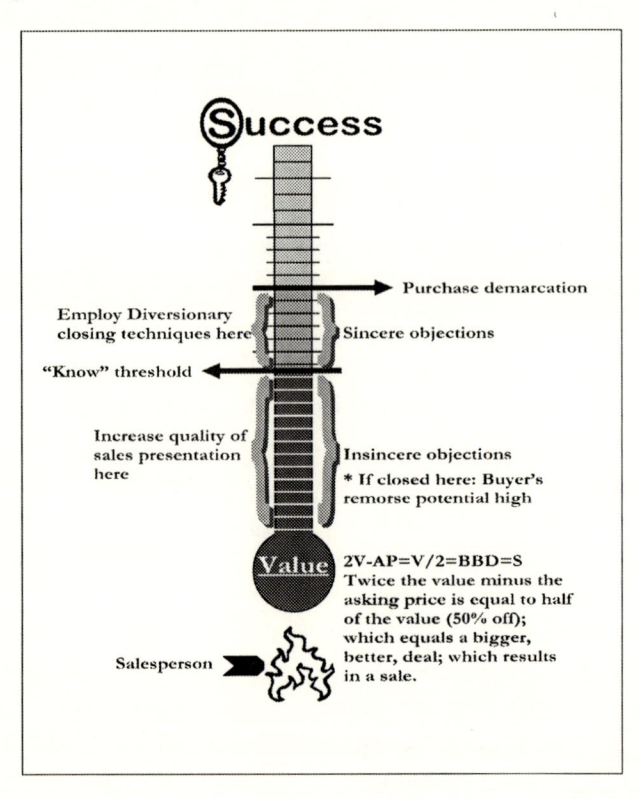

Success

→ Purchase demarcation

Employ Diversionary closing techniques here

Sincere objections

"Know" threshold ←

Increase quality of sales presentation here

Insincere objections
* If closed here: Buyer's remorse potential high

Value

2V-AP=V/2=BBD=S
Twice the value minus the asking price is equal to half of the value (50% off); which equals a bigger, better, deal; which results in a sale.

Salesperson ▶

In this event, the buying temperature will remain above the purchase demarcation point and thus the customer is not likely to experience any buyer's remorse.

Let's consider another example of value. Suppose that the product you were selling was a twenty-dollar bill. You explain that it has a serial number to differentiate it from all other twenty-dollar bills. You show the security and counterfeiting measures which have been taken to ensure its authenticity.

You explain that it was produced at the mint and bears the images of Andrew Jackson and the White House. It is reversible and constructed of very durable paper. You go on to explain to your potential customer that it is worth twenty dollars but that you are only asking ten dollars for it. You ask the potential customer how many they would like. They respond appreciatively and say, "As many as you can get!"

You ask them how they would like to pay for the bills, explaining that you accept cash, credit cards, and even offer financing. They agree to purchase ten thousand of your twenty-dollar bills, but admit that they do not have the hundred thousand dollars it would require. You offer them financing terms which, when calculated, add an additional dollar to the cost of every bill.

Does the potential customer flinch at the interest? Nope, they are happy to sign the contracts just the same. Even though the product (consisting of 10,000 X $20.00) can be delivered in two days, the customers will be asked to pay a monthly payment of five hundred dollars per month for several years. They do have the option to pay off the loan early without penalty. Quickly calculated, the potential customer will be paying one hundred and ten thousand dollars for two hundred thousand dollars' worth of bills. This would be a difference of ninety thousand dollars in favor of the customer.

The customer doesn't hesitate over the interest or other semantics, because this is an example of a BBD (Wilson, 1991).

Let's now consider another scenario: Suppose that the product you were being asked to sell was a ten-dollar bill. You explain that it has a serial number to differentiate it from all other ten-dollar bills. You show the security and counterfeiting measures which have been taken to ensure its authenticity. You explain that it was produced at the mint, and bears the images of Alexander Hamilton and the US Treasury building. It is reversible and constructed of very durable paper. You explain to your potential customer that it is worth ten dollars, but that you are only asking twenty dollars for it. You ask the potential customer how many they would like. They respond with surprise (sometimes called "sticker shock") and say, "We're not interested!" You inquire as to why they would not be interested in such a great product. After all, we all need money! They reply that they need to think about it.

Do you really believe that the potential customer in this scenario is actually going to sit down and meditate on whether or not they should purchase the ten-dollar bill for twenty dollars? Of course not!

This is what we call an insincere objection. It cannot be reasoned upon because it is not the genuine reason why they are not purchasing. Perhaps the potential customer might say, "We really cannot afford it!" If you are truly selling to your target market, is this possible? Would you believe that they do not have twenty dollars?

Suppose you offered to finance the purchase. Based on the numbers in the previous scenario, this would end up costing them twenty-two dollars for every ten-dollar bill, because of interest. Do you think that would persuade them to purchase your product? Perhaps they will come clean with the truth and state simply that, "Your product costs too much!" Rephrased, this means, "The value does not meet the price!"

Although you are not likely to be asked to sell currency, you can look at your product/service in the same way. Will you be selling twenty dollar-bills for ten dollars or would you rather sell ten-dollar bills for twenty dollars? Depending on your sales presentation, you will be, in essence, doing either one or the other.

Note how insincere objections cannot be reasoned with, and also how the potential customer may in fact miscommunicate their reason for not buying. When questioned or asked to explain this behavioral pattern, potential customers will usually say that the reason they did not openly communicate their genuine objection to purchase was because they did not wish to hurt the feelings of the salesperson. In other words, they wanted to let the salesperson down easy! In other cases, the potential customer did not state the actual reason because he knew that he and his spouse did not feel the desire to purchase and they were unsure how to decline the order tactfully. So they instead used phrases of dismissal that had been successful with other salespeople in the past, even though, when subjected to reasoning, their objection may not be logical. If the potential customer communicates an objection which he knows is insincere, he will not wish to be questioned in any way. If questioned he may become easily agitated, aggravated, or even hostile; a sort of Dr. Jeckyl/Mr. Hyde transformation.

The easiest way to avoid insincere objections is simply by not putting your potential customer in a position to have to give them to you. Perform a good, value-building presentation. Sell twenty-dollar bills for ten dollars and watch your sales begin to skyrocket.

Finally, don't forget the major question that potential customers are thinking while watching sales presentations: What's in it for me? The benefits that build value are the answers to this question.

This is the conclusion of The Sales Savior's Six Fundamentals for Selling. Let's review them:

1) The Cycle of Success
2) Personality
3) The Need-Greed Factor (NGF)
4) Build the problem & Solve the problem (BS)
5) Little Details, Big Difference
6) Building Value

With the knowledge of each of these fundamental grapes of wisdom you have laid the foundation for your legacy. In the following chapters we will begin to explore and advance in the magical realm of professional sales.

I say professional because the only real difference between amateurs and professionals is what's in your head and how much is in your pocket!

You have learned secrets in the length of time it has taken you to read this far that most people will have taken a lifetime to learn and squandered a fortune to barter for. This gift is both priceless and worthless! It is priceless to all those who have the courage to step forward and the determination and perseverance to see it through, and worthless to those who would have their ears tickled by its wisdom but lack the drive and willpower to be anything more than ordinary.

I wish to bestow this gift on you this day. Now it is up to you to do something great with it.

Far better it is to dare mighty things, to win glorious triumphs, even though checkered by failure, than to take rank with those poor spirits who neither enjoy much nor suffer much, because they live in the gray twilight that knows not victory nor defeat. (Roosevelt, 1899, See *Goals* section)

Chapter 9

Enthusiasm & Salesmanship are Greatness

- **Doppelganger Effect**—A term used to describe the behavior and communication mutation of a salesperson who has had to face an objection.
- **Pace**—A measurement term used to describe the forecasted number of sales that will be achieved if a specific amount of consistency is achieved

As illustrated on p. 130, the word enthusiastic entails much more than an excited feeling. There is more to it than zeal and a smile. It is with enthusiasm that the real professionals sell.

Let's explore what it really means to be ENTHUSIASTIC:

"**E**" signifies the need for the sales presentation and the sales person to possess *enthusiasm*. Enthusiasm is quite probably the single most important factor when it comes to making the sale now!

"**N**" stands for *nice attire*. "People buy from pretty people" (Lamb 1991). Take care when you are getting prepared for sales presentations and remember that old adage, "You never get a second chance to make a first impression" (u.a).

"**T**" stands for *timeliness* or punctuality. If you have an appointment, never keep your potential customers waiting. Nobody likes waiting.

"**H**" stands for *hire*. Offer the potential customer an opportunity to profit by getting into your line of work. This is especially important to those wanting to build an organization. By offering to hire the potential customer and providing the ability to join you in selling, you will also build integrity. The potential customer will be assured that you are engaged in an honest sales presentation simply because if you were practicing a deception, and they joined your business, they would uncover your dealings. Even if your intentions were not to realize the fulfillment of obtaining a larger sales organization, it is recommended that you, at the very least, offer to hire a prospective customer merely for the added integrity.

"**U**" stands for *uncomplicated* sales presentation. In sales, a good rule of thumb is to always KISS: Keep It Simple, Stupid (u.a.). You don't have to use a lot of big words when little words will do. Don't try to appear too clever at your potential customer's expense. It's best to communicate in a manner in which your potential customer can easily understand and identify with. Leave out the technical jargon and mechanical intricacies unless your customer asks about these things. Chances are, the customer won't be familiar with the terms and the use of them would likely cost you the sale. Most people do not need or want to know every detail of a product in order to benefit from it. You don't need to be an electrician to appreciate turning on a lamp in your home. Sell the benefits, not the product!

Also, try to keep your stage for the sales presentation uncluttered. When things appear cluttered or lack organization, it is easy for the potential customer to become confused and overwhelmed. This can cause them to feel that the product is too complicated, and that they may not be able to enjoy all its benefits, which in turn makes them likely to reject the sales process.

"**S**" stands for *sellable*. Make sure that your sales presentation follows the instructions given in chapter eight on building value.

"**I**" stands for *interesting*. Interesting is the opposite of boring! Your potential customer should feel like they're on the edge of their seats throughout the whole sales presentation. If your potential customer is continually yawning, fidgeting, or looking at their watch you are probably not that interesting. Some ways to create interest include using your prospects' first names, making eye contact, changing tonality and facial expressions, using hand gestures, illustrations, humor, and audience participation. If the potential customer has an opportunity to get involved in the sales presentation while having their senses stimulated (try to include all five senses if possible) the sale has a higher probability of being made.

Consider watching two movies: the first movie is three hours long, but completely entrancing; the second is entitled "Dirt Doesn't Move" in which you see slide upon slide of dirt, not moving. After finishing the first one, you cannot believe that three hours have passed by and you even begin to think of alternate endings, mentally continuing in the fantasy. The second one, however, will quite possibly feel like the longest hour of your life. Similarly, if your sales presentation is not interesting and the potential customer is bored, it won't matter how long your presentation is, it will seem too long to the potential customer.

"**A**" stands for *ask* the two basic questions[1]:

1) "(Insert potential customer's first name), if you had the (insert the product name here), would you use it?
2) (Insert potential customer spouse's name here), if (insert potential customer's name here) would appreciate and use the (insert product name here) would you support him/her in getting one?

For example: "Mary, if you had the vacuum, would you use it? Bob, if Mary said she would appreciate and use the vacuum would you support her in getting one? This method of asking for the order is excellent for direct sales because it accomplishes two critical exploits. In direct sales, there is a common phenomenon in which the potential customer and their spouse shift the responsibility of the purchase back and forth. This is largely due to an agreement, arrangement, previous argument and or beliefs that, though they have not been spoken aloud to you, the salesperson, they are understood (or misunderstood) between the potential customer and their spouse.

Such a situation might occur if Mary told her husband Bob that she really liked a patio set that she saw at a local department store. He asked

---

[1] The Two basic questions are based on Meyers, 1991.

her how much it was. When Mary told Bob it was four hundred dollars, he scolded her for an hour. He asked her if she didn't fully grasp their financial situation and asked her about their plans to save for a vacation. He talked about the layoffs at his workplace even though he knew his job was not in jeopardy. He talked about the kid's college fund, which they had not started (Their children were five and six years old). He talked about the car repairs he had been putting off, and the upcoming taxes.

Mary felt hurt and stupid for asking. She was very quiet for the rest of the evening and quietly complied with all of Bob's wishes.

Two weeks later, Bob received a call from a water softener salesperson. Bob agreed to see the presentation and invited the salesperson over one evening after work when both he and Mary would be home. The salesperson put on an excellent presentation. It was enthusiastic, interesting, sellable, humorous, and entertaining.

Bob and Mary had a great time while watching the show. They were both really impressed with the benefits of putting a water softener in their home. They recognized that they could save on detergents, possible plumbing repairs in the future, the durability of their clothes, and even the health of their skin. The salesperson asked for the order, but instead of eagerly agreeing like she wanted to, Mary held back, saying that it was very nice, but that it was up to Bob. Mary didn't want to get excited and have it all fall apart like it had with the patio set.

Bob was about to say, "Yes, let's get it!" but he held back, sensing that Mary was not all that impressed because she didn't sound as excited as when she talked about the patio set; and because Bob remembered what a big scene he had made when he scolded Mary for even thinking of buying anything. Essentially, Bob's previous behavior was about to rob them of the great feelings they would both enjoy if they were to go ahead with the purchase of the water softener.

Bob said to the salesperson that it was up to Mary. Mary looked at Bob trying to figure out if this was some kind of a test. She responded by saying that Bob was the one who earned most of the family income and therefore it was really his decision. Bob assumed that Mary was trying to remind him of what he had said and done two weeks ago, so he told the salesperson that they would have to think about it.

What Bob really meant was that it would take some private time for him to try and tactfully find out how Mary really felt about the water softener without having to lose face. The salesperson ended up leaving without the sale because of this teeter-totter effect. Can you see why the potential customers might pass the responsibility of a purchase back and forth?

Sometimes potential customers will make an agreement with each other not to purchase anything no matter how much they like it in order to budget toward an agreed upon goal or purchase. They do not expect to feel the desire to purchase anything very strongly when they enter into the agreement.

After a successful sales presentation, the potential customers may wish to break the agreement because the product is so appealing. They hope that their spouse feels the same way, so that the spouse will not hold it against the one that is agreeing first. This is another reason they will sometimes pass the responsibility of the purchase back and forth amongst themselves. By asking the two basic questions above, the invitation to purchase is communicated, and the cycle of passing responsibility can be broken and replaced with a joint decision to purchase.

Can you see how this strategy can be very effective? Try it and I think you will be pleased with the results.

The second "S" stands for *see the objection the way you would like to see it*. What does this mean? First, it assumes and predicts that objections are sure to be a part of your daily communications at the conclusion of your sales presentations. It is best to believe that this is true of the nature of sales rather than believing that every sale will miraculously jump into your lap at the end of the show.

Many apprentice salespeople have undergone a seemingly horrific transformation in the eyes of the potential customer, a transformation I call the "*doppelganger effect*", once the potential customer has communicated an objection to the purchase. The salesperson started out being enthusiastic, excited, confident, charming and entertaining. However, upon hearing an objection they mutated right before the potential customer's eyes. They became agitated, disheartened, argumentative, and even rude. Their smiles quickly turned into looks of disappointment and even scowls. The potential customer often reacts to this doppelganger effect with something I call "mirroring."

Potential customers often engage in mirroring throughout the sales presentation. They tend to emulate the feelings and facial expressions of the salesperson during the presentation. When the salesperson is smiling, the potential customers smile. When the salesperson is laughing, the potential customers laugh. When the salesperson frowns, the potential customers frown. Those who tend not to mirror are usually not impressed by the salesperson, the presentation, or the sales process. These are often observed displaying a perfunctory attitude, and seldom participating in the sales presentation.

If we anticipate and actually incorporate the mirroring effect into our sales presentations, then we have to abstain from undergoing the doppelganger transformation or else we will have to bear the responsibility for its negative backlash when the potential customer begins to mirror the effect. This is the purpose of *seeing the objection the way you would like to see it*. If a salesperson hears, "We can't afford it!" she is certain to become disheartened and feel rejected. This could trigger the "doppelganger effect."

But if the salesperson instead interpreted this as, "We would love to buy this satellite package from you. We both feel that this would be far better than the cable we have installed now, and we like the parental control we can exercise. You are a great salesperson. You did everything right! We have never seen a more impressive sales presentation, but right now we are not sure that we can fit the new satellite package into our budget. You're a pro, though. You must have heard this before. Can't you say something that would convince us that we could comfortably fit the new satellite into our budget? If you can, we are going to go ahead and purchase the package from you today!"

Do you think that if the salesperson were to hear this, she would immediate undergo the doppelganger effect? Would she scowl at the potential customers and act rudely? Of course not! She would probably smile and think of what more she could say to convince the potential customers that they could comfortably afford the new satellite package. Notice the huge difference between the doppelganger effect and seeing the objection the way you would like to see it. The way a salesperson interprets his potential customer's objection will have a direct and profound impact on the eventual outcome.

"T" stands for *throw in*. When the potential customer objects, they might also be concerned that the salesperson may find the objection stupid or inappropriate. That is why I have always taught my classes to follow the ABCs of closing. ABC stands for Agree, But Close (Meyers, 1991). In other words, throw in with the potential customers. Show empathy, but not sympathy! It has been observed that on too many occasions the salesperson engages in a power struggle after undergoing the doppelganger effect. They say things like, "Haven't I proven the case?" or "Didn't you say (   )?" I recommend the following example.

"Bob and Mary, I can understand how you feel and I agree that if you feel (repeat their objection), then you should not go ahead with the purchase." Notice I said I can understand how they *feel*—I did not say I *agree* with how they felt. I said I agree that if they feel (their objection), that they should not purchase the product. The key here is for the salesperson to effectively change this feeling to a feeling that is more conducive to obtaining the sale. Thus it is permissible to "throw in" with the potential customers and yet still assertively pursue the sale. By agreeing instead of fighting the potential customer, the salesperson can avoid raising the potential customers' defenses. Remember that when the potential customers become defensive they no longer maintain the ability to listen or reason effectively and the sale is sure to be lost.

"I" stands for *inform*. Potential customers do not always have enough information to make the decision which you are asking them to make. At this point, they require some additional value building by the sales presentation and some assertive illustrations and reasoning. In chapter eleven you will be instructed on the various forms of communicating this much needed "information."

However, consider the following cause and effect with regards to Scott, who was considering the purchase of a new sound system for his home theater. He went to an electronics store where he had seen some systems. The salesperson began trying to build value by explaining to Scott the differences between the various systems they had. The salesperson understood the differences between the systems very well and assumed that Scott knew and could appreciate his technology inspired lingo.

Scott, however, was confused about which system would be the BBD he was looking for. Scott objected to the salesperson and left that store and went to another where he met a salesperson who may not have been as technically proficient as the other salesperson, but who was able to put things into terms and illustrations that Scott could easily understand, and Scott purchased a new sound system. Scott did not say, "No," that he did not wish to purchase to the first salesperson. What he said was "Know" (Wilson, 1991). I simply don't "Know" enough to say "Yes!" When the second salesperson explained the sound systems in a manner that Scott could easily understand, Scott was able to appreciate which system he thought was the BBD he was looking for and he made the purchase. This is where the information becomes necessary.

"C" stands for *come back*. Come back to what? Come back to the two basic questions. In Chapter 11 on "Overcoming Objections" you will see exactly how this is performed and be invited to participate by using your own creativity to construct informative closes tailored to your avenue of business.

E nthusiasm
N ice Attire
T imely
H ire (offer opportunity)
U ncomplicated
S aleable (2V-AP=BBD=S)
I nteresting
A sk the 2 basic questions
S ee the objection the way you want
T hrow in (agree with prospects)
I nform
C ome back

The Acronym ENTHUSIASTIC and its explanation are by Tom Lamb, 1991.

Keeping Pace

Now that we have discovered the importance of being enthusiastic in sales, let's examine a record-keeping tool which is very effective.

"The true spirit of delight, the exaltation, the sense of being more than Man, which is the touchstone of the highest excellence, is to be found in mathematics as surely as poetry" (Bertrand, 1917, See *Mathematics*).

The following formula is an effective way of predicting the number of gross or net sales that will be generated in a specific period of time. Let's be more specific and set up a scenario. Suppose you wanted to track the number of sales you would generate in a month, and this particular month consisted of thirty-one days.

THE SALESMAN'S BIBLE

(X/Y)Z=P

X (The total number of sales generated until this date) **divided by Y** (The number of days in the month, which have expired.) **multiplied by Z** (The total number of days in the month.) = **P** (Pace, the total number of sales {maintaining the standards used in obtaining the data} that will be generated by month's end.)

One Month Pace Calculating Form Example

Date	# of Demos (day)	# of Demos (mos)	# of Sales (day)	# of Sales (mos)	Close % (day)	Close % (mos)	Pace
1	2	2	1	1	50	50	30
2	3	5	1	2	33	40	30
3	1	6	1	3	100	50	30
4	5	11	3	6	60	55	45
5	6	17	3	9	50	53	54
6	2	19	2	11	100	58	55
7	4	23	2	13	50	57	56
8	1	24	0	13	0	54	49
9	0	24	0	13	0	54	43
10	0	24	0	13	0	54	39
11	2	26	0	13	0	50	35
12	4	30	2	15	50	50	38
13	1	31	1	16	100	52	37
14	1	32	1	17	100	53	36
15	3	35	1	18	33	51	36
16	5	40	4	22	80	55	41
17	3	43	1	23	33	53	41
18	2	45	1	24	50	53	40
19	0	45	0	24	0	53	38
20	1	46	0	24	0	52	36
21	2	48	0	24	0	50	34
22	0	48	0	24	0	50	33
23	0	48	0	24	0	50	31
24	1	49	0	24	0	49	30
25	3	52	2	26	67	50	31
26	2	54	1	27	50	50	31
27	3	57	2	29	67	51	32
28	2	59	1	30	50	51	32
29	3	62	1	31	33	50	32
30	5	67	2	33	40	49	33

For example, if you had generated one sale on the first of the month and you wanted to know how many sales you were on pace for, you would simply input the figures in the formula and you would arrive at a pace of 31. How? One sale divided by the first of the month (one) equals one. One multiplied by 31 (the number of days in the month) equals 31. Suppose that on day two you generated three sales. You would add up the sales from day one and day two: three. So, three (sales) divided by the second day of the month (two) multiplied by 31 (the total number of days in the month) equals a pace of 46.5.

Your pace would now be adjusted from thirty-one to forty-six point five. It is not unusual to observe increased pace results during the first quarter of the month, however as you enter the fourth quarter of the month you will observe a figure closer to what the actual achievement will result in. This is where consistency plays a big role in the achievement of your goals, as stated in chapter seven of this book under the heading "Little Details, Big Difference." (See p. 87.)

It is permissible to modify the Pace formula to encompass larger time spans, such as to track the pace of sales made in one year. Calculate the pace using the total number of sales generated per week divided by the number of weeks expired and multiply by fifty-two (the number of weeks in a year). Calculating the pace can also be referred to as forecasting. This formula will prove useful when forecasting a business plan. If you want to calculate the pace for net sales then you only need to use net sales figures when inputting the data into the pace formula.

If you keep records on both the gross sale progress and the net sale progress it is possible to graph the various closing percentage/average totals. If the first graph (the number of gross sales percentages) were superimposed on the second graph (the number of net sales percentages) it would clearly illustrate how the number of gross sales has impacted the number of net sales. The relationship between the two graphs would affirm the relationship between the net-gross ratios (See p. 134).

What is the importance of the net/gross ratio? The gross number of sales is the number of times the salesperson was able to convince the prospects to place an order. Cancellations (sometimes referred to as BRs: buyer's remorse) or applications that are turned down for financing are the contributing factors in developing the number of net sales. Cancellations can be caused by a variety circumstances such as an imbalance between the twin powers of selling—emotion and logic, or if the salesperson is obtaining the sale using cancellation as a closing technique. Let me explain. Salesperson Terry was conducting a sales presentation at Rhoda's. When he was almost finished, Rhoda began to explain that she had some reservations. Terry told Rhoda to go ahead with the purchase because she had ten days to cancel if she didn't like the product or changed her mind. Rhoda knew she didn't really want to purchase Terry's product because the presentation hadn't completely convinced her, but she really liked Terry a lot and wasn't sure how to tell him that she would not be buying. Rhoda reasoned that she could fill out the paperwork for the order and then a few days later when Terry had already gone it would be much easier to cancel the order over the phone, so she filled out all the paperwork.

Terry was excited because he reasoned that he had obtained the sale because of his sales skill. He did not realize that by offering a method of cancellation he was in fact inviting one. When customers request cancellation information the salesperson should immediately interpret this to be unresolved reservations on the part of the potential customers. This is a great time to be frank and ask the potential customer if they have any reservations or if they are, in fact, planning to cancel. If the potential customer reassures you that they will not be canceling, this solidifies the deal in their mind. If they change their mind and decide not to purchase, consider it a favor. You don't have to go to all the trouble of filling out paperwork and getting your hopes up for nothing. You will not have to face the customer again to repossess the product you sold them (this is especially helpful with consumable products or products which can be easily damaged or caused to become cosmetically displeasing).

The final reason for a cancellation is interference, when a third party is successful in negatively influencing the customer for various reasons, usually self-serving ones.

Regardless what their intentions may be, it is necessary to consider these valid cancellation factors. Now we should also consider what factors influence finance applications which have been turned down. Instead of considering why some people have less than perfect credit, we should consider how we obtained the lead and why we were performing the sales presentation for potential customers who, for obvious reasons, should not have been part of our target market. Using proven lead acquisition and qualifying techniques, a salesperson is able to filter the lead pool in order to reach his true target market.

It is true that it may not be possible to completely filter out a questionable lead, however this will only appear as a small deviation between the gross sales percentages and the net sales percentages (See illustration p. 134). Any consistency in deviation between these two graph lines is cause for concern.

Another possible factor in consistent credit refusal is geographical demographics. For example, I once visited a direct sales organization in West Virginia, USA, when I was working as a marketing support director for a leading direct sales company. I had an opportunity to talk with a once highly successful sales organization leader. Her gross sales volumes were formidable, and deserving of as much recognition as any of our top volume distributors. I questioned her about her sinking orders.

She explained that more than seventy-three percent of her gross sales were turned down when examined by the finance companies. (She often would send applications for financing to several finance companies.) She revealed to me that the majority of her customers were financially frustrated coal miners. For various reasons the coal miner's income had become unstable and inconsistent, and thus they were experiencing financial difficulties. These difficulties had a negative impact on their credit ratings and thus trickled to the salespersons who were co-dependent on their incomes to generate sales.

Sample of Net/Gross Sales Graph

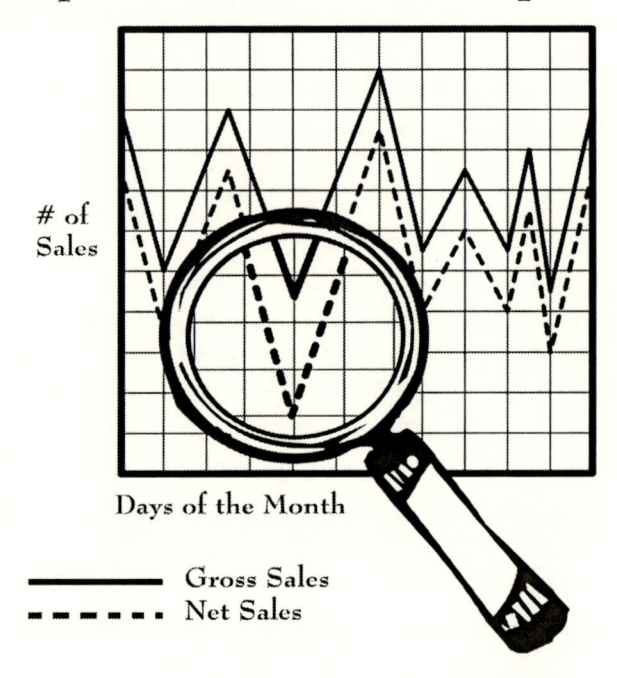

# of Sales

Days of the Month

——————— Gross Sales
– – – – – – Net Sales

Note: Areas where the net sales graph line increases in distance from the gross sales graph line are considered problem areas; the greater the distance, the more serious the problem. A perfect net/gross ratio (meaning every deal was an approved, paid, delivered, and finalized purchase) would appear as a single line.

The net sale graph line cannot exceed the gross sale graph line. Therefore, when you're graphing, if you discover this phenomenon, you will need to recheck your plots.

The consistent deviation by the net sales percentage graph line from the gross sales percentage graph line illustrated these geographical demographic environmental influences on her sales organization.

She was not able to retain her salespeople because they could not generate enough net sales to compensate for the effort necessary to acquire the gross sales. In other words, they could not generate enough net sales to adequately compensate them for their work efforts. This illustrates what a profound effect the net/gross ratio can have on a salesperson. Any and all influences directly impacting the sales force will likewise have a heightened and even more recognizable effect on a sales organization as a whole. This will then be transferred eventually to the manufacturers in the form of decreased sales volume. Thus, training and teaching the sales force is of direct concern to all levels of the distribution chain, and ultimately to every employee and shareholder in a company. Remember the basic theory of supply and demand.

An unusually and consistently high net/gross average (one in which the net closing percentage graph line perfectly shadows the gross sale percentage graph line), may be attributed to human error. If the record keeper only records sales that have been financially resolved by an acceptable method of payment, this will most certainly be the result.

"I read, I study, I examine, I listen, I reflect, and out of all of this I try to form an idea into which I put as much common sense as I can" (Lafayette, n.d. See *common-sense*).

What Every Distributor Needs to Know about Financing

There are a lot of considerations about financing that all would-be distributors should know, and those mentioned here will undoubtedly change over the next few years, but the root of this understanding will remain the same.

Most direct sales companies use third-party financing sources and act as an agent of these companies when the consumer wishes to make payments on an item. Thus, the distributor receives a check or funding on the sale within a few days and up to two weeks. Here are some important questions to ask when considering whether or not you're dealing with a finance company that's right for you:

- ✓ How long will "funding" take? You do not want your check being delayed because this corresponds to how long you will have to delay the dealer/sales representative's check, as well as your repurchase cycle.

- ✓ Will it be payable by check or direct deposit? If you are a new business, deposits electronically sent to your account do not usually have a hold placed on them by your bank. However, company checks (even finance companies' checks) can be held by your branch/bank for as many as ten business days (or even longer).

- ✓ How soon will you know if your deal is approved? Some finance companies offer instant approvals. You call a toll free number and give the consumers' credit information over the phone (while you or your representative is still in the prospects' home). Within a minute you get an approval or denial. This is especially important if you are planning to leave your product with the customer when you sell it (this cuts down on buyer remorse/cancellations). Without this service, you may have to send your sales representatives back to houses to pick up product that has been delivered but turned down at the finance company (very awkward for the sales representative). If your attrition rate is extremely high and you are a distributor, you'll have to take of this job personally.

- ✓ Is the financing full recourse, partial recourse, or non-recourse? Full recourse is a type of financing whereby the distributor agrees to buy back all or part of the credit extended to customers in the event of non-payment or delinquency. I strongly advise against any recourse style financing.

    It is a fact that there will be some delinquency. When this happens, the "payback" to the financing source could topple your business. Imagine you're selling a hundred $2800.00 vacuums per month and 10% go delinquent after 3 months, and another 5% go delinquent after 4 months, followed by 3% after 5 months. In month six you could be buying back 18% of one month's contracts. Most of the finance companies functioning in this manner want all their money right away. So they will seize the funding from your future sales. That means you won't even have the sales representative's commission when pay day rolls around.

Now the sales representative wants to quit and starts a panic throughout your business. Partial recourse is exactly what it sounds like. With partial-recourse financing (unlike full-recourse financing), you are only responsible for paying back part of the money issued to the consumer on credit.

Here's a question to ponder: If the distributor is responsible for paying back the credit issued to consumers, then isn't the distributor in effect co-signing with every one of his customers? Why should the finance company even have an approval or denial process? The distributor is responsible no matter what happens anyway, isn't he? Non-recourse financing is definitely my choice for direct sales financing. If the financing source has checked the credit, verified the deal with the customer, and paid the distributor, it should be the responsibility of the financing source to collect on delinquent accounts, not that of the distributor!

✓ What is the annual percentage rate (APR)? Customers don't like paying high interest. Yet most finance companies with a broader range of acceptance (contributing to higher delinquencies) charge higher interest rates (to compensate for the higher risk).

Is the interest calculated on the declining balance? If so, what is the highest amount of interest a consumer would pay? Is this an installment plan with fixed payments and interest, or a revolving credit plan like the credit card companies use? Revolving credit plans usually offer lower payment options and have no fixed time limit for repayment.

Therefore, if you only made the minimum monthly payment every month, it could literally take several more years before you were able to pay off the loan, as opposed to a fixed-term installment contract. Some financing companies that offer revolving credit will charge a percentage to the distributor (deducted from the funding) and give the consumer an interest-free loan. The credit card the customer receives can later be used for other purchases (at other vendors if it carries the Visa/Mastercard logo). Then the interest rate jumps to 18-29%. This form of financing seems to be excellent at helping a bank get their cards into customer's wallets while providing direct sale distributors with a valuable and effective financing service.

- ✓ Many financing companies will offer distributors a percentage of all their contracts as a quarterly bonus (call it a volume discount if you like). If you don't mention it to the financing company when you're setting up your account, don't expect them to.

- ✓ A lot of finance company decisions are negotiable if the credit is marginal, so remember that before agreeing to a certain acceptance condition.

Some finance companies agree to buy all different kinds of contracts from low to high risk, with a condition that they will only buy/pay out a percentage of the contract based upon the risk factors of the consumer. An example: High risk may only pay you 50% of the contract. On a $2800.00 vacuum you might get $1400.00. On a marginal sale you might get 75-80% of the contract, and on a great credit deal you might get 100% of the contract. Minus, of course, the standard deductions for paperwork processing, administration fees, and whatever other reasons they can think of for keeping some of the money.

When dealing with this type of situation you need to establish a rapport with the finance company "buyers" so you can argue for each of your contracts and subsequently get them funded at a higher percentage, or perhaps even get some of the fees waived.

"Remember that the squeaky wheel gets the grease"(Wasyliniuk, *Personal Communication*, 2000).

- ✓ You may wish to acquire credit checking software or a special machine called a retail machine for checking consumer's credit yourself. This service is offered through all the major credit agencies like Trans Union, Experian and Equifax. This is especially important if your financing source doesn't offer you instant approvals.

- ✓ Finally, you can usually tell if a deal will be approved by examining the key areas that the finance companies look at when making a credit assessment. First, do they have credit cards? If yes, you're headed for an approval under the theory that "if other people will lend you money, so will I." If they have absolutely no credit, it's not looking good. Look at how much they make per month. How long have they been at their job? A long time on the job means stability and a short time means risk. How long have they lived at the same address? More than 2 years looks stable, whereas less than 2 years looks suspiciously like risk. Look at the amount of bills they have. Fifty percent free income looks good on paper; eighty-five percent or more of their money going to pay credit cards and mortgage, etc., looks like risk. You and your sales representatives can be trained to spot potential bad deals and this is of particular interest when trying to determine whether or not to leave the product with the consumer while you await an answer from the finance company.

Why is this important to a salesperson? If your distributor makes poor decisions regarding financing, you will be caught in the middle. Hopefully your distributor was promoted based on a healthy and successful demonstration of this knowledge and you can concentrate on the fun stuff: selling! If your distributor is unaware of all or part of this information, perhaps you're just the leader he's looking for; someone who can help implement strategic change.

Chapter 10

Asking for the Order & Closing the Sale

➤ **I&W Technique**—The "If & Would" Closing Technique.

The task of asking for the order and closing the sale is the reason behind why many feel that they would not be good candidates for a sales-oriented career. When people say, "I'm not a salesperson," what do they really mean? Do they mean that they are incapable of getting a product out of the packaging? Do they mean that they do not believe they could talk about some of the features of the product? Do they mean they could not smile and act enthusiastic?

No, this is not what they mean at all. What they really mean is that they are not confident that they could successfully ask for the order. This is not limited to those who don't even attempt sales. Many who attempt selling have difficulty asking for the order and closing the sale. But you should know that feeling uncomfortable is entirely natural for those lacking the familiarity gained through experience.

During the entire sales presentation, an inexperienced salesperson might be able to speak with precision, knowledge and zeal. But when the presentation is finished that inexperience might lead them to freeze up, or worse, engage in verbal diarrhea. This is because throughout the sales presentation, silence has been connected with boredom or other negative influences. When the salesperson runs out of things to say, he mistakenly expects the potential customer to initiate the sale by saying, "We'll take it!"

Instead of allowing the potential customer a few minutes to reflect and conclude that the purchase is right, the salesperson will often begin trying to induce the sale by suggesting that he is finished, assuming that this will communicate to the customer that it is now his/her turn to reciprocate some form (hopefully positive) of response like: "We'll take it!".

If this sounds familiar to you, there is nothing to fear because your problem isn't as big as you might think. You simply have to come to the realization that less than one percent of potential customers will ever initiate the sale. You must be proactive at this critical time. "Don't wait for your ship to come in; swim out to it" (u.a.).

It is also important for you to remember that silence is a great motivator. While I agree that silence during the demo is not always a good influence, it can be vital during the asking-for-the-order-and-closing-the-sale phase.

So what is the number one reason why the sale is lost? I have heard that question many times, and my answer has always been the same. Simply put, because the salesperson does not ask for the order. So how can salespeople be proactive when they wish to ask for the order and close the sale? What must be in place in order for this to work? The right mental attitude!

> There ain't no free lunches in this country. And don't go spending your whole life commiserating that you got raw deals. You've got to say, "I think that if I keep working at this and want it bad enough I can have it." (Iacocca, n.d.)

Not only must we maintain perseverance whilst acquiring this wisdom, but also optimism, self-confidence and belief. Take heart from these words of wisdom:

"Keep a green tree in your heart and perhaps the singing bird will come" (u.a.).

Never think that you're not good enough yourself. A man should never think that. People will take you very much at your own reckoning" (Trollope, n.d. ¶30).

"The thing always happens that you really believe in; and the belief in a thing makes it happen" (Wright, n.d.).

What follows are a few methods for easily and effectively asking for the order.

The Two Basic Questions

Remember again the two basic questions associated with the letter A in the acronym ENTHUSIASTIC:

1. Mary, if you had the product, would you use it?

2. Bob, if Mary said she would appreciate and use the product would you support her in getting one?

Even if you do not choose to use this technique on every presentation, you should always be prepared to use it if you observe the prospects passing the responsibility of the purchase back and forth between them.

The Choice Close

The choice close option is very effective. It is easy to learn and understand how and why it works. Basically, at the end of the presentation the salesperson asks the potential customers a question where the answers are limited to a choice in which either would essentially involve the agreement to purchase.

For example, Salesperson Mike is selling two thousand dollar child scholarship funds. Mike finishes his sales presentation for Potential Customers John and Kim. He has been exciting, enthusiastic, informative, interesting, and humorous. Mike has also built enough value to excite John and Kim about the BBD. Mike has run out of words, and realizes it is time to ask for the order.

He asks John and Kim *how many* they would like to purchase, <u>two or three</u>? Mike is silent patiently waiting for their answer (with a sincere expression). He knows that, in a manner of speaking, whoever speaks first loses.

"I think just one would be enough," replies John. Kim nods in agreement, and Mike begins filling out the necessary paperwork. The sale is made! This is the perfect illustration of a successful choice close.

Mike's experience may have told him that one sale is what is normal, however he did not ask for one sale. He asked for two or three. Consequently, since Mike began using this choice close he has, on several occasions, broken company sales volume records for most sales in a month, week, day, and even on a single presentation. He has taken orders for two and three sales on many, many occasions and his co-workers often ask him what his secret for closing the sale is. When he reveals his answer, it is so simple his colleagues are dumbfounded.

The secret to selling is merely the courage to ask for the order and the self-confidence to remain quiet long enough for the potential customers to say, "Yes!"

The choice close method is easily modified to incorporate other products in which higher quantities are the norm. For example, a liquor salesperson who normally delivers four cases of rum might ask the potential customer if they would like a half dozen or a dozen cases. It is true that the potential customer may object or merely take the four cases, which is usual. However, by using this method consistently, a salesperson is likely to find that he is generating a greater number of sales. By the end of the year, it is not unfathomable that a salesperson could have increased their total volume of sales by as much as twenty-five percent.

The Assuming the Sale Method & the Yes, Yes Method

This method of closing and asking for the order it seems is easier to adjust to for someone who has had great difficulty in the past with this phase of the presentation. This is because the salesperson never really asks for the order directly with this method. Because they do not ask for the order directly, they are not required to endure any awkward silence while the potential customers contemplate a decision.

How is this method practiced? When the salesperson is finished with the product presentation they ask the potential customer how they would like to pay for the product. This is usually a good time to offer the various acceptable methods of payment. Credit card, cash, check or perhaps a financing method might interest them. Some salespeople have modified the question "How would you like to *pay* for this?" to "How would you like to *invest* in this?" They claim that this subtle difference may have an effect on obtaining the order. People don't really like paying for things, but they like investing in things.

When the customer chooses a method of payment they have usually mentally purchased the product since no such method would be necessary for someone who was not intent on purchasing. When using this method, it is necessary for the salesperson not to seem as if the purchase wasn't expected. Otherwise the potential customer may develop reservations believing that the salesperson's behavior is abnormal. Also, when the potential customer provides a method of payment, it is also important for the salesperson to immediately assert action. Don't wait around for an objection or you're likely to get one.

For example, if the potential customer replied that they would pay by check, the salesperson should say something which motivates the potential customer to take action, such as, "You go ahead and get your checkbook and I'll start filling out your warrantee card." If the salesperson does not motivate the potential customer to take action then an awkward silence can develop while both parties are waiting for each other to do something.

The potential customers are not sure what they are supposed to do and the salesperson is waiting for the potential customers to act. When they do not act, the salesperson often mistakenly interprets this behavior as a form of stalling or a non-verbal objection.

Remember that in general people do not make all that many decisions in their lives. For most people, the two biggest and most controversial decisions they will make on an average day are what they will eat and what they will wear. In today's speed-of-information age, many people rely on others to tell them what to do rather than consciously deciding things on their own.

It is either through action or inaction that we all find ourselves in whatever environment we are currently in, whether good or bad. We could even say, "By not making a decision, we're really making one."

Procrastination is another common reason why potential customers do not take action when perhaps their communication indicates they should. Most people have been taught all their lives to procrastinate (remember the PWEC principle). Every year, adults panic when tax season rolls around because they have procrastinated when it comes to preparing their taxes.

When you think about it, there are essentially three ways to dodge spontaneous responsibility. One is to not make any decisions, the second is to put off making a decision, and the third is to have someone else make the decision for you. In the last case, you can later hold the decision-maker responsible if the outcome is not desirable.

This does not mean that people don't know what they want. They just don't want to be responsible for a negative outcome if what they "want" turns out to be a bad choice. Just listen to a couple argue over where they will eat dinner:

Man: "Would you like to go out for dinner?"
Woman: "That sounds like a great idea."
M: "What kind of food do you feel like?"
W: **"I don't care. Whatever."**
M: "How about Mexican food?"
W: "Again? We had that last week."
M: "Alright what about a burger?"
W: "I thought you wanted to eat somewhere nice?"
M: "What about seafood then?"
W: "You know I don't really like seafood."
M: "I thought you said you didn't care where we ate."
W: "I don't. I just don't want that."
M: "What about steak?"
W: "You know what, let's just not bother."
M: "Well where do you want to eat?"
W: "What about Chinese food?"
M: "Okay, Chinese sounds great!"
W: "But only if that's what you want."
M: "That sounds great let's get Chinese food."

Observe that the woman first claimed she did not care where or what they ate. But her later communication indicated that she knew exactly what she wanted. She just didn't want to take responsibility for making a decision that might be criticized. As you can see, she initiated the idea of the Chinese food but directed the communication so that the man would ultimately be the one making the decision.

An average person simply doesn't make that many decisions but are instead essentially told what to do. The alarm clock tells people when to wake up. Their career choice tells them what type of dress is appropriate. Their boss tells them what work they need to do, and their car tells them when to put on their seatbelts and refuel. The list goes on and on. The average day consists of a constant cycle of being told what to do. It is not odd, then, to see why people have such poor decision-making skills today.

A good salesperson recognizes and respects this behavior and its effect on the closing of the sale. This behavior demands that the salesperson be willing to tell the potential customer when to act, and this is especially true when practicing the assumption method for asking for the order and closing the sale. The assumption method goes very well with the *"Yes, Yes Method"* for asking for the order and closing the sale.

The *"Yes, Yes Method"* requires the salesperson to ask questions throughout the sales presentation which the potential customer would probably answer, *"yes"* to. The salesperson would also encourage mirroring by effectively nodding his head in affirmation of the potential customer's "Yes" answers. This method argues that the potential customer will both physically and mentally have a more difficult time saying "No" when later asked for the order.

Even though the assumption method does not require the salesperson to verbally ask for the order, it is implied when the potential customer is asked which method of payment they would prefer. Generally, if there is going to be an objection, it will be when the potential customer is asked for their preferred method of payment or when they are asked to take action.

If there is an objection when you ask the potential customer how they would like to pay for the product, it is beneficial to then rephrase the question to sound as if you're speaking hypothetically. This is because in some cases the method of payment is, in fact, the reason behind an objection; as is the case when a person wishes to finance an order believing that a down payment may be required, which they do not have or cannot afford at the time.

Regardless of whether a potential customer agrees or disagrees to the purchase, always determine how they would have paid for the product if they were to in fact purchase. This will aid you when you move into the Overcoming Objections phase discussed in the next chapter.

Another way of practicing the assumption method is by asking the potential customers to go to the kitchen table (if you're not already there; this is supposing the sales presentation was performed in the living room). At the end of the presentation the salesperson might say, "Let's go into the kitchen and sit down at the table where we can better fill out some of the necessary paperwork." Don't wait for the potential customers to get up. Simply turn as if to walk to the kitchen. A slight glance behind you should confirm whether or not the potential customers are following. If they are, in fact, following you, continue as if this is what you expected. Go to the kitchen and begin filling out the necessary forms to complete the purchase. Always begin with the least important forms first.

When asking the potential customer for his signature, always refer to his signature as his autograph. Signature sounds a little abrasive and formal (even intimidating) whereas autograph sounds much more fun and implies that the potential customer is of importance.

If the potential customer does not immediately follow you to the kitchen, don't panic. Turn around and say, "Oh, did I forget something?" The potential customers will either give you an objection, or they will communicate that they did not understand what you wanted them to do. Repeat your invitation to come into the kitchen and sit at the table where you can fill out some paperwork.

A third method of practicing this technique is to present the potential customers with some accessory items which they might enjoy purchasing. These items would be best if they were unusable without the initial product, which was the center of the main sales presentation, but any incentive that would be of value to them will work.

Marionette was once asked to see a presentation of a steam cleaner. She was very impressed with the product and the salesman, Steve. Steve wasn't new to selling but felt intimidated by Marionette's strong, assertive personality and overwhelming beauty. He was afraid to ask for the order directly, so he decided to utilize the assumption method for asking for the order and closing the sale.

Steve showed Marionette a fantastic accessory called a four-inch upholstery steam wand, which was great for cleaning couches, chairs, stairs and even cars. He explained to Marionette that this was worth a hundred and forty-nine dollars, but that if she purchased the steam cleaner that night, he would give the wand attachment to her for half price.

Marionette said yes to this and Steve began filling out the paperwork for both the steam cleaner and the four-inch upholstery steam wand. Marionette had mentally purchased the steam cleaner the moment she agreed to purchase the four-inch upholstery steam wand since the wand attachment was of no use to her without the main unit. Thus the sale was made.

The I&W Method

This technique is probably the one I recommend the most. It involves asking two questions and is very effective when combining asking for the order and overcoming an objection. First, the salesperson asks the potential customer a question starting with *If* and then a second part beginning with *Would*. Consider the following question.

"*If* I can get you this (insert product here) for only (X) dollars, *would* you get it tonight?"

This technique, also known as the If & Would Method (I&W), is easy to adapt to any product or service.

It asserts that the potential customers are getting a BBD by purchasing now. It is important to recognize that potential customers need to be able to justify any and all BBDs in order to feel completely secure when purchasing. This is to say that if a salesperson does not justify a BBD the potential customer may feel that the salesperson was prepared to overcharge them, and that the BBD being offered is actually the bottom line price. This would have a negative effect on the sales process.

How can a salesperson come up with the proper if and would statements? The salesperson would do the presentation and refer to the sticker price, sometimes referred to as the suggested retail price. At the end of the presentation, the salesperson would then explain that he might be able to do something special for the potential customer in order to entice them to purchase that night. Remember to justify your BBD before using the I&W method.

An example: Salesperson Gary was performing a sales presentation for Potential Customers Crystal and Joel. Gary asked Crystal and Joel if they liked the new television he had just presented to them, and they both agreed it was much nicer than the one they had at home and that they had been considering replacing it for some time now.

Gary mentioned that he might be able to get Crystal and Joel a deal on the television because it was their first time shopping at the store and perhaps the manager would like to do something special for them to entice them to shop there again. He asked them *if* he could get them fifteen percent off the price of the television, *would* they buy it?

Crystal and Joel agreed and Gary called his manager to inquire about the deal. A few minutes later, Gary returned and informed Crystal and Joel that he had been able to negotiate the deal for them. Crystal and Joel happily purchased the television, shook Gary's hand in appreciation, and promised to come back and shop there again.

Notice how Gary justified the reduction in price by using the first time shopping there to his advantage. This is a good illustration of turning a possible negative into a verifiable positive. It is possible that Crystal and Joel may not have purchased the television there because they had never shopped there before and may not have felt secure about the company. However, because of Gary's justification, this was averted and the sale was made.

Let's look at another scenario. JJ showed a vacuum cleaner to an elderly woman named Beatrice. Beatrice was impressed by the sales demonstration and thought that at her age, she certainly deserved a good vacuum cleaner.

JJ told Beatrice that he might be able to get her deal on the vacuum if she purchased it that night. He explained that he believed the company had a "seniors special." This was a discount reserved for people sixty-five years of age and older.

He explained that he would need to see her driver's license in order to verify her age, and that if she met the qualifications, he would ask his manager to give her the deal. He said that many seniors he had dealt with in the past had taken advantage of this offer because they had been on fixed incomes. This would mean Beatrice would be able to buy the vacuum for five hundred dollars off the *"suggested retail price."* This "lower price" was the price at which JJ would receive his full and regular commission check (normal/regular deal).

He asked Beatrice, "*If* I can get you the senior's special, *would* you get the vacuum tonight? Beatrice agreed and JJ called his manager.

In JJ's case, he already knew he would be able to get the deal for Beatrice because the reduction was only from the suggested retail price he had shown her, not from the bottom line. In other words, Beatrice was paying the normal price of the vacuum. Yet when JJ returned to tell Beatrice that he had got her the senior's special, Beatrice was so happy she purchased the new vacuum for herself.

Why was Beatrice so happy when she ended up paying the full and actual price of the vacuum? Beatrice felt special because she was getting a BBD as a senior. She felt as though JJ understood what it was like to be living on a fixed income, and that he had offered her the best possible deal in order to meet her financial limitations.

JJ was happy, too, because he had earned six hundred dollars in commission and could care for his family.

This sale is an example of a win-win scenario. This is the right way to sell! Some may argue that the right way to sell is to always give a better price, but that is not the case. Great selling is when both the salesperson and the customer complete the transaction feeling good! A reduction in price does not guarantee this will be accomplished.

It's wise to be careful with this method, however, and make sure to justify the discounts and only mention them after the sales presentation is concluded. Consider Salesperson Martha's scenario. She was selling sleep-sets at a furniture store. She approached Potential Customer Rick and began a sales presentation on several of the models in the store. Rick seemed particularly interested in one set, so Martha continued with it. <u>She asked Rick *if* she could get him the box spring and stand for the mattress for free, *would* Rick purchase the mattress.</u>

Rick seemed to hesitate and appeared to have reservations about the purchase. Martha offered to lower the price by one hundred more dollars. Martha knew she would have to forfeit the hundred dollars from the three hundred dollar commission she would receive if Rick were to purchase the sleep set. Still, Rick did not seem satisfied, and moreover, he did not appear to be all that interested anymore. Martha felt like she was losing the sale so <u>she asked Rick *if* she could get him an additional one hundred and ninety-five dollars off the price, *would* he take the sleep set.</u>

Rick agreed reluctantly and Martha wrote up the order. When Rick got home, he was not all that happy about his purchase and he wondered if he should cancel the order. Martha was excited at first that she had made the sale, but her excitement quickly faded when she realized that she had only earned five dollars. She reasoned that it was better than nothing, but she did not fully enjoy the sales experience. The next day Rick cancelled his order for the sleep-set.

Martha approached another couple that were looking at the sleep-sets and did the same sales presentation. Only this time, she spoke only of the suggested retail price and never talked about what a great deal she might be able to make them. They seemed to really be interested in a particular sleep-set, and appeared to be on the verge of making the purchase. Martha finally broke her silence and tried the I&W method again. <u>She asked the couple *if* she could get them a twenty-five dollar discount, free pillowcases, and sheets to go with the sleep–set, *would* they take it.</u>

The couple agreed and Martha said she would inquire with the manager about the deal. Martha came back and affirmed that she had, in fact, negotiated the deal for the couple. They were both happy and smiling. They had received the BBD they were looking for and could not believe that Martha had even thrown in a set of sheets and pillowcases.

Martha was excited and reassured the couple that they could count on her for all their future service needs. Martha had earned her full three hundred dollar commission plus an additional fifty dollars. She would have been able to bring the price down a hundred dollars from the suggested retail price but she did not. Instead she offered the couple a twenty-five dollar discount and a set of sheets that cost her another twenty-five dollars. When all was said and done, Martha had made the sale for fifty dollars more than her lowest price (her full commission).

The reality of great sales is not how little the customer pays, but rather how good they feel about whatever they do pay.

The I&W method is very versatile and can be effective in overcoming objections and asking for the order. Let me demonstrate: Salesperson Luke finishes his sales presentation and begins by using one of the various assuming-the-sale techniques. His potential customers, Jill and Jamie, have reservations and object to the purchase. They claim that they need to think it over. Luke knows that Jill and Jamie do not plan to sit for days and meditate on whether or not they should purchase his product. He knows that if he does not write up the order while he is there, it is likely that he will never be writing it up. Luke needs to find out what is really stopping Jill and Jamie from buying the product, or else he will lose the sale.

Luke asks Jill and Jamie if they were given a couple of days to think about the purchase and they decided not to go ahead with it, what the predominant factor would be. Jamie replies that it would probably be finances. Luke asks Jill and Jamie how they would pay for the product, hypothetically, if they were to make the purchase. Jill and Jamie both agree that they would have to pay with monthly installments. At this time, they had neither the down payment nor the budget for another monthly payment. They say that things will be better a year down the road when they finish paying for the washer and dryer they bought last year. Luke asks if there's anything else besides the finances which is stopping them from getting the product and Jill and Jamie both say, "No."

Luke asks Jill and Jamie, "*If* I could arrange it so you did not have to pay any down payment, and I could get you low monthly payments you could afford, and that you didn't have to start paying those payments for the first year, until the washer and dryer were paid off, *would* you get the product tonight?"

Jill and Jamie agree that they would take the product but only if they can defer the payments for one year. Luke calls his manager and asks if such a thing is possible (He already knows it is.) and when he returns he smiles and says, "Congratulations!" Jill and Jamie also smile and they all begin filling out the necessary forms over a coffee.

Notice in this scenario how Luke began using another closing technique, but after hearing an objection switched to the I&W method. As you can see he was successful at not only overcoming their objection, but also in obtaining the sale.

A variance of the "I&W method" is stated like this: "*If* I could get you (X), could I *appreciate* your business tonight?" (X) Represents the solution to their objection, or a BBD. The "I&W method" integrates well into third party closing.

Third Party Closing

Third party closing is when a third party is introduced to help negotiate the sale. Often this person is the manager or owner of the business, or other person of some authority. Using a third party can be highly effective in obtaining the sale if the salesperson realizes that it is his responsibility to obtain an I&W commitment from the potential customers prior to contacting the third party and requesting the BBD which would satisfy the potential customers' I&W commitment.

Without a commitment, the third party is no longer being asked to aid in obtaining the sale, but rather requested to ask for the order because the salesperson is afraid to. This is not nearly as effective as when the salesperson himself asks for the I&W commitment because the potential customers have already come to the conclusion that they like and trust the salesperson, where as they have not necessarily made that assumption regarding the third party.

Often, if the third party is solicited to ask for the order, he must then introduce a fourth party in order to obtain an I&W commitment.

Consider the following illustration: Mathew was a new salesperson at the company. He was very nervous about selling and felt unsure of himself. He wasn't sure whether or not people would really pay the asking price for his product because he had never sold anything which cost as much. When he was performing the sales presentation, he tried to sense whether or not the potential customers were getting excited; trying to test their buying temperature. The prospects seemed frigid and unresponsive. Mathew began to realize that his sales presentation could really use some work. He was afraid to ask for the order because he felt intimidated and helpless.

He called his manager and immediately began explaining how the sales presentation went. His manager asked Mathew what the potential customers' payment method was. Mathew said he wasn't sure, but he could ask. He cupped his hand over the phone as he asked the potential customers. When he got back to the manager he interjected that the customer would like to speak with the manager. The manager introduced himself and asked how they liked the sales presentation. The potential customers explained that they thought the product was good but that they would not be buying anything that night. They explained that it was their policy never to buy anything on the spur of the moment.

The manager asked them how they would have paid for the product if they were to have purchased. They explained that they were unsure as they really hadn't considered purchasing, but probably cash. They couldn't stand to pay the "crazy interest" charges that the finance companies were charging. They then confided to the manager that they just did not have enough cash saved to go ahead with the purchase that night.

The manager said that there might be something he could do to help them. <u>He asked them *if* he could manage to obtain financing for the couple, with monthly installments they could afford, but with absolutely no interest charges at all, *would* they purchase the product.</u>

He explained that for such a BBD, he would have to ask the director of finance for authorization (notice the fourth party being introduced because the sales representative deferred the I&W commitment). Before requesting the BBD from the director of finance, the manager wanted their commitment.

Keep in mind that when the number of parties being asked to get involved in the I&W process increases like this, the potential customer may feel overwhelmed and become agitated with the whole thing, resulting in the loss of the sale. Also remember that the I&W method can be used multiple times in the same presentation, all to help eliminate and overcome the various obstacles a customer might have. The "I&W technique" works like magic!

Why not try the I&W method on your next sales presentation? I think you'll be pleasantly surprised at the profound effect it has on your negotiating skills.

"Shoot for the moon. Even if you miss it you will land among the stars" (Les Brown, n.d.).

"Destiny is not a matter of chance; it is a matter of choice. It is not a thing to be waited for; it is a thing to be achieved" (Bryan, n.d.).

Chapter 11

Overcoming Objections

- **Wall of Reasoning**—A term used to describe what potential customers are communicating when they give all the symptoms of an objection rather than an actual objection so the salesperson will feel that the reasoning behind the objection cannot be overcome.
- **Reverse Closing Technique**—The art of closing with communicative reasoning and without exerting excess pressure on the potential customer.
- **Diversionary Reasoning**—The art of overcoming objections by misdirecting the potential customers with a story for the purpose of reasoning out a successful conclusion whose outcome has been predetermined to be supportive and conducive to obtaining the sale.

"If I were asked to give what I consider the single most useful bit of advice for all humanity it would be this: Expect trouble as an inevitable part of life and when it comes, hold your head high, look it squarely in the eye and say, 'I will be bigger than you. You cannot defeat me.' (Landers, n.d.)."

Why do People Object?

Overcoming objections is a topic that an entire book could easily be written on. However, in this chapter we will be specifically analyzing how closing techniques really work, and the seven-up approach to overcoming objections. Let's begin by talking about the "Six Reasons that Potential Customers Object" (Francoeur, 2002, *Personal Communication*).

- ✘ No Money
- ✘ No Desire
- ✘ No Trust
- ✘ No Hurry
- ✘ No Need
- ✘ No Value

Once a salesperson realizes that these are the roots of any and all objections, the entire process of closing the sale and overcoming objections seems much easier. The number one reason that potential customers do not purchase is still, believe it or not, because the salesperson simply doesn't ask for the order.

In the past, the typical salesperson would begin a power struggle with the potential customer as to why they ought to purchase the product whenever an objection was given, the *doppelganger effect* mentioned in chapter 9.

The byproduct of the doppelganger effect is *pressure*. In time, the potential customers begin to develop resentment toward the salesperson who employs pressure tactics to try to get them to purchase. The customer becomes empowered and the slogan, *"The customer is always right"* became the new catch phrase. But this didn't seem to be enough to prevent the stereotypical salesperson from preying on the meek.

That is why today, most states and provinces have legislation which allows the potential customer a cooling-off period in which they may choose to cancel the order of a product sold to them through direct sales. This has forced the direct sales industry to carefully examine their sales techniques and adopt new approaches to acquiring sales.

For many years now I have advocated reverse closing techniques. Reverse closing is really the opposite of pressure selling. It generally requires a better sales pitch and quality products. Reverse closing requires patience and perseverance. It is essentially earning the right to ask for the order because the potential customer has been so impressed by the sales presentation that it is their desire to purchase the product or service.

The 7-Up Approach to Closing and Answering Objections[3]

The seven-up approach to closing and answering objections follows seven simple steps. These are:

- Listen
- See the objection the way you would like to see it
- Repeat the objection
- Agree & Reverse
- Isolate the objection
- Inform
- Ask for the order

Step 1. Listen

You might think that simply listening to an objection is not all that important; that it is easy. However, when the salesperson has invested many long hours practicing and manipulating his presentation, the realization of a possible rejection can be disheartening.

Because the average salesperson does not know all the secrets to successful selling, he may not wish to hear any objections for fear that this will somehow lead to his exposure as someone who isn't really prepared.

I have observed many times, while I was training in the field, that most salespeople are ill-prepared to handle objections because of a lack of commitment to their sales presentation, despite their seemingly genuine desire to improve. I have been asked repeatedly to diagnose why a salesperson lost a sale. I have observed, throughout my experience, that it is always the result of some area of weakness in the salesperson's presentation. I have taught for years that the easiest close there is, is a good

---

[3] (Based upon a sales meeting conducted by Tom Lamb, 1989).

value-building presentation! If the customer says, "Great we'll take it!" there is not a whole lot of closing necessary.

As you read the informative closes and answers to objections, please be advised that these are merely band-aids, and they do little to address the core causes of any objection. While they are effective at obtaining the order and boosting your income and total overall closing percentage, consistently having to use them means you are missing some important mechanics in your sales presentation. You should not only determine what the real problem is, but you must also create a solution that will be more than just a temporary fix.

Even throughout my own sales career, I started out young and inexperienced, and gradually, along the way, I learned each of the closes you will read about. The more I learned, the better I became at performing my sales presentation. Eventually, I learned that *a fantastic sales presentation transcends the need for closing*. Facing objections and confidently answering them is something that great salespeople should possess an affinity for. It is, after all, one of the greatest "highs" to ever be felt by man. It is not a drug, but the effects of selling have many amazing properties.

The most successful salespeople have not claimed to leap tall buildings in a single bound, but they have boasted of an endless source of energy and renewed enthusiasm for life. They have talked about how much of the stress in their lives has seemingly dripped from their fingertips and negative forces were easily dismissed and cast aside. They have found more precious time to be with loved ones, and some have even begun to dream again.

A continuous cycle of underachieving has robbed us of our dreams. As children we were never too old to embark on the achievement of our legacy. We were never too tired to reach for the cup of life. We were never too downtrodden that we would not accept the invitation to make our dreams come true, despite what conventional logic or even the opinions of those around us maintained. We were willing to dare, and our destinies would not be denied us!

Learning the first step in the seven-up approach can be difficult for those who thought the ability to talk was the only prerequisite to great sales. The ability to listen, reason on, and read all forms of communication, including body language and tonality, is an asset to every great salesperson. Some claim to have mastered this skill so well that in many cases they feel they can tell you whether or not a potential customer will buy their product after they have performed only a quarter of their sales presentation (some, even sooner).

Of course, this is not an exact science and others have used this to proclaim that it is impossible to get a sense of whether or not a potential customer will buy, and that one should leave the psychology to the psychologists.

However, good salespeople really do have the ability to sense the imminence of a sale. However, there are always exceptions, and the issue behind this is that there are those who use their "ability to sense" as an excuse as to why they did not make a sale when, had their presentations been better, the sales would have been made.

For example, consider Jennifer, a carpet salesperson with a few months of experience. She had just had a very long day in the field and was tired. She missed her children, her husband, and the comfort of home. She didn't really want to perform her next sales presentation. At this time, she was training a rookie named Darlene. As Jennifer prepared everything for the day's final presentation, she excused herself to go out to her van where she kept the samples of the various tapestries.

Darlene accompanied her to the van and when they got there, Jennifer told her that she was only going to perform a quick presentation because she could sense that the potential customers were not the buying sorts. Darlene wondered how Jennifer knew this since they had just arrived and hadn't even really spoken to the potential customers.

Since Jennifer was still fairly new at sales, it's unlikely that she could really tell at this point whether or not her customers would purchase. She was instead trying to justify why she was not going to give her all when performing this sales presentation.

In this type of scenario it is not unreasonable to conclude that, far from being a science one can apply, this art of reading buying signals and judging customers' tonality and body language is nothing more than an elaborate rouse perpetrated by salespeople wanting to introduce an air of mystery into the process.

However, for those "doubting Thomas's," isn't closing the sale as much a science as the study of human behavioral patterns? We can often predict certain behavior patterns when introducing certain stimuli. This is also true of sales. Now consider the following illustration and decide whether or not you believe the potential customer's response could have been predicted.

Salesperson: "This is the tuberculosis virus magnified. We found tuberculosis, streptococci, and even hemolytic bacteria in just one thimble full of the dust inside this vacuum bag. We also found that there were over five million germs. The objectionable odor emanating from the vacuum is caused by the incubation of the germs and bacteria inside. Germs and bacteria need three favorable conditions in order to breed and multiply best. They need a warm area, a dark area, and a filthy place. Inside your vacuum bag is it warm?"

Potential Customers: "Yes."

Salesperson: "Is it dark?"

Potential customer: "Yes."

Salesperson: "Is it filthy?"

Potential customer: "Yes."

Salesperson: "So what you're telling me is that we don't all own great vacuums, but we do own great incubators. And how do we know the odor is not simply the dust? Because it stinks! If dust smelled as bad as your vacuum bag, wouldn't your whole house stink? After all, it's covered with dust. The only time we notice the odor is while vacuuming. That's because as we vacuum we suck the air of our homes in, force it through a bag full of germs and disease, and blow it all over our homes. When meat begins to decay in the fridge, how can you tell it's bad without eating it?"

Potential customer: "By smelling it."

Salesperson: "What about sour milk?"

Potential customer: "Smelling it."

Salesperson: "What about a rotten egg?"

Potential customer: "The smell."

Salesperson: "Let me ask you a question. Does this sound healthy, or unhealthy?"

What do you think the potential customer will respond, that it's healthy or unhealthy? As you can see, the potential customer's responses can be predicted to some degree if the right stimulus is given prior to the questioning.

An oversimplified version of this can be seen in this question. "When was the war of 1812?" While the answer may be obvious to you, you might be surprised at some of the answers given by a group of people from a variety of societal and educational backgrounds. Far from all of them would be able to tell you that it started in 1812.

In my sales classes, I experimented with this very question. Believe it or not, on the odd occasion I heard a student say, "I don't know, Sir. I wasn't that good in history." Another time I heard a student say, "How am I supposed to know?" On still other occasions, the student asked to have the question repeated so they could have more time to think about what the answer might be.

The reason I explain this is that your sales career is very much like this experiment. Although it can be very scientific, and even predictable, there will always be deviance in the behavior patterns of certain individuals. This may arise from a lack of comprehension of the material being discussed, ignorance, a lack of interest, or simply not listening.

The final reason that some unpredictability may occur could be due to the potential customer's need for attention, or a held resentment toward the salesperson. If we reckon that our sales communication has a specific effect on a potential customer's response, than we are responsible for the acquisition or loss of a sale. We also must understand and reason on our potential customer's communication, including, but not limited to, physicality and tonality. This means we must, as salespeople, possess the ability to listen intuitively and effectively.

If the salesperson conveys some factual information or stimuli and the potential customer rolls his eyes, is this kind of non-verbal communication relevant? Yes! Every bit of the potential customer's communication is relevant and should be considered. This ability to read potential customers is sometimes called "street smarts" and it is an asset to all great salespeople.

Now that we have determined that there are several forms of communication, listening and interpreting their message becomes that much more important. It is also important not to interrupt their communication. Many salespeople have had the tendency to stop their prospects in mid-objection:

> "I know what you're going to say, but let me say…" This can cause several things to happen. First, you offend the potential customer because you interrupt them. Second, you may not know what they are going to say, and third, you…[cannot] …interpret… [the seeds for the objection's solution]. (Meyers, 1991)

"Every problem contains the seeds of its own solution" (Arnold n.d.).

Step 2. See the Objection the Way You Want to See It.

Seeing the objection the way you want to see it makes it much easier to listen to the potential customers' objections, even when you feel that there is no good reason for them. Customer objections can sometimes be interpreted as insults to the salesperson, especially if the salesperson feels that the sales performance was one of their personal best. However, remember that your mission in listening is to reveal the seeds of the solution to their objection. This is difficult when you are busy feeling sorry for yourself. Instead of interpreting the objection as an insult, look for the solution.

"When the door of happiness closes, another opens; but often we look so long at the closed door that we do not see the one which has been opened for us" (Keller, n.d.).

Objections aren't personal! The potential customers are not attacking you or your presentation. They are merely reacting to stimuli and behavioral programming. They are reacting to your image and your communication. This is important to remember, since a person cannot change who they really are for every sales presentation. Those who have claimed to, have only demonstrated their failure to know themselves. Yet it is possible to change one's image merely by making adjustments to the sales pitch.

For example, think about movie actors who have played convincing roles as both villains and heroes. If we had only seen them in villainous roles, we might believe that's how they are in real life, until we see them in heroic, kind roles, and realize they are merely adjusting their presentation of themselves as a character.

Similarly, potential customers react to the role we play as salespeople, and not to who we are as individuals. Remembering this may make it easier for you to listen to your potential customers' objections sincerely. This is a critical step in resisting the doppelganger effect.

"Do you know why that cow looks over that wall? I will tell you. She looks over that wall because she can't see through it and that is what you must do with your troubles—look over and above them"(u.a.).

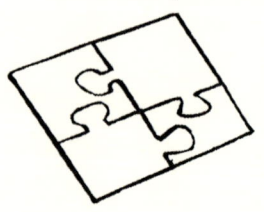

It is best to see the customer's objection as an invitation or challenge for you to close. An objection is very much like a puzzle. You must first examine the puzzle to understand how it works. Then you can come up with a solution. So let's try to understand a few facts about our puzzle. First, people love to shop! They love the feeling of buying new things. They love the feelings of a satisfied curiosity.

Men and women both love shopping. The main difference I have observed is that men enjoy the gratification of the purchase, whereas women enjoy the entire process of the sale, including all the debate and reasoning that precedes it.

If the salesperson views an objection as a request for assistance in attaining the necessary thoughts, beliefs and emotions required to attain the sale, than the doppelganger effect is likely to be averted and more peaceful strategies for a solution employed. This is the aim of seeing the objection the way you would like to see it. Maintain the same physical and mental attitude, and be enthusiastic and use confident tones in your communication.

Step 3. Repeat the Objection

Repeating the customer's objection aloud ensures a misinterpretation has not occurred. It is recommended that you rephrase the objection but maintain its original meaning so you can reveal whether or not your interpretation is correct. Consider the following example: the potential customer objects to the purchase by saying, "We can't afford it." The salesperson listens objectively, and replies, "So it's just the money then" (This is an example of repeating an objection). Notice how the salesperson repeated the objection, and though it was rephrased, it maintained its original meaning.

The salesperson would now observe the potential customers for signs of acknowledgment and agreement. The potential customers are usually sincere about this because they believe that this is an objection that cannot be easily ignored. It is also possible for the potential customer to voice more than one objection. Another common method of objection by potential customers is to build a *wall of reasoning*.

A wall of reasoning is when a potential customer feels some anxiety that the salesperson may in fact possess enough sales ability to overcome the objection and generate the sale despite it. To combat this anxiety, the potential customer will not communicate the objection outright, but instead will communicate a mountain of symptoms that imply the objection. This is illustrated in the following scenario: Salesperson Casey asks his potential customers for the order. The husband, Don, began to object in the following manner.

"We'd love to buy, but you wouldn't believe what happened today. On the way home my car broke down. I took it into the shop and the mechanic told me that it was going to be a very expensive job. While he was looking at the engine, he discovered a serious problem with the transmission and I don't know how we are going to pay for it. I've got two kids going into college and my youngest needs braces. My wife Marie just told me that the washing machine is on the fritz and my tool belt broke today while I was on the job. You understand, don't you Casey?"

In this example the potential customer did not communicate the objection outright. Instead, Don built a wall of reasoning, using symptoms of the problem (lack of money) rather than communicate the problem itself. He reasoned that the salesperson would not be able to overcome such a mountainous objection, and therefore Don felt secure that he and his wife would not be buying anything after having given such an objection.

Don liked the product, but had vowed that he would never purchase anything again from a direct salesperson, since he felt that a pressure-salesman had taken advantage of him two years earlier (something Casey was unaware of).

Casey repeated Don's objection, "So it's just the money, then?" Don's wall of reasoning had been reduced to a single brick with that one line.

Don appeared deflated, but stood by his now seemingly small objection. Casey had maintained his composure and sincerely listened to Don's entire verbal objection. He patiently waited for his opportunity to seize the sale, but he knew that he would need to extract the seeds of the solution from Don's objection.

Step 4. Agree & Reverse

This is a very important step in the Seven-Up approach. No matter what the potential customer says, it is very important for the salesperson to calmly agree and back off. There is a method for agreeing and reversing without giving up any power in the sale. For example, if Don were to say, "Yeah it's just the money," Casey could reply, "_If right now you feel as though you can't afford it_, then don't get it. Because if you were in my home showing me the product and I _felt like I couldn't afford it, then I wouldn't get it_. But I want to thank you, Don and Marie, for having invited me over to show you both the product."

At this point, Don and Maria both smile and shake Casey's hand. Casey appears to be accepting defeat graciously, and both Don and Maria admire him for that. They may even begin to feel some guilt over not buying, because they both realized that the reason they were objecting had nothing to do with Casey or his presentation, and that they both really liked the product.

Notice that Casey *did not* say that he agreed with the objection that Don and Maria couldn't afford it. As noted by the underlined portion of the text, Casey said he agreed that if they *felt* like they couldn't afford the product, then they should not get it.

This catches the potential customers off guard because they are not expecting this response. For the entire presentation, Casey had promoted his product and reasoned with Don and Marie on the benefits they could receive for having purchased. So when Casey boldly proclaimed that if they felt this way they should not purchase the product, both Don and Marie were confounded. In the past, they had argued with salespeople and even been forced to extremes, e.g., getting rude and throwing the salesperson out of their home.

It was like a breath of fresh air for them when Casey calmly agreed and reversed. Often, potential customers will, in such a situation, find it easier to relax and be themselves.

You may be wondering how the sale will ultimately be achieved if it appears as though you are leaving. Remember that things are not always as they appear and many a sale has been earned through what I call *diversionary reasoning*, which will be discussed in more detail in point 6 below.

Note: Reversing does not involve putting on your jacket, packing up your products, and leaving. Reversing is merely a pressure release valve which allows the potential customer to communicate an objection without feeling like they need to become defensive.

Step 5. Isolating the Objection

Step five is one of the easiest steps of the Seven-Up approach, and yet one of the most frequently forgotten and critical steps in the closing procedure. Isolating the objection is the name given to the protocol for committing the potential customer to a specific number of objections; usually one, but on rare occasions, multiple.

Asking the potential customers if there is any other reason why they would not purchase the product performs this. Consider the following question made by Casey.

"Don and Marie, apart from the fact that right now you feel as though you can't afford the product, is there anything else preventing you from purchasing tonight?"

"No just the money," replies Don.

Casey confirms this by saying, "So if you could afford it, you would have definitely purchased tonight?" Don and Maria both agree.

This is an excellent example of Casey isolating the objection. Perhaps the potential customer will give another objection during this phase. If this happens, be happy, because the potential customer has provided even more of the seeds necessary for the solution of the objection. It is best to get all the objections out on the table right away so that you know what you're dealing with. For example, Casey asks Don and Marie if there is anything else besides the money preventing them from purchasing. Don and Marie explain that they would consider financing options, but that Casey has come at an awkward time. Marie has been out of work on maternity leave for the past two years and has just started back. She thinks that things would be better down the road.

Casey explains that these things happen to everyone, and that he understands completely. In this case, when Casey went to isolate the objection, he was given another. Notice that Casey did not panic, but merely listened and appreciated everything that Don and Marie had to say. He was now ready to close the sale with diversionary reasoning.

Before we move on I want you to consider the outcome when this step is skipped. The salesperson uses the diversionary reasoning technique and successfully closes the potential customers. As he is writing up the necessary paperwork, the potential customer comes up with another objection. This is also called *switching*.

The salesperson follows all the steps in the Seven-Up approach, except to isolate the objection. Again, the salesperson is successful in closing the potential customers and begins with the paperwork. Before the potential customers are willing to sign the contract, he objects again. As the salesperson begins (what has now become a cycle of objection and closing) the Seven-Up approach, the customer appears overly defensive and does not wish to cooperate in the closing procedure. The potential customer begins to feel pressured and the whole purpose of reverse closing has been lost.

Step 6. Inform (Diversionary Reasoning) A Practical Analysis

It is this stage in the Seven-Up approach that most salespeople find intriguing. Let's examine an example of diversionary reasoning and see if we can find out why it is so effective.

Customers Bob and Mary give the objection that they need time to make a decision as to whether or not they will buy the air cleaner from Salesperson Erica. Erica follows all the steps in the Seven-Up approach and decides to use the diversionary reasoning technique. She decides to try the Time & Money Close. She asks Bob and Mary a question.

"From what you learned from my sales presentation, would you say that having this new air cleaner would save you time and money?"

Bob and Mary are not sure where this line of questioning is leading, but they believe that it sounds harmless enough, so **they agree** that they both feel that having the new air cleaner would, in fact, save them time and money. Erica proceeds.

"When is the best time, for you to start saving time and money?"

"Right now!"

"That's why nobody puts off purchasing this fantastic new air cleaner. Congratulations!"

Erica reaches out and shakes Bob and Mary's hands. She then invites them into the kitchen to fill out the necessary forms.

In this scenario, we can begin to understand where this technique gets its name. The first part of the communication begins with a non-threatening diversionary question or story told to the potential customer. Armed with the correct answer or solution to the initial objection, the salesperson then asks a question which effectively causes the potential customer to overcome his own objection. Then the salesperson simply asks for the order again.

Now let's consider some more complex illustrations of diversionary reasoning. Salesperson Brian just finished a vacuum cleaner demonstration and his potential customers John and Nicole objected to the purchase by saying that they could not consider buying Brian's water trap vacuum system because they had recently (six months earlier) purchased a conventional name brand vacuum for fifteen hundred dollars. They claimed that they had too much money tied up in the vacuum cleaner they already owned. They knew, however, that it wasn't doing the job they bought it to do, and they really enjoyed the machine that Brian had shown them. Brian followed all the steps in the Seven-Up approach and decided to use diversionary reasoning to help close the sale. Brian uses the Vitamin story (Lamb, 1991).

"Have you ever taken vitamins, John and Nicole?

John and Nicole wonder what vitamins have to do with his vacuum cleaner, but the question sounds innocent enough, so they decide it is okay to answer. John says that they have taken vitamins many times, especially around "cold season." Nicole says that it helps them to fight off various forms of sickness.

Brian continues, "Suppose you went down to the local pharmacy to buy some vitamins and you saw a pickle barrel full of your favorite vitamins on sale for a hundred dollars. It seems like a lot of money, but you realize that you'll be saving over time. So you go ahead and purchase the vitamins.

When you get home, you announce to your family that you got a really good deal on vitamins and that you would like everyone to take one every day. You decide to be the leader and take the first one. Everyone else in the family supports you and also takes a vitamin. About an hour later, you all begin to come down with painful stomach cramps and nausea. Everyone feels sick and in discomfort. It lasts for over an hour, but then it goes away.

The next day, shortly after taking your vitamins, you all come down with the stomach cramps and nausea again. It wouldn't take you too long to realize that every time we take these vitamins we get sick, would it?"

"No."

"So you call up the pharmacy, but they explain that you bought the vitamins on a clear-out special and that no return or refund is possible.

"Would you say to your family, 'Well I know every time we takes these vitamins it makes us sick, but I've got a lot of money tied up in these vitamins, so we're just going to have to eat them?'"

"No."

"What would you do with the vitamins?" asks Brian.

"I'd throw the vitamins out!"

"Yes, because if they don't do the job you bought them to do, the money is wasted! It doesn't make any sense to punish your family for a mistake does it?"

"No."

"It's the same thing with a vacuum that can't clean. If it doesn't do the job you bought it to do, the money is wasted! So if you would throw out the vitamins, what should you do with this?" (*Pointing at their vacuum.*)

"Get rid of it, I guess."

"Well, John and Nicole, it really wouldn't matter if you had one vacuum or a thousand vacuums, if they can't clean, they're equally useless. Besides, if you wouldn't use this new machine, it would still be a bad deal. So let me ask you this. If you had this new vacuum/steam cleaner, would you use it?"

"Yes, of course!"

"Who does most of the cleaning?"

"Nicole does," replies John.

"Fine, if Nicole said that she would appreciate and use the new vacuum/steam cleaner, would you support her in getting one, John?"

"Yes."

"Let's go to the table where we can fill out your warranty," concludes Brian.

In this illustration, Brian effectively used diversionary reasoning and then came back to asking for the order with the two basic questions from p. 125. He then incorporated an assuming-the-sale technique and took them to the table. Notice how Brian was able to get the potential customers to effectively overcome their own objection.

There is a simple logic behind why this closing technique works. It is because of the assertion that "the customer is always right!" Who better than the customer to overcome his objection? It is difficult and silly looking to argue with oneself. Only the potential customer knows whether the objection was genuine and sincere, or just an excuse to rid them of a poor salesperson.

Some have asked if diversionary reasoning is always successful, and of course I remind them that in sales there are rarely any absolutes. However, diversionary reasoning has been responsible for the gaining of thousands, perhaps even millions of otherwise potentially lost sales.

Considering the alternatives to diversionary reasoning, which usually include the doppelganger effect, pressure, or simply accepting defeat and rejection, I would say that it is certain that any technique which effectively offers the salesperson another shot at the sale has merit. The basic laws of probability insist that this technique can and will improve your closing endeavors.

This particular close can be modified to work with many different products. In the next few pages you will have the opportunity to view several more of these closes. Keep in mind that they are not tailored to your business until you customize them.

"The Fifty Cent Pay-Cut Close" (u.a.)
(*We can't afford it!*)

"Where do you work, Bill?"
"I work at Smile Safe Airlines."
"How much do they pay you per hour?"
"I make twenty-eight dollars an hour."
"Let's say that Smile Safe called you and all the other airline personnel into an emergency meeting. There, they explained that due to the decline in passengers since the September eleventh terrorist attacks in the US, the Smile Safe Airline Company had lost a large portion of its customers, and as a result would have to layoff everyone in the company.

"Wouldn't you panic a bit? Wouldn't you call your wife and tell her what was going on? I bet you would wonder how you were going to pay the mortgage, or your daughter's college tuition fees wouldn't you? You might even call your wife and tell her not to purchase anything. Heck, take the braces off the kids!

"But what if they called everyone back into the assembly hall and explained that they had come up with a way to save the company. The accounting department has assured us that if everyone in the company were to agree to take a fifty cent pay cut, the company could pay off its deficit in three years. At which time everyone could resume his or her normal pay.

"They required everyone to vote on this decision. What would you do? Take the cut, or join the unemployment line?"

"I'd take the cut!"

"Wouldn't you call your wife back and tell her everything's okay? You would, wouldn't you?"

"Yes."

"If you could have afforded (insert product), you would definitely have bought one from me tonight, right?"

"Of course, if I could afford it."

"Well let's go back to the fifty cent pay cut. Wouldn't you be relieved that it was only fifty cents?"

"Yes."

"Honestly, would you have to change your standard of living for fifty cents an hour?"

"No."

"So you're saying that fifty cents an hour wouldn't take food off your table?"

"No."

"How many hours in a week do you usually work?"

"Forty."

"So fifty cents an hour times forty hours per week is about twenty dollars right?"

"Yes."

"And that would not take food off your table, correct?"

"That's right."

"How many weeks are there in the average month?"

"Four."

"So twenty times four is about eighty dollars per month right?"

"Yes."

"So what you're telling me is that the most you could afford, without taking food off your table or changing your standard of living, is about eighty dollars per month right?"

"Yeah, I guess so."

"So, if I could get you this product for under what you said you could afford a month, you'd honor your word and go ahead and get it wouldn't you?"

"Yes, but it would have to be less than eighty dollars per month."

"Well, let me call my manager and see if there's anything we can do. But before I do, I have to ask you this. If you had this product in your home, would you use it?"

"Yes, of course."

"Because if you wouldn't use the product, it wouldn't really matter whether it was eighty dollars per month or five dollars per month, because it would still be a bad deal. So, you would use it?"

"Yes."

"(Prospect's name) if (insert spouse's name) would appreciate and use the (insert product), and I can arrange this deal for under eighty dollars per month, would you support him in getting it?"

"Yes"

"Okay let me call my manager and see what we can do."

"Now, promise you won't be mad at me if I can't get you the deal, okay?"

"No, we won't be mad if you can't manage it."

"Just before I call my manager, if I can convince him to make you this deal, you will for sure take the (insert product here), right?"

"Yes."

"Okay, can I use your telephone?"

"Sure."

In this scenario, the diversion came from the potential customer's work place. Notice how the salesperson commits the potential customer to an amount which he can afford, essentially inviting the potential customer to overcome his own objection. Then the salesperson relates everything to the current situation.

Just when he has the potential customer where he wants him, the salesperson relaxes the tension and follows up with the two basic questions as shown on p. 125. Then the salesperson employs a third party closing technique and makes sure to solidify the commitment one last time before calling his manager. Also, it is important to note that the salesperson attempts to make the potential customer feel special should the deal be struck, by asking the potential customers not to be angry if he is unable to meet their requirements.

"The Mortgage Close" (u.a.)
(*We can't afford it!*)

"Do you have a mortgage on this home?"

"Yes."

"Suppose the mortgage company called you and told you that they had made a mistake when calculating your mortgage. Apparently, your monthly payment was supposed to be a hundred dollars more than what you have been paying. What would you do? Would you call your realtor, and sell the house?"

"No. I'd just pay it."

"Would you still be able to eat and smoke cigarettes?"

"Of course, it's only a hundred dollars a month."

"Okay, well let me ask you this: *if* you could have afforded the (insert product here), *would* you have purchased it tonight?"

"Yes."

"So *if* I could get you the (insert product/s) for less than a hundred dollars a month, which is all you could afford, you *would* you get it, right?"

"Yes."

In this scenario, the diversion comes from the mortgage. When the potential customer has overcome or solved his own objection, then the I&W technique is used to wrap it up, shown in italics.

Another common objection with "We can't afford it" is "We didn't really plan for this." This close can easily be modified to encompass this possible scenario. Consider the following example:

"Do you have a mortgage on this home?"

"Yes."

"Suppose the mortgage company called you and told you that they had made a mistake when calculating your mortgage. Apparently your monthly payment was supposed to be a hundred dollars more than what you have been paying. What would you do? Would you call your realtor, and sell the house?"

"No. I'd just pay it."

"Would you still be able to eat and smoke cigarettes?"

"Of course, it's only a hundred dollars a month."

"Okay, well let me ask you this: *if* you could have afforded the (insert product here), **even though you didn't really plan for it**, *would* you have purchased it tonight?"

"Yes."

"So, *if* I could get you the (insert product/s) for less than a hundred dollars a month, which is all you could afford, you *would* you get it right?"

"Yes."

As you can see by the bold underlined text, introduced into the mortgage close, it can easily encompass other scenarios. Notice that the potential customer's own words are used to overcome the objection. This illustrates well how the seeds of the solution are inherent in the original objection.

"The Reduction to the Ridiculous Close" (u.a.)

(*It costs too much!—lack of value building*)
*Calculator required

"How much too much would you say that the (insert product here) is?

"I think it's about one thousand dollars too much!"

"If it wasn't too much, would you have purchased the product?"

"Yes."

"Well, let's consider if the product really is too much? You said about a thousand dollars right?"

"Yes."

"All right, let's look at the product. It was designed to last you a lifetime, but let's say that you abused it and it only lasted you ten years (Use calculator. Punch in 1000 and divide by ten).

"Then what you are saying is that it is about one hundred dollars a year *too much* for every year that you have it, right?"

"Yes."

"Okay, how many months are there in a year?"

"Twelve." (Use calculator and punch in one hundred divided by twelve).

"So what you're telling me is that this product is about eight dollars and thirty-three cents too much for every month that you would enjoy it, right?"

"Yes."

"Now, how many days in an average month do you work?"

"About twenty." (Use calculator and punch in eight point three, three divided by twenty).

"So what you're saying is that this product would be about forty-two cents a day too much for you and your family to enjoy all the great benefits. How many hours a day, do you work?"

"Eight." (Use calculator and punch in forty-two divided by eight).

"So what you're saying is that this product would be about five cents too much for every hour that you work while you and your family enjoy the benefits of it, right?"

(Potential customer begins grinning)

"Can you see how the (insert product) would provide great benefits to you and your family?"

"Yes."

"If you owned the product, would you use it to benefit your family?"

"Yes."

"When you think about it, is providing your family with these benefits, for only five cents an hour, really too much?"

"No."

"Well, it really wouldn't matter whether the (insert product) was a thousand dollars too much, or just five cents too much, because if you wouldn't use it, it would still be a bad deal. So if you had the (insert product), would you use it?"

"Yes."

"If (insert prospect's name) would use the (insert product), would you support his/her decision to get it?"

Spouse: "Yes."

"Let's go to the table and fill out the papers."

In this scenario, the length of time the product will or will not last is the diversion because the potential customer cannot associate what this has to do with the product costing too much. Then, the salesperson relates the answer to the objection to the story and overcomes it.

The "Yes, yes" method is also introduced. The two basic questions are asked, followed by a version of the assumption close.

"The Prescription Close" (u.a.)
(*We Need to Think About it*)

"Let's say that your child were to get sick and you decided it was time to take him to the hospital. After the doctor's examination, he explained to you that your child had an infection and would require a course of medication. The doctor begins to write out a prescription and hands it to you. Is it likely that you would hand the prescription back to the doctor and tell him that you would need to think about it?"

"No."

"Because when it comes to the health and welfare of your family, that's not something you really need to think about, is it?"

"No!"

"Now, when you consider this new (home security system/similar product), which is going to protect the health and welfare of your family, is that something you really need to think about?"

"Well, not really."

"You don't have to think about it, because you already know that their protection is important to you, right?"

"Yes."

"But you know it really wouldn't matter whether you thought about it for ten minutes or ten days, because if you wouldn't use it, it would still be a bad deal. So let me ask you this: If we were to install the new security system would you use it to protect your family?"

"Of course."

"(Spouse's name), if your husband/wife went to the trouble of installing a home security system for your protection, would you support his/her decision?"

"Yes."

"Well, congratulations and welcome to our home security family!"

"Switching Close" (u.a.)
(*We Need to Think About it*)

"How long would you need to think about it?"

"Just a couple of days."

"Let's say that we waited a couple of days while you thought it over and you decided not to get the (insert product), what do you think the biggest factor would be that prevented you from getting the (insert product)?"

The potential customer is likely to answer "money" or some other underlying cause of objection. The salesperson may choose to switch the closing technique to one that better addresses the potential customer's real objection. [Example: *The Fifty Cents Pay-cut Close.*]

"The Kid and Scooter Story"(u.a.)
(*We Never Buy on the Spur of the Moment*)

"Let's say that you were driving down the road in a residential neighborhood and suddenly a child riding a scooter jutted out from behind a parked car. At the spur of the moment, you were forced to make a decision. Either you hit the brakes and save the child or you continue and hit the child. What would you do?"

"I'd hit the brakes."

"So you are capable of making a decision on the spur of the moment. The real question is, was it the right decision or the wrong decision to save the child?"

"It was the right decision!"

"Now, is having the (insert product) and all the benefits it can provide in your home the right decision or the wrong decision?"

"Well, I think it's the right decision."

"Great! But it really wouldn't matter whether you decided right now or ten years from now, if you wouldn't use, it would still be a bad deal. So, if you had the (insert product) would you use it?"

"Yes."

"(Insert name), if (insert spouse's name) would appreciate and use the (insert product), would you help him/her get it?"

"Yes."

"Great.

"Let's go to the table and I'll show you how easy it can be."

In this scenario, there is a double diversion. The child on the scooter is the first diversion and the issue of whether or not this decision is the right one is the second. The salesperson relates the potential customer's answer to his objection. Then the salesperson follows with the two basic questions, and an "Assuming-the-sale" technique.

"Live Forever Close" (u.a.)
(*I'm Too Old Objection*)

"Let's say that you didn't purchase the cookware from me tonight. If anything were to happen to you, you would probably give the money to your children. After all, you never see a Brink's Truck following a hearse, do you?"

"No."

"You can't take it with you. How long do you think it would take for your child to spend two thousand dollars?"

"Not very long."

"If you were to buy the cookware tonight and anything was to happen to you, you would probably give the cookware to your child. How long do you think the cookware would last?"

"Forever!"

"That means that every time your child cooks a meal, they would think of you. In other words, you can live forever!

"But it really wouldn't matter whether you bought the cookware or not if you didn't use it. To buy it and never use it would be a bad deal. So if you had the cookware, would you use it?"

"Yes."

"If you could benefit for the rest of your life from this cookware, live forever and pass it on to your family, wouldn't you like to enjoy the benefits of this fantastic cookware?"

"Yes."

"Great! Let's go to the table and I'll show you how easy it can be."

"The Honeymoon Close"(u.a.)
(*Husband doesn't support wife's desire to purchase*)

"How long have you two been married?"

"Fifteen years."

"I bet you really love Sarah. If Sarah would have whispered in your ear just before she said "I do" and asked you to buy her this washing machine, I bet you would have bought her ten of them wouldn't you?"

"Yeah, I bet I would have."

"Well, Charles, after fifteen years, aren't you willing to get her this washing machine and show her that you still love her at least one tenth as much?"

"Yes."

"Fantastic! But Charles, it really wouldn't matter if you bought Sarah one machine or ten machines, because if Sarah wouldn't use the machine, it would still be a bad deal. Sarah, if you had this new washing machine, would you use it?"

"Yes! I would make sure that all his shirts were always nice and clean."

"If Sarah said that she would appreciate and use the new washing machine, and showing her that you still love her as much as you did the day you married her, you would support her, and help her get it wouldn't you, Charles?"

"Yes."

"Great. Let's just go over to the table and we'll have a coffee and fill out your warrantee card."

"Puppy Dog Close" (u.a.)
(Potential Customers are on the fence.)

"Listen, Keri and Glen, why don't I leave the product here with you. Try it out and see if you like it. I'll come back in a few days, and if you fall in love with it, we'll write up the paperwork. If not, I'll pick it up. How does that sound?"

"Okay, we'll try it and see how we feel."

This close is so named because of its similarity to the following story: Ned was moving into a new apartment where pets were prohibited. He did not know what he was going to do with the puppy he had bought two weeks earlier. He knew that if he couldn't find the puppy a home, he would most likely have to give the dog to the animal shelter where many animals that did not find homes were put to sleep.

Ned knew that his sister Karen could provide a good home for the puppy, and that her children would love the pet. Ned went over to Karen's and asked her if she would care for the puppy for a week while Ned was out of town on business. Ned explained that he was trying to find a home for the puppy and had hoped that he would be able to before the puppy would have to be put to sleep. Karen asked what the puppy's name was and Ned told her he had not named him yet. Karen agreed to watch the puppy while Ned was away.

After a few days, Karen began calling the puppy Spots. Karen's kids also began to fall in love with Spots. When Ned came back to pick up the puppy, Karen explained that she didn't want to let Spots go. So Spots had found a new home with Karen and her family.

When a salesperson uses the puppy dog close, I have observed that it is because they usually do not possess any other closing techniques, or they are too afraid to ask for the order. They are hoping that the potential customer will ask them for the sale so they don't have to ask the potential customer for the order.

This close is not the most effective and lends itself to an increased number of Buyer's Remorse situations. It also results in products whose appearance has been tarnished cosmetically because some individuals will use the product(s) knowing that they have no intention of purchasing.

In this way, they are taking advantage of the salesperson, the company, and the situation. In other scenarios, the potential customer only agrees to keep the product because they feel that it will be easier to make an excuse for not buying at a later time when the salesperson is no longer supported and fueled by a sales presentation whose arguments and reasoning seemed compelling at the time.

It is important to keep in mind that some potential customers, upon learning new information which might compel them to purchase a product or service normally, may enter into a state of psychological denial in order to subvert the sales process. Others may simply be stubborn.

I have observed potential customers who verbally reversed themselves or said things contrary to their earlier reasoning, simply because their suspicions led them to believe that by completing the sales process they would in some way be accepting a psychological defeat.

It is important to conclude that all closing techniques are methods for reasoning with your potential customer, and as such, they require that the potential customer be willing to reason. A good example of this has been demonstrated in some of my seminars when a former student had bragged to another student that I possessed the amazing ability to close any objection.

The student asked me if I would be willing to attempt to reason with him over an objection. I began a role-playing session with the student.

He was playing the role of his potential customers and I was playing the salesperson. It began fine until I asked a question that he had not thought to ask his potential customers. He paused and realized where he had been mistaken. However, instead of explaining that he had noted the deviance in his line of questioning, he continued. I continued to reason with him using Diversionary Reasoning techniques.

The problem was that whenever an obvious answer presented itself, he would purposely say something contradictory or argumentative in order to prove that these techniques could not be effective. After a few power struggles, I realized what was happening and discontinued the communication.

For this reason I wish to tell you that in order for your closing techniques to be effective you must be dealing with potential customers who are willing to reason. This would also be important to realize while practicing your closing techniques on friends, relatives, or work associates.

If & Would
(*Effective for almost any objection*)

The I&W technique was described in chapter ten and is a very effective tool for overcoming objections.

Take the following situation: the potential customers tell you that they only pays cash for items, but they do not have enough at this time to purchase. This usually brings three possible scenarios to mind. First, the potential customers do not like to pay interest and therefore only wish to purchase things with cash (Some may argue that not wanting a payment could be a factor). However, phone service, heating, home mortgage, car payments, and insurance indicate that, in most cases, payments are a reality of life. If the potential customers have any such things, it is obvious that when they feel they really want or need something, they are willing to pay by installments.

The second possibility is that the potential customers have poor credit and do not wish to tarnish their appearance to the salesperson by having a credit investigation expose it.

The third possibility is that the potential customers are not being sincere about the objection and are merely using this form of communication to make an excuse to the salesperson for not buying. They reason that this is better than explaining to the salesperson that their performance was not adequate enough to generate the sale. To add insult to supposedly invisible injury, the potential customers patronize the salesperson by saying, "Despite the fact that we're not buying, you're a good salesperson! We were really impressed."

When the potential customer is sincere, and there is a possibility that they simply do not like paying interest charges, than there is a possible I&W phrase which may be effective.

Some banks offer financing terms with no interest charged to the potential customer. If such terms exist with your finance company or bank you may say, "*If* I could get you the product for this price, on monthly installments you can afford, and there were no interest charges at all, *would* you take the product?"

Another scenario would be to agree to pay the interest charges and finance the contract over the shortest agreeable time so that the interest charges/loss can be minimized. The If & Would phrasing would remain the same.

The customer does not need to know whether or not you are accepting a loss with the agreement. However, some may feel that the explanation of this loss may actually help the potential customer to visualize the BBD that they are receiving. Other scenarios for I&W phrases would be no interest and no payment scenarios, also sometimes known as deferred payment options.

It is important not to nonchalantly offer BBDs but instead to always use a BBD to get an I&W commitment. This would also include questions by the potential customers such as, "Are the taxes included?"

At first, if they are not, you should explain that they are not included truthfully, but anticipate that this may turn into the root of an objection which can be easily solved with an I&W commitment. "*If* I could get you this product, for this price, tax included, *would* you get the product?" If the answer to this question is "No," then you can immediately dismiss this as the cause of the objection, and you will have to discern what is really causing the objection before you can solve it.

Keep in mind that you may have to be creative when using the I&W technique. Consider the following example and see if you can think of a solution to the potential customer's problem that will not cost any of the salesperson's possible commission, and yet effectively solves the potential customer's objection. Explain how you would phrase your I&W questions.

Patrick and Rose watched a sales presentation for new windows in their home. Patrick worked for the airport as an airplane mechanic and Rose was a stay-at-home mother of three. Patrick made good wages but had been laid off for several months because of cutbacks since the September eleventh terrorist attacks in the United States of America. Patrick had returned to work, but both he and Rose had their reservations about the stability of Patrick's job. They really liked the new windows but they knew that it would be three months until they would be caught up on their bills.

They had good credit because they had budgeted wisely in the past, so they objected to the purchase because it wasn't a good time for them.

Salesperson Tyler offered Patrick and Rose the following methods of payment:

- Cash
- Check
- Credit Card
- Monthly Installments

Patrick and Rose did not have enough money on them or in the bank to pay for the windows. They did not have enough room on their credit cards and they always liked to leave a little for emergencies. They felt that monthly installments would be the method of payment they would prefer, but that this wouldn't be feasible for another three months. Patrick and Rose thought that they could afford about one hundred and twenty-five dollars per month.

When Tyler made the calculations for the windows they wanted, the monthly payment only came to one hundred dollars per month. Tyler had heard of companies that offered no interest, no payment options, but unfortunately, the financing company that he dealt with did not offer such plans. Tyler knew that if he didn't walk out of their home with a signed contract, the chances of obtaining this sale later would be greatly diminished. He needed to come up with something fast. He needed to overcome their objection and solve the puzzle within the next thirty seconds.

If you were Tyler, what would you do to overcome Patrick and Rose's objection and get the order using the I&W technique? Stop reading and see if you can solve this problem before continuing to the solution on the next page.

Think Outside the Box

"Patrick and Rose, *if* I could get you the windows for a monthly installment under one hundred and twenty-five dollars per month, and you didn't have to come out of pocket for three months, *would* you get the windows tonight?"

"Yes, we would."

"My finance company doesn't offer any no-interest, no-payment options. However, I think I may be able to come up with something for you. The total cost of the windows is thirty-five hundred dollars. Your monthly payment on that amount would be one hundred dollars per month. Perhaps I could finance three months of payments for you.

"By adding three hundred dollars to the price of the windows, your adjusted monthly payments would only be one hundred two dollars and seventy-seven cents per month. When the finance company pays us for your contract, we could give you a check for three hundred dollars, which we would call "cash back." When your first payment comes due in a month, you can pay the finance company with one hundred of the cash-back dollars. You could do the same for the next two months and you wouldn't have to pay anything out of your own pocket for three months. This way, you can take advantage of the sale we're having on the windows and begin enjoying the benefits of them right away. Of course these conditions would all be in writing.

"If I could arrange this deal, would you go ahead and get the windows tonight?"

Patrick and Rose smiled and shrugged their shoulders and nodded. "If you can get us that deal, we'll take them."

Tyler said that he would have to call his manager and see. Just before Tyler called in, he recommitted Patrick and Rose. He said that he would not want to go to all this trouble if Patrick and Rose weren't serious about the windows. They agreed again and Tyler called in to the financing department of the office. After some quick calculations, the manager agreed to the deal since the company would not be losing any money. Tyler was excited because he had earned a thousand dollars on the sale. Later, Tyler realized how quick and creative thinking saved the sale.

How did you do? Were you able to think up a quick and creative solution to save the sale without making any adjustments or assertions which were not described in the storyline? If not, don't beat yourself up about it. That is what this exercise was all about. This illustrates how creativity and thinking fast on your feet can help you to solve potential customers' objections, increase your closing average, and your yearly salary. Remember that the first answer may not always be the correct one and the logical answer may not be the obvious one.

Critical & Strategic Thinking

There is an exercise, a brain teaser, which I sometimes ask my students to perform which helps to illustrate this point well. Imagine you are walking on a path through an alien planet. There are only two kinds of aliens that reside on this planet. They both resemble humans, except for the color of their skin and their reasoning methods. The red aliens always tell lies and the green aliens always tell the truth. After a while, you come to a fork in the road. One path leads to immortality and the knowledge, wisdom, and riches of all great salespeople since the beginning of time. The other leads to poverty, ignorance, and death.

In the middle of the fork stands a figure in the shadows. You are permitted to ask the figure only one question to determine which path you will take. You do not know which path is the correct one and you cannot tell if the figure is green or red, but you have determined that the figure is a native of the planet. What question would you ask that will determine the correct direction to take and solve the problem?

You see that overcoming objections does require some problem-solving skills. The answer is always on the tip of your tongue once you've heard it explained by someone else. You can feel it. You know that if you could just clearly picture it and articulate it, the problem would be solved. This is sometimes what sales are like. Sure you could give up now and chalk it up to experience, but what if sales like this one could be saved? What if, with a little logic and practice, you could possess the key to all the closed doors and all the hearts and minds of potential customers everywhere? Solve the puzzle of objections and you will unlock the door to financial riches and personal growth within your sales career.

Have you solved the alien planet "objection"? Many of my students thought that the right question would be, "Are you red or green?" But the answer to that question does not solve the puzzle, nor does it direct us in either direction.

Some students suggested that the question should be, "Should I go this direction?" However, if the alien is red, then he will lie, and if it is green, he will be honest. That still does not help us to determine which road to take.

If you can only ask the figure one question in order to solve this problem it should be this: "If you were green, would this be the correct path?" If the alien was red and he were asked to answer from the perspective of a green alien, then the individual would have to tell the truth, and whatever answer that was given could be relied upon. If the alien were of the green race then he would answer truthfully anyway, and their answer could still be relied upon (u.a.). Not only is this an interesting illustration, but it also encourages us, as salespeople, to be mentally prepared to be creative and be free thinkers when in the field.

Even if you felt that the previous two illustrations were difficult, do not simply presume that sales are not for you. On the contrary, believe that, as a salesperson, you will undoubtedly be faced with many challenges that serve various purposes and overcoming them will make you even better at your job. The challenges will give you a deeper respect for your chosen profession and they will hone your determination and skill at problem solving, constantly giving you the courage to press on.

Remember, even the greatest salesman who ever lived, Jesus Christ, did not sell everyone. As the record shows, those he did not convince of his message not only persecuted him but also delivered him unto death. It is comforting to know that likely the greatest tribulation you will encounter while selling is a "rejection."

Since his death, Jesus has continued to live, breathe and sell among us. More copies of the bible have been sold throughout the world, and in more languages, than any other book in the history of mankind. His trademark closing technique has never been a mystery, and is a strong endorsement for "third party" closing. Jesus never professed to be the source of his dealings, but maintained that all things he was able to arrange came through means of his father, the creator of all things.

While I was teaching in Atlanta, Georgia, I had an opportunity to meet a young man who was eager to learn the craft of salesmanship. He had witnessed me successfully writing up deals in the organization, when I was not teaching and motivating others. I explained that I would teach him what I knew if he would tell me what the initials on his bracelet stood for. The bracelet read, "WWJD?" He explained to me that he wore the bracelet to remind himself to ask "What Would Jesus Do?" in times when he was unsure what he should do. I thought about this question from a salesperson's perspective and realized that when things seemed to get a little tough out in the field, this is exactly what every great salesperson should ask. "What would Jesus do?" As the greatest salesperson who ever lived, he knew what the potential customers wanted and needed to hear. He saw their needs and fulfilled them. He worked whatever hours were necessary and never complained about the payment he received. He never gave up even though he surely faced rejection after rejection. He reasoned using illustrations that the people could easily understand and never engaged in power struggles with potential customers. He was honest in his dealings; never deceitful.

If I could recommend a mentor or a teacher for which admiration and respect among salespeople alike should flow, it would be that of the life of Jesus Christ.

There was never an objection that he did not overcome with a smile and softly spoken illustrations for the "potential customers" to reason on.

Who would have imagined that such revelations might come from one small hand-woven bracelet worn by a student seeking knowledge and experience. Although this bit of genius perhaps meant more to me than it did to him at the time, the young man seemed happy and eager to write down everything I told him. Perhaps it is due in part to this young man that I am writing this book now. For it is certainly a great honor for me to have the opportunity to pass on these secrets and strategies for selling and I sincerely hope and pray for your success and lifelong achievement in the pursuit of your dreams in this magical realm we call "sales."

Tailoring Closing Techniques

Now that we have discussed closing and answering objections, and we have discovered how they work and what makes them effective, it is now our responsibility to begin the real work. Perhaps some of the diversionary reasoning closes will work for you in your sales career. The ones that do not seem as snug a fit should not be quickly dismissed. With some modifications, many can be tailored to your specific type of business.

If these options are not permissible, perhaps you can learn from the architecture of these reasonings and create some original diversionary reasoning closes of your own. If you find some to be effective, please write to me, so we can share them with others.

Step 7. Ask for the Order Again!

After we have successfully informed the prospects, then reasoned with them that the key to overcoming whatever issues may have been preventing them from making the purchase is in fact to make the purchase, then we must ask for the order again.

I find the best way to do this is to use the If & Would technique. It is advisable to mention how the previously stated issue (reason for not purchasing) has now been resolved. For example, (Using the "We cannot afford it" objection solution & The 50 Cent Pay Cut Close), step #7 would sound something like this:

"Now that we have agreed that you can afford at least $80.00 per month, if I could get you this deal, would you get the product?"

Courageously persevere until you have solved the problem and you will write up more sales than your competitors every time!

> "I think a hero is an ordinary individual who finds strength to persevere and endure in spite of overwhelming obstacles" (Reeve, n.d.).

Chapter 12

Recruiting In-Home, Casual Recruiting & Ad Hiring

- **Residual Income**—A term used to describe income that continues to be generated long after the initial work has been performed.
- **Infrastructure**—The underlying foundation or basic framework (pertaining to a system or organization).

A Natural Progression

It is a natural progression for most successful salespersons to become interested in the obtaining of greater sales volumes and profits through the growth of a sales organization. This is accomplished through the recruitment, orientation, training, and perpetual coaching of individuals with similar sales-oriented goals.

Fueled by their sister-like companies in network marketing, direct sales executives have sought to benefit from the demonstrable increase in sales volumes which networking companies enjoy by turning their salespeople into customers; or perhaps seen from a different perspective, turning their customers into their salespeople.

For example, it is interesting to note that most direct sales companies will encourage their sales staff to purchase the product(s) they wish to sell for themselves as a way of establishing and supporting their belief in the company and its products/services.

Duplicatability

The first and primary consideration of anyone wishing to grow a direct sales business is *duplicatability*.

The processes chosen to acquire leads, sales, and future recruits, must be simple enough for the average person to be able to model. For example: Suppose a large part of the reason an excellent sales representative is successful is because of their charismatic personality and great looks. Expecting that future recruits will have developed that same charismatic personality, and that all of them would be extremely good looking, is unrealistic. This model would not be the best one to pattern your business on.

If the method for generating leads is so complicated that even seasoned veterans have difficulty adapting to it, what will become of the new recruits whose ability to remember even the most rudimentary facts is often negated by their immaturity in the business?

The product presentation and procedures that a business will require its sales representatives to carry out on a daily basis must be uncomplicated, clear, and simple.

It is not enough to be able to justify that your best sales representatives are able to successfully use the systems, or that you have personally tested the systems and found them to be excellent. Remember, not everyone will be as talented and success driven as you are!

It is very important to think about, analyze and theoretically test, the business systems you plan to duplicate. The best systems will accommodate small groups (such as when your business is just getting off the ground) and large groups (such as when you have two hundred or more sales representatives). Otherwise you will have to teach your whole organization new systems to accommodate your growth and compensate for the failing systems that once worked, but are now impractical because of your size. Never underestimate the value of forethought, especially since new businesses can be extremely needy when it comes to your limited capital resources, and they seldom forgive error.

Here are some questions that you might consider when it comes to duplicatability. Can the average sales representative build enough value in the products to justify their price? (This would be very important when determining the price of a product.) To many direct sales distributors, the question seems to be defined largely by whether or not they think they could personally get a certain sum of money for their product, and without consideration for duplicatability. A good gauge might be to reflect your competitor's pricing if their products are comparable and they are doing decent sales volumes.

How long will the sales presentation or demonstration take? Over the years the most successful direct sales representatives have developed into the manufacturer's distributors. They have learned an enormous amount of information that they can resource quickly and accurately while engaging in what amounts to be a psychological cat-and-mouse game with their prospective customers; the victor getting the spoils.

A one hour demo could last for four hours if the sales representative had an enthusiastic method for maintaining the prospective customer's interest. In the end, if they were to be continually successful at obtaining the sale, who would question them? This is where the problem may arise. This successful sales representative grows into one of the manufacturer's distributors. He then begins trying to grow an organization, but his people never seem to be able to duplicate his results. They are, however, duplicating the length of the demo, which seems has now been extended to five hours, because they are not as polished at the presentation. Go out and observe these presentations and you are likely to become ill. Not only are they long, but what's more, they're boring! All hope for a sale has been lost after the first thirty minutes, and the idea of the prospects giving leads and contacting them becomes almost an absurd notion.

"Which of your friends would be willing to sit and watch this pitiful marathon (four to five hour) demonstration?" So we can conclude that the leads will no longer be generated (at least not on a consistent basis), and soon the sales representative will be out of business (and not by choice).

If we duplicate this system, what we will end up with is high attrition among our sales representatives, a generally poor assessment by the public of our company and products, and a distributor who has invested untold capital and valuable time into building a dream that rather closely resembles their worst nightmare. We have to be careful that we don't adopt business systems and practices that at first glance appear to be sufficient, but will later be proven faulty by the very persons that will be asked to carry them out.

Perhaps a better question is who should be responsible for setting up these systems, practices, and procedures? Many distributors make the assumption that the manufacturer has performed this diligence long before they arrived. In a perfect world this would be true. But we don't live in a perfect world! Our world is full of imperfections, assumptions, miscommunications, and assertions.

If you are a would-be distributor or even a seasoned veteran distributor, never assume that someone else did the work for you, let alone did it correctly. As we learned earlier in this book, demographics could drastically change what works from one location to another. Therefore, it is the responsibility of each individual distributor (even sales representative) to thoroughly evaluate the procedures and properties of these protocols in each area, making whatever necessary changes are demanded by the business for its own success.

If you want to grow a big business, it is your responsibility to ensure that the model you wish to see duplicated in order to achieve growth is in fact duplicatable. Remember, more people have been successful at duplicating failure than success.

Let's examine what some of the possible pitfalls are, and how we can avoid them. The first thing we should examine is what is most valuable to a distributor.

The Most Valuable Possessions

Recruiting is the act of obtaining more people to join your cause. In sales companies the expression that "people are your most valuable commodity" is omnipotent. The most popular methods for recruiting I have seen were through newspaper ad hiring, in-home recruiting while on a demo, or word-of-mouth recruiting/casual recruiting. The difference between these methodologies is substantial and some claim that they may even oppose one and other.

Network marketing seems to contain an *infrastructure* that many direct sales companies find attractive. Thus you may notice similarities in their growth forecasting. Both network marketing and direct sales involve the creation of sub-distributors which, in turn, generate sub-distributors. These go on to generate sub-distributors, and the process continues through as many levels as the current distributors are capable of perpetuating.

Usually, each distributor is required to purchase a certain amount of product each and every month in order to retain his purchasing level rights. In this way, a constant income stream called *residual income* can be earned by the distributor's up-line (**Note:** residual incomes can be reduced to the significance of how often your sub-distributors can accomplish the sale).

Often the manufacturer organizing the distributor/customer infrastructure determines the degree and depth of this residual income that the original distributor will be entitled to. In some cases this liberty is permitted to the distributors themselves. A problem can arise when the down-line distributors communicate amongst themselves, since purchase price/level of distributorship is a natural bragging point. This can lead to infighting and an argument for a change in distributor status by the offended party. For example, "You're charging so-in-so blank, but I've been with you for longer, and I'm paying blank. It's not fair!"

Remember that not all direct distributorships (paralleling multi-level marketing companies) have the same purchase requirements, bonus and advancement structures, or pay percentages. Also the structure of their distributor infrastructures may range dramatically.

The typical structure and perhaps the forefather of network marketing is a pyramid structure as shown on p. 201. In this diagram, you will also see the process of growth illustrated. Concentration is focused on recruiting and the sale is seen as a byproduct of growth. The more people in an organization, the greater the sales volumes. Thus people, and those who recruit them, are a valuable commodity to manufacturers and to the up-line distributors whose incomes are directly influenced by their growth (for this reason, don't expect to get a fair assessment of a competing company from your current distributor or company echelon).

This is true of most companies that manufacture products and then sell them to self-employed distributors and their affiliates. Instead of competing for sales, manufacturers actually compete for the people. Whoever has them, sells more!

I have often taught that the only difference between a salesperson and a distributor is people. Regardless of whether an individual has obtained a higher rank or position (title within the pyramid), and thus a lower purchasing price, without people he is merely a salesperson with a price/commission that corresponds to his rank.

If you want a piece of advice with regards to building and maintaining a sales organization, I would admonish you to "Keep Your People (Lamb, 1991)."

The act of keeping your people is also known as retention, and it is the reason why any sales organization experiences growth. Stated another way, a lack of retention is the number one cause of failure. Consider the following illustration: you are successful at convincing ten of your associates to join your selling conglomerate, pyramid, or business tree. After one week, five of them have decided to quit. The next week you lose the remaining five people. Now you are the only one in your business tree. You successfully convince five more people to join your business tree. These five were considerably more difficult to acquire because you did not know them before speaking to them regarding your business. A week later, four of these quit and now you have one. Your business tree appears to be more of a shoestring. The following week, this person too quits. You are determined to succeed and you bring in ten more people. The cycle continues and within weeks you have also lost these people.

Let's take a closer look at what has happened. In total, you have generated at the very least the sale of twenty-five product orders (It is encouraged that you sell the product to your recruits. If not, you have generated no sales). You may have received a small income and you have zero possible dollars of residual income to look forward to. This is because the down-line distributors, sometimes referred to as dealers, are no longer with the company and are therefore no longer selling/ordering products on a monthly basis. Because your commissions are based on the purchases of your down-line, when your down-line diminishes, or you experience a lack of retention, your expectations of residual income from these must also diminish.

In the above illustration, this may happen to the degree that these residual incomes become nonexistent. The key to real success under this pyramid umbrella is to retain all or part of your recruits longer than the length of time it takes you and the sum of your pyramid down-line, to increase the number of persons joining your organization by a number greater than those who are leaving. In this way the organization will experience true growth.

The realization and commitment to this growth must entertain that there will be some "wheel spinning." This means that those involved in such an enterprise should expect a certain amount of loss with regards to the sum of persons involved in the business tree at any given time.

Individuals considering this type of career/self-employment will have to make a decision as to whether to pursue their sales organization goals full-time or part-time.

Many have quit their conventional jobs to work at this type of pyramid/business-tree building full time with little consideration given to the consequences, such as whether their business will take longer than they anticipate to attain enough growth to adequately compensate them for the loss of their original income.

Some believe that the average individual with little or no experience in this arena will enter it, believing he can attain a large organizational growth rate within ninety days due to the encouragement from a motivational sales meeting, only to have things go awry. Others have even falsely argued that this type of organization is not profitable at all. To the contrary, if enough effort is used, I have not found a business anywhere in the world that is more financially rewarding. The revenue stream can roll in, and in a very short time as well. There are many examples of those who have exceeded their sales expectations and earned literally millions of dollars. Even when I was the lowest level distributor, I was able to generate over a million dollars in sales per year, and this at moderate sales volumes. Keeping your overhead down, earning a hundred thousand dollars in income per year is a trifle.

In this respect, this type of sales business is not unlike any other sales-oriented business. When you're not earning what you want, the fault seldom lies in the vehicle, but rather in the individual whose efforts are required to fuel it.

Think Before You Leap

You've read and heard about this before but it's worth another mention if you plan on opening your own distributorship, "Location, location, location!"

With regards to location, you should consider several factors. First, if your competitors *are not* operating in an area, is it because you are the first person to open your brand of business in the area (seldom the case) or is it because some unique demographic has caused others who have attempted to conduct a successful business there to fail? If it is the latter, you may wish to spend time, effort, and money gathering increased intelligence in order to be sure an area will support your business before committing to opening there. Consider this intelligence gathering an investment; an insurance premium paid in advance of the undoubtedly larger investment you will be committing to when you open your business and begin cultivating it.

If you are planning to run an ad in the newspaper in order to hire some people, the following is crucial to your success: check the unemployment rate, average rate of income (for the middle class), foreign immigration influences both positive and negative, local paper costs and drawing areas. For example, a newspaper ad in the general Help Wanted section in Atlanta, Georgia in the late '90s would get you nowhere fast since the unemployment rate was so low. In contrast, selling in this area was particularly good, since so many in Atlanta were gainfully employed. Also note, however, that a similar newspaper ad in an area of high unemployment would not really be more beneficial if the applicants from sales all possessed poor credit histories. There is an easy way to observe unemployment demographics. Just look at the number of local businesses with "help wanted" signs in their windows. If you see a lot, then hiring by newspaper ads will be difficult and the labors may outweigh the rewards because this generally signifies that businesses are competing for employees.

When recruiting, it is also important to know the general number of foreign immigrants in an area and what kind of culture they come from. In Brampton, Ontario, Canada, a similar newspaper ad would fetch you calls (150, sporadically over a week) from the East Indian people who have moved to the city. Their ability to communicate effectively in English is somewhat compromised as English is often their second language, and their ability to sell upscale vacuums seems negated by their desire for a bigger better deal. The same ad in McAllen, Texas, on the other hand, would bring in around eighty calls (all at once in one day for around $60). The Hispanic people who live there also speak English as their second language, yet they love to buy things and word-of-mouth advertising there spreads faster than butter at a pancake house.

Consider the following illustration: Todd wishes to open a franchise with a successful restaurant in his hometown. He has seen the success of this restaurant in many cities he has visited and so he purchases a franchise without any consideration of the demographics in his area. He spends a lot of money setting up his restaurant and even builds a drive-thru lane for customers in a hurry. He runs a help wanted ad in the local newspaper and waits patiently for the money to roll in.

He's not getting the recruits he hoped for, however, and in time he realizes that even with the bulk of the town frequenting his restaurant, he is unable to generate enough revenue to continue to meet his staff payroll requirements and keep the restaurant open. Within a year, his franchise is closed and Todd has lost all of the money he has spent on the venture. Todd ends up declaring bankruptcy because he cannot repay the debts incurred while attempting to establish the business. Todd's friends and relatives conclude that the franchise was over-rated and not a reliable business vehicle.

Todd has since visited many cities where franchise operations belonging to the same company, not even as organized and well-funded as his, are succeeding far beyond his own original expectations for his restaurant. This makes Todd change his position on the franchise, and he now believes that the reason his restaurant franchise did not succeed was because he failed to consider the demographics of his area, along with some other related factors. He wishes he could do it all again, because he is certain that he could have succeeded with the franchise had he better understood that simply having a vehicle to succeed does not guarantee success.

Many people have their ears tickled by the promise of unimaginable material wealth, and seldom a consideration for the efforts, which surely must have preceded them. This illustration helps us to conclude that while one should consider the products/services to be sold as a determining factor when seeking to become involved, there are many other considerations which can dramatically impact the success of the endeavor. These would most certainly include the rate of attrition, the confines of the company's infrastructure and commissions, financing, any governing factors which relate to demographics, language and cultural factors, timing, financial concerns, behavioral patterns, and the projected length of time for an adequate income to be generated considering your expected effort level throughout the foundation of the business and your level of commitment to the project.

Another unrealistic expectation made by those wishing to get involved with most direct sales distributorships/companies is that of tangible profits during the first year of business. Consider that if your growth went as predicted and planned, you would need to reinvest much of your profits from sales, into more equipment, demo related supplies, and promotional gifts/items.

One unique manufacturing company consigns products to its distributors, as well as providing a constant financing source, thus successfully navigating around this issue, but this is a rare instance. Most manufacturers want their cash up front, and with good reason. If the attrition rate is high among distributors and the selection process for those distributors is not really scrutinized, the future would not be financially appealing. And for some distributors, having big-brother so woven into your business may not be all the advantageous.

I have observed among new would-be distributors an unwavering belief that their business will grow far greater and faster than most others, and that finances won't even be a consideration once the myriad of sales start washing up in their laps. (Usually, doctors cannot even test these new distributors' pupil dilation because the Ferraris and dollar signs that have replaced them keep getting in the way.)

Yes, you can make what modern "employed middle-classmen" would consider obscene amounts of money every month, but just remember that the money is tied directly to your individual priming efforts. It is so exciting when you start calculating your profits based on everything over your cost of equipment rather than conducting business.

It seems that these new distributors do not believe that the history of small or even big business indicates record losses during the years involved in establishing the business. This is demonstrated by the decline in businesses that succeed beyond the five-year threshold. It is evident that many of the individuals seeking to enter into such a business have scarcely the commitment to endure the short-term pangs of a "childlike" business in order to benefit from the long-term pleasure that a successful "full-grown" business can provide.

This is not written to discourage entrepreneurial liberty or creativity, but rather to encourage the continued success of the entrepreneur by helping those who

Network Marketing & Direct Sales Model Infrastructure Diagram

Global Thinking + The Company + Technology to Organize Infrastructure = Success

The Process

Potential Customers + Current Distributor; Customers; Sales Representative = Enrollments as new customer; sub-distributor & payment for product; service received = New Self-employed Business Owner; Distributor; Sales Representative

Duplication — Sales Organization Growth

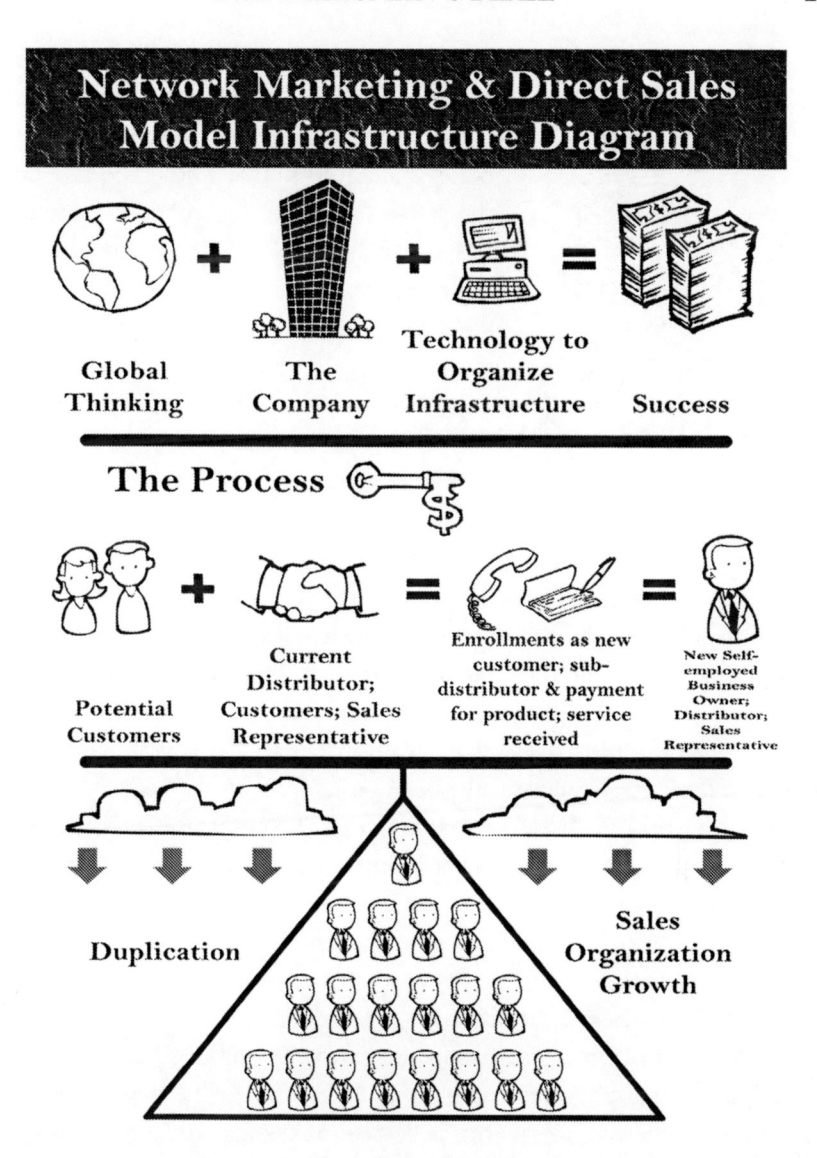

possess the spirit to enter into the marriage of business ownership with the wisdom required to realize the fulfillment of their dreams. There are many rewards for the self-employed and those whose view and expectations are not contaminated by the emotion of lofty presumptions.

With this in mind, one can better determine whether or not a sales business should be entered into on a full or part-time basis. A safe position when in doubt is always to begin and maintain balance. Therefore, you may wish to consider beginning such an endeavor on a part-time basis while still keeping your current method of income intact.

Using this part-time method as a springboard for your new entrepreneurial activities is a consistent approach. This does not mean that any less effort should be expended in the pursuit of your entrepreneurial adventure, but it can help you to accept the realism of your results and maintain a positive view of your sales organization, rather than running the risk of failure based on exaggerated expectations based on the apparent success of some others.

What's important is not what level of success others have obtained, but the degree of success that you will obtain. While the success of others is certainly encouraging, it has no reflection on the measure of which your success will be based. Your goals should be exactly that: yours! In the future, your aim should not be to out-perform others, but to measure your success by how well you are able to out-perform your own previous achievements. In this way, if you should you exceed those around you, you will not find yourself without adequate self-motivation, creating for yourself a sort of "Zen and the Art of Successful Sales"—out-perform thyself!

Perhaps you have performed your due diligence and feel that now is the time to plunge whole-heartedly into your entrepreneurial ocean and full-time is the way to go. If so, you may find comfort in the saying that those whose backs have been against the wall have accomplished amazing results.

More than once, I have observed individuals who have pursued a new business full-time, (with emphasis on the full) and have used their expectations to fuel their efforts. This has enabled them to work longer hours, expecting, in some cases, little compensation, or even losses, while maintaining their course and their determination to succeed despite any and all mental or physical obstacles. Remember that you are capable of far greater a measure of success than any current level of satisfactory living you may now enjoy. The real difference between the successful entrepreneur and those that live with the realization that they could achieve more *if only*... Is one word: action! There is a simple yet powerful distinction between knowing something and practicing it.

Salesperson or Customer?

What is the distinction between a salesperson and a customer? Some may claim that the salesperson assists or acts as a liaison between the company and the customer. The customer exchanges a financial sum for the product or service he receives. Certainly in the past this distinction has been clear, however with the integration of the network marketing infrastructure into direct sales distributorships, this distinction has become clouded.

For many, the beginning of a self-employed status type business begins by establishing oneself as a customer; either as an end user, or in the case of distributorship, a customer of the manufacturer or up-line.

Some direct sale distributorship manufacturers require you to produce a certain amount of volume in order to even participate in the compensation plan. Basically as a distributor, you have to be a good customer of the manufacturer (this is what distributors want from their salespeople: a good customer, one who sells a lot). So while you may have thought you were getting rid of the middlemen by buying direct (distributor level), this is likely not the case. More and more, these middlemen are fading into the shadows and collecting their cut directly from the manufacturer, after the fact (in the old days, you paid your money to them and they purchased for you). It's not worth any time spent commiserating over how much your up-line is making anyway. Especially if you were initially happy with the price you were presented. For sales representatives, consider your price the selling price of your product, minus your commission.

If you're now feeling jaded, perhaps your business practices are causing your business to generate fewer sales than you predicted. I have noticed that when people are not making as much money as they need or think they deserve, desperation can convert a good heart and good intentions into a stubborn individual with more than his fair share of character flaws. So try to recognize where the blame for these feelings really lies. Remember, success has never been synonymous with ill feelings, whereas failure...

Keep in mind that residual incomes are based on the foundation of down-line sales. This epiphany points to the obvious, which is that up-line distributors have to be receiving a percentage of the money you are paying to cover the cost of such products or services (middlemen), unless you are at the very top of the distributor food chain. I suppose residual income actually acknowledges the receipt of payment to a multitude of middle people. However, this infrastructure is necessary to create the residual income that most business builders are initially attracted by. In the end, every purchase should be viewed as an investment in your business rather than a savings opportunity as some might assert when making their initial purchase.

Some direct sales companies make it a mandatory requirement for all sales representatives to purchase the products/service that they wish to promote. The sales representative thereby profits from the difference between their purchase price and the price the end consumer pays. These companies, however, usually wish to obtain their sales representatives from their customer base. In this manner, training and belief in the products/services are considered to be substantially easier to develop within the customer-turned-apprentice salesperson. So this begs the question: Is there still a distinction between the customer and the salesperson? Since the business model is logistically a chain, everyone involved is a customer to their up-line, and the end user is quite literally the end of the line.

Is Up-Line Behavior Consistent With Logic & Growth

If we view down-line distributors and self-employed sales representatives as valued customers because of our interdependencies, do we (up-line distributors & manufacturers) behave consistently with this assertion? Some up-line distributors have attempted to employ negative reinforcement when wishing to motivate down-line customers to produce greater sales/purchasing volumes. How effective is this strategy?

In my observations, it is best to conclude that, although these customers/lower-level distributors do shoulder the bulk of the burden for their business success, it is of no consolation to the up-line if the down-line distributor/business owner becomes discouraged by such acts, regardless what their intention. As absurd as it would be for a retail clerk to act rudely with potential customers, is the pretense that by applying some form of discipline the up-line can motivate the down-line?

What about the scenario of direct sales businesses who view their salespeople/lower-level distributors as those whom they have in some manner provided for by offering the opportunity of involvement with the company? These should consider reversing their views to ones, which maintain that although the former is derived from some truth, their salespeople/lower-level distributors are actually their most loyal customers. Maintaining that these individuals are customers may help you to view their accomplishments (both meager and great) as beneficial to the fulfillment of your dreams. A salesperson who sells ten units per month would be seen as a customer who has returned on ten different occasions to purchase from your business, plus one who provides you with a residual income.

This is often a direct result and repayment for your own hard work, motivation, training and coaching efforts. With this view it is easy to maintain a positive perspective with regards to even your weakest volume salespeople. Ask yourself if your actions, with regards to your sales staff, reflect how much you value them as customers? If so, what more can you do to genuinely help these customers succeed in their sales aspirations? It is via this perspective that you are able to father the principals of teamwork within your sales organization. Remember, TEAM stands for Together, Everyone Achieves More! (u.a.)

The Psychology for Sabotage

If teamwork is so important in this type of sales-oriented business, why have some up-line distributors been observed sabotaging the positive mental state of their successful down-line affiliates? This is accomplished by adjusting the lower-level distributor's purchasing price, and thus creating a ripple effect with regards to their profit percentages so as to increase the up-line's own profit-margins. There are two main contributing factors to this often-illogical behavior. The first is jealousy. Some up-line distributors have sought to sabotage the serenity of a successful down-line distributor by attempting what is known in the corporate community as a hostile take-over. In effect, the up-line distributor becomes complacent with their level of satisfaction derived from the financial percentages being paid them. They, in turn, view the down-line distributor (perhaps receiving the bulk of the compensation) as an obstacle preventing them from receiving a greater share of the revenues. They believe that it is easier to take over the foundation of their down-line's business than it would be to extend (build through hard work) their own. Rather than viewing the down-line's business as an extension of their own, they rationalize that because the opportunity was obtained through them, they have a right to make adjustments to the compensation plan according to how successful the down-line distributor is. They reason that it is unfair for down-line distributors to generate any profit greater than their own. For this reason, some up-line distributors have sought to keep the identities of down-line customers secret from their up-line distribution. In this way, they are able to take credit for their down-line's purchasing volume.

The second reason behind such acts of sabotage is one that we can agree is not unfamiliar to a wide variety of the populous in today's material-driven society. It is, quite simply, greed! As referred to by the preceding explanation, although these negative acts are in contrast to true business building, it would be derelict for today's entrepreneur not to acknowledge their existence and potential for undermining their true business goals.

The adjustment of compensation by up-line distributors is usually only predominant in direct selling organizations where the establishment of these parameters is left solely to the discretion of the distributors, since most manufacturers do not recognize all levels of distributorship as customers. Many only recognize a select few distributors as customers, and thereby create a legal firewall or distinction between themselves and the actions of their customers/select distributors. In this way, they cannot be held responsible for the actions of sub-distributors or their sales practices (suggesting a few bad apples may have crept in; beware).

Since many direct sale distributorship infrastructures are based upon network marketing logistics, there exists a risk directly from the top. In many network-marketing companies there is a provision for something called break-aways. This is when the manufacturer has concluded that a leg of your down-line, usually a very profitable one, should be liberated from underneath your volume collection umbrella. You will no longer receive your commissions on this leg's volume of purchases, but in some cases you are provided some compensation for the loss. This would be of particular interest to anyone serious about building a substantial network-marketing based direct-sale distributorship.

Upward Mobility

Another element to consider when becoming involved in direct sales distributorship is upward mobility. In many established direct sales organizations, territory has been divided by the manufacturer between select groups of individuals/companies. These then subdivide their territories, and so on. This can pose a potential problem in the future as your sales organization attempts to spread its wings. What if there is no place to grow? Naturally, the territories with the best demographics are the first to be selected.

One possible reason for a territory becoming open may be due to product saturation or other factors which could cause a sharp decline in sales in that area. This would be of concern to potential new distributors who might be considering opening a distributorship there.

Don't expect the manufacturer or your up-line distributor to be watching out for your best interests. It would seem logical that these people would be concerned about your future in the business since that determines how long you will be a customer of theirs. However, in my travels it has become clear that many of these up-line distributors have witnessed far too much attrition and have given up hope for any long-term solutions. You're likely to hear only positive affirmations rather than realistic assessments of your location choices. I suppose a word of caution at this delicate time would be contrary to the genuine smile and confident handshakes which generally precede your initial purchases. All new distributorships opened appear to be a crapshoot equal to the previous with one exception. They still have money!

Of course, the success or failure of any business is dependent upon those who open it. Yet it can be said by most who have failed, that a lack of education in some area of the business was at the root of the cause. "If I only knew then what I know now!" seems to be an underlying theme with those who have endured failure and persevered to reach ultimate success.

For this reason, I have concluded that the most powerful and direct relationship between those organizations that have a history of opening successful distributorships and those that do not is the genuine level of marketing support that the manufacturers provide and promote to their sub-distributors. Some of these tools include professionals who have previously succeeded in opening a distributorship(s) who would frequent your distributorship, evaluate, diagnose, and recommend courses of action. Videotapes or DVDs that can be reviewed and or used to assist in the training of your sales staff would be included in this arena. Audio tools, like CDs, are also helpful. Posters and record-keeping tools and recognition systems are also crucial. Legal advice and accounting services may also be provided.

Before opening a distributorship in any new geographical location, it is highly recommended that you personally practice selling the product there. Although many companies would have you believe that all territories are equal because the product is the same, do not be easily misled. The difference between demographic considerations from one area to the next might easily be compared to your marketing of an entirely different product. This alone could be the difference between success and failure!

Relatively new manufacturers may not have a credible history that you can investigate, and although your emotions may conclude that you are ready to take on this challenge by yourself, it is a strong credit to you if you reserve your judgment until a comfortable long-term strategy can be made available to you.

Learning from the experience of others is often less costly than experiencing them for yourself. Just remember that in all business there is risk. However, the degree of that risk should be carefully and conservatively measured against its corresponding reward.

Upward mobility is something that every would-be distributor should inquire about and investigate! With that said, there is one factor that can ultimately propel you and your organization beyond any obstacles. That factor is you! It is important to be aware, but *not* to become engrossed in any negatives.

Recruiting as a Lead Source

There are many different methods for generating leads. If a distributor moves into a new location and has no personal leads to get started with, he may opt to recruit as a form of lead generation. A distributor can easily afford to pay the commission earned by a new dealer/sales representative and make a handsome profit. A distributor may therefore choose to recruit people through casual recruiting or ad hiring, and then offer to train them in the field by allowing them to watch the distributor sell to their personal circle of leads (friends & family). In this scenario everybody wins. The new trainee/dealer could not ask for more hands-on training than that.

Contacting Potential Recruits

Before attempting to contact a potential recruit, the accomplished distributor has to have a thorough knowledge of what basic principals motivate others to become involved in an organization. The distributor knows what the potential sub-distributor wants and needs to hear.

When considering the recruitment of an individual, these basic principals should be your utmost consideration. It is not simply about money, as some are accustomed to believe. What are the basic methods for contacting a potential recruit?

You could use the old fashion approach, which is always effective, i.e., contacting them in person. Many people are now using other information mediums such as the internet or the newspaper. Of course the telephone is also very effective. Let's see how some of these methods work to establish a growing sales organization or network.

In-person recruiting works best when combined with a sales presentation. In that way, you follow the same basic steps to set up appointments and then visit with them. When you perform the sales presentation, you would do well to ask the prospects to participate and compliment them on how well they do. This will help to encourage them when you invite them to learn more about your opportunity.

Never prejudge anyone, and always talk about the ways that the opportunity has helped to change your life. Remember to under-promise and over-deliver. Show pictures of people having fun, winning prizes, and making money at your office. Show copies of checks people have earned and be sure to include yourself!

Another method of direct recruiting I have found to be effective was to recruit people for a self-employed position using the *employment-oriented* approach to a self-employed position. To clarify, I am suggesting that you use an approach that mimics traditional employment in order to bridge the psychological gap between self-employment and traditional employment. This will ease the transition for new recruits. A fundamental shift in thinking is required when you consider the financial differences between commission-based pay and that of hourly compensation. This difference is only one of many.

For example, consider the following scenario: Michael was interested in growing and expanding his sales force. He devised an approach which proved very effective. Michael targeted college campuses where he knew there would be a steady supply of individuals looking for extra income. He approached John and Marsha, who were talking in a common area.

"Excuse me. Would either of you two know anybody who might be interested in a part or full-time job?"

"Yeah. I might be" replied John. Marsha also looked interested.

"What would I be doing?" asked John.

"Well, my name is Michael and I represent (Company name), we're looking for some talented individuals to act in live commercials. Have you ever done any acting before?"

"No, but I am sure I could."

"Well it doesn't pay all that much for this type of work. I have earned upwards of twenty-five dollars and fifty cents per hour when I figured it out, but do you think you might be interested?"

"Are you serious?" asked John.

"Yes, I am completely serious. In fact part of my job is to recruit the next superstars of our business. I have been involved for (# of years) and I have come to really love my job. I can't promise you a job, but I may be able to get you an interview, or perhaps get authorization to perform the interview myself."

"What would I be selling?" inquired John.

"Our company carries the following products, (insert your products and some value building.) But don't worry, there's no experience necessary and if you are selected, we will provide you with complete company training and support. Would you be interested in a part-time position, or a full-time position?"

"Part-time! I have classes four days a week, but I am usually done by three-thirty pm."

"That's perfect, John, because most of our work is performed in the evenings and on weekends! This is my business card. If you have any questions you can feel free to call me. Perhaps I can also take down a number where you can be reached, just in case something comes up, or I can manage to get you an interview."

"Okay my phone number is (XXX) XXX-XXXX."

"Do you think I could give you my name also?" asked Marsha.

"Sure. As I was telling John I cannot promise you a job, but I will try and arrange an interview for you okay?"

"That sounds great thanks a lot!"

John and Marsha appeared to be talking about the possibility of acting in these "live commercials" as Michael walked away.

Michael began to target persons that were working lower paying and often dead-end jobs. He would talk to people working at gas stations and convenience stores. He talked to people at restaurants, including cooks, waiters and waitresses, and even hosts and hostesses. He talked to employees in the mall, as well as other sales people. Michael compiled a large list very quickly.

A few days later, he began calling people and arranging interview appointments. Soon Michael had sixty-three people scheduled to interview with him. Some of them even asked if they could bring friends along who also might be interested. Michael was excited and confident that his sales organization would soon be growing. He especially liked that there was little initial capital required before he began his networking campaign. He simply had to dress his part.

He envisioned a recruiting officer at a big corporation to be a confident, well-dressed individual. So whenever Michael went out recruiting, he always looked like a million bucks! He was clean, smelling fresh, and radiating enthusiasm for his occupation.

He realized that if he made it enticing enough, and yet did not make it seem overly easy to become involved, his success was assured. He also noted that the less he said about the position during this initial and brief encounter, the better his results were. He reasoned that this initial encounter was merely to create curiosity and compile a list of candidates. He purposely kept these first meetings brief, but exciting.

There were, of course, some people who simply were not interested, but he was supremely surprised at how great his results were. For this seemingly glamorous position, many confided that they would be willing to leave their current employment if necessary to obtain the position.

So how did Michael make the transition from what these individuals imagined the position to consist of, and what it really did? You can read about how this is done in this chapter under the subheading "The Ultimate Sale."

The newspaper is another effective method for recruiting individuals. However, it certainly requires a much greater amount of effort and know-how than in-home recruiting. **Please note**: in some instances, newspaper hiring has thwarted the efforts of in-home recruiting. This is because people will often duplicate their own experience. Say, for example, a personal friend or relative brought you into the business. It is likely that you will also attempt to bring in a friend or relative in a similar manner. In contrast, if you were brought into the business via the newspaper, it is likely that you will not have your heart rooted deeply in recruiting. Of course, there are always exceptions, so I encourage every method that you find works for you!

Newspaper recruiting is time consuming and has some initial costs associated with it. However, it is effective at targeting specific areas for growth. You will be empowered by the knowledge of the newspaper's circulation and potential for contacting your target market. There are more kinds of advertisements for the newspaper as you can possibly imagine. Some examples whose effectiveness I have personally witnessed are included on p.216.

By seeing how these ads are constructed and understanding how they work, you can create your own examples and use them to begin building your business network. Some of the important factors when designing newspaper advertisements are job titles, work hours, salary expectations, transportation requirements, job duty explanation, experience and education conditions, and anything you feel might attract an individual and entice them to call you.

It is also important to note that the public in general tends to fall back on stereotypes and be judgmental concerning commission sales positions and so it is important to use a measure of vagueness and creativity when designing such advertisements. A greater and more genuine explanation of the position can be explained over the phone or (most recommended) when you are able to perform your polished sales presentation. This is because the individual may be more easily enticed by the position of selling/distributing your products if they are completely sold on them and naturally, it is easier to create this level of belief and inspiration if you are able to perform your presentation for the possible recruit.

Having samples of tangible products is recommended, since these are easier to demonstrate value and samples are also more exciting to viewers. When designing advertisements, you will usually find the "less is more" approach most effective. Remember what people are looking for. You do not want to appear to be a small, home-based business because people want to be involved in something that they think is greater than themselves. If they assume that you are a large corporation when they call because you have a four-digit extension (existing or not) this serves your benefit. Your only goal at this point is to generate the greatest call volume from your advertisement.

How will you explain and make the transition easy for your possible recruits? This will be discussed in depth under the heading "The Ultimate Sale" in this chapter.

Newspaper Contact
(Direct Sales Business)

If you are using the newspaper to recruit, you will need a script to guide you when they call in. You will need to determine what types of lead sources you will ask the new recruits to use when they get started, and you will also need to determine how you will perpetuate these lead sources.

Keep in mind that your recruits will fail to recruit and sell one hundred percent of the people they don't see/contact. As we learned in The Sales

Savior's Six Secrets for being the Best Salesperson, leads must precede everything but preparation.

Having the Lead Program First

Since a lot of effort is required to train and coach individuals, you would certainly not want to lose large numbers of people due to a lack of leads, which is often the number one cause of attrition among properly trained and motivated salespeople. In many cases, you may plan to target the leads that have proven in the past to have the greatest closing percentage, double-income home owners for example. If your product requires financing, the finance company will almost certainly appreciate the stability of home owners. The fact that both the husband and the wife have a good income will also predictably impact your sales ratio as well, and if it is possible, you may even wish to predetermine their credit worthiness by finding out if they already use credit cards.

Can you think of what type of lead would permit the greatest closing percentage and hold-up ratio? Of course, it is the *personal* lead: the friend, the neighbor, the relative, the co-worker, the people you associate with on a regular basis. First and foremost, you already know if they can afford your product and whether or not they have the credit (if necessary) to purchase your product. These people already like you, and likely even trust you. These are known as your inner circle.

The only down side to a person's inner circle is that they run out. Some may have an expanded inner circle, but for most, the inner circle consists of ten families or fewer. One way to effectively perpetuate inner circle leads is the successful act of recruiting. Consider the following example: Peter recruited Margo and trained her on how to sell and recruit. He also recruited others from his own inner circle. When his inner circle was depleted he began helping Margo recruit and sell to her inner circle. Peter encouraged Margo to train and aid her recruits. When Margo had completed her inner circle, she took a more active role in helping her recruits to recruit and sell in their inner circles. This continued until there was an upside-down "tree/down-line" (often illustrated by network marketing based companies) beginning to expand and create volume under both Peter and Margo. They were both very excited. One of the factors that helped boost their retention was that their personal recruits had each recruited several people with the coaching of their up-line, and were receiving residual incomes.

Although these were relatively small residual incomes, they were just enough to turn on some light bulbs in the minds of their personal recruits. This is because they could start to envision how they, too, could create a lasting and expanding business for themselves.

In most network marketing companies an infrastructure is already prepared. In contrast, most distributorships in direct sales leave the company infrastructure to the discretion of the distributor, and thus a wider crevice emerges between those experiencing success and those who are challenged.

In direct-selling distributorships, an infrastructure needs to exist at least mentally in the individual initiating the effort. When you begin to consider this infrastructure, you should always participate in mental rehearsals. Pretend that your proposed infrastructure is in place and that you are succeeding beyond your imagination.

Will this infrastructure be strong enough under the weight of your incredible expansion? Another way to look at it is to say to yourself, "Whatever is disorganized now, with very few participants, will be multiplied by the number of added participants". Then you must decide whether what you are doing now (your method of organization) is going to be effective with ten people. Will it still be effective with fifty people? Will it be as effective with one hundred people? The best infrastructures are just as effective with one person as they are with one hundred people.

Assuming that you have considered a company hierarchy, recognition and rewards programs, training, lead sources, lead perpetuation, administration, stock issues, shipping & handling, application to financing delay, management style and interoffice communication, the next step is answering the call of your potential recruits. This is quite literal when dealing with the newspaper as an advertising and recruiting medium.

If you have chosen a "blind ad" such as those illustrated below then you will have to take special considerations. The response script would need to choose an ultimate direction because while a blind ad may be used to initiate interest, the response script will need to supply a greater sum of information, but this information should include only that which is considered crucial for most people in determining whether or not they are interested in your positions.

Blind Advertisement Example I

Customer Service Representatives Wanted
$18.00 per hour
No experience necessary
Must enjoy working directly with the public
Must have a car
Call now
(555) 555-5555
ext. 1701

- Minimum wage at time of Ad running was $7.00 per hour
- Saves time when answering calls
- See It Big

Blind Advertisement Example II

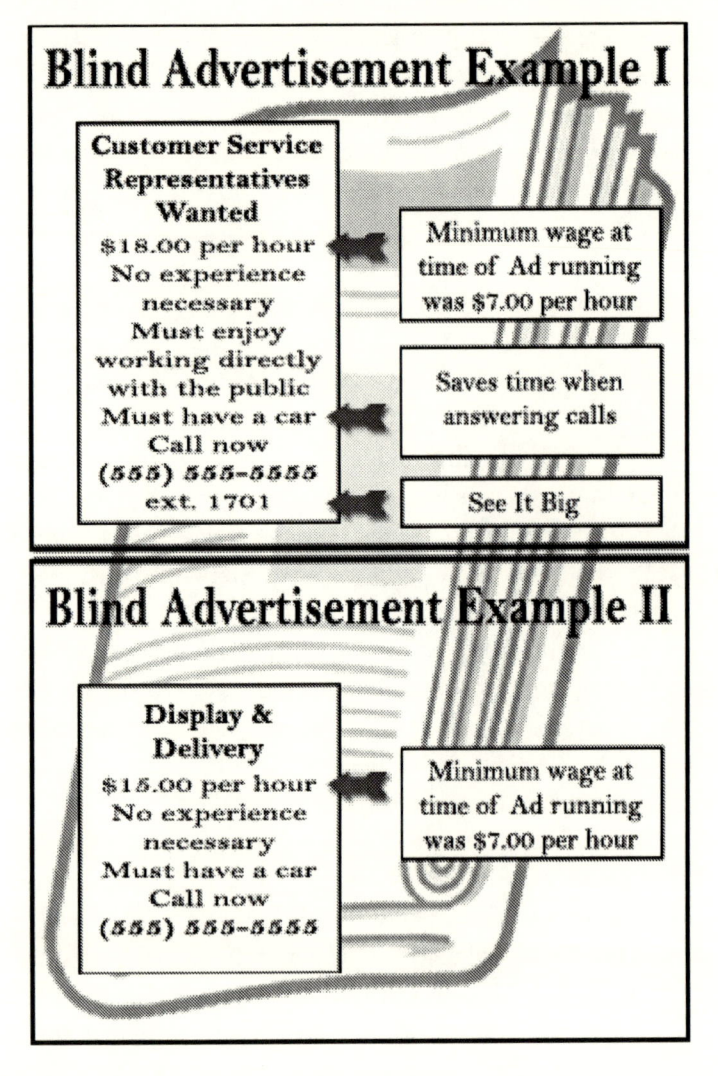

Display & Delivery
$15.00 per hour
No experience necessary
Must have a car
Call now
(555) 555-5555

- Minimum wage at time of Ad running was $7.00 per hour

A response script that is purposefully vague and elusive usually accompanies a genuine blind ad. It should appear to provide information while maintaining interest and curiosity. The crucial determining information will be reserved for the ultimate sale or presentation. This presentation should be performed by the person who is most qualified to generate the sale (yourself, or your best salesperson). It is often performed for groups to prevent repetition.

If you have determined to run the process blind until the presentation, a very brief explanation is required as a newspaper advertisement response script. 'Blind' is the description given to this type of hiring/recruiting because the potential recruit is kept very much in the dark about what their duties will consist of, and what kind of product(s) they will be selling. (This is of particular interest if a greater percentage of respondents would choose not to participate with the company without first having been sold on the product, which is generally the case. Being in direct sales in some areas is considered almost like being a bottom feeder in the ocean of career opportunities, while in other areas, it is a respected and sought after career opportunity.) This is especially true of products that carry stereotypical baggage with them. These might include vacuums or used cars. In some cases the product may hinder the recruiting process because people may not want others to see them as the stereotypical person that they imagine selling such products. Hence, the demand for blind advertising and some purposefully vague practices is created.

To see some examples of the way non-vague and blind advertising can look, consider the following headlines and ask yourself if the average person was asked to consider one of these to call, which one they would:

First: **Local Vacuum Store**
  Seeks commission salespeople

Second: **Customer Service Representatives**
  Wanted
  $18.00 per hour

If you had limited options and really needed the work/money, consider which would be most appealing to you. If you believe that you, and most of the rest of the population, would rather choose the Customer Service Representative position you probably understand the stereotyping I was referring to. To a lot of people searching for employment, image is everything!

If you have decided to keep the process completely blind until the sales presentation, you should expect a greater rate of attrition (after the presentation), but a higher hold-up percentage for the presentation. This is because once they obtain the necessary information to be able to make an informed decision as to whether or not they wish to participate, it is usually after the sales presentation has satisfied their curiosity. Some recruiting professionals select this method because they believe that their sales skill will have a greater opportunity to impact the individuals viewing the sales presentation, rather than just hearing about it over the phone (obviously the case since you can use more forms of communication in person). As a result, there is a higher probability of successfully recruiting the potential attendees.

Another school of thought held by recruiting professionals is to be blind with the newspaper advertising to generate a higher call volume, but to perform some level of verbal presentation which maintains or increases the potential attendees' curiosity but provides some critical information that can help those with little or no interest to make this determination before attending the sales presentation. I recommend this method because you can negate a negative shift in momentum should some of the attendees choose to leave before or during the presentation. Reducing the potential for disruptive and outwardly negative individuals to impact the group of attendees as a whole is very important when attempting to maximize the successful results of your recruiting efforts.

Say, for example, that you speak to one hundred callers inquiring about the job. You keep the process blind and seventy-five callers claim to be attending the sales presentation/interview. When the day arrives, only thirty people actually attend the presentation.

Halfway through the sales presentation, ten people get up and walk out. The remaining twenty are still listening. Many are planning to follow the others but do not wish to be impolite. At the end of the presentation, only a couple of them show some genuine interest. In the parking lot outside, some of those who were less interested are talking about the opportunity with your company. A loud, negative individual claims that he has tried something like this before and it is not a very good opportunity.

Later on, when you go to contact the people who claimed to be interested, only four agree to participate. Of these four participants, only one shows up for your training seminar and you realize the devastating effect of attrition on your recruiting success.

Now, consider a similar situation using a blind newspaper ad but with a more thorough verbal explanation when the first contact is made by callers inquiring about the job. You speak to one hundred callers and forty state their interest in attending the sales presentation/interview. Of that forty, nineteen actually show up for the presentation. This group seems to be a little more informed than the last group so they do not engage in very much communication about what type of job this may be. Throughout the presentation, everyone participates and enjoys him or herself until the conclusion. Three of the attendees claim that they are not interested in the opportunity and leave quietly but politely. Of the remaining sixteen, four seem very excited and zealous to get started, and the remaining people, though a little more reserved, still show a desire to become involved. On the first day of training, twelve people attend and the rest claim to be able to start soon.

In this illustration the latter methodology proved to be more effective, though of course the results could just as easily been shifted. If the hold-up rate for attendance at the sales presentation was extremely poor because too much information was given, or it was given incorrectly, then it may be more encouraging to employ a completely blind process.

A sample script of a blind ad call response for a satellite provider may sound like this:

"Hello can I help you?"

"Yeah, I'm calling about the ad in the paper."

"Okay, and what is your name?"

"My name is Cathy."

"Hi, Cathy. My name is (Your name) and I'm with the Human Resources Department here at (Company name). I need to ask you a few quick questions to see if you meet our basic qualifications. Do you have a car? Do you enjoy working directly with the public? Do you have friends and family in this area that would keep you anchored here? Are you looking for a full-time job, or a part-time job?

"Okay, you do meet our basic qualifications. The whole reason we have the ad in the newspaper is because of our recent expansion in your area, and we are looking to fill several positions. These include people for our warehouse, administration and marketing departments. We deal mainly with the marketing of satellite television service and installation. Do you know of anybody that has satellite television service? Great! As you probably already know it is a fast growing business. We can provide our viewers with a unique viewing experience with over three hundred channels to choose from. We are scheduling interviews for (day). Would you like me to see if we still have room for another person? Hold on, while I see what's still available okay? (*Book appointment.*)

"This interview will consist of a short personal interview and a group presentation. Because we only have a limited amount of seating I would like to know if you can commit to this appointment? Fantastic then, Cathy, we'll look forward to seeing you on (day). Because this is a business interview we ask that you do dress in business attire and bring a pen and paper just in case you want to jot anything down. Bye."

Let's define the real position/openings: salespeople for satellite service. This illustration would be considered blind because the caller still is not sure what position she is applying for. Notice that warehouse and administration were mentioned, so people who would enjoy working as laborers and forklift operators would still feel comfortable applying for the positions, and also people from accounting backgrounds and secretarial positions and personal assistants have not been alienated. Finally, positions in the marketing department were mentioned, so people with sales backgrounds also feel comfortable.

Another point of interest was the question, "Do you have friends and family in this area that would keep you anchored here?" This question appears to be searching for the stability of the caller, but in actuality is attempting to ascertain whether or not the potential recruit possesses any "personal leads" with which to get started should she become involved with the company. The respondent also makes the company appear large by indicating they have a Human Resources Department and by having to check and see if they have enough room to invite the caller for an interview. After the appointment is made, the respondent explains what type of dress is expected. This is important for the presentation. If a person is permitted to attend the sales presentation poorly dressed, the remaining group of attendees may perceive the company as being desperate to hire anyone. However, if poorly dressed or even outwardly negative persons are asked to leave prior to the presentation then the remaining attendees will associate more value to the position for which the hiring is being conducted. This translates to a greater desire to attain the positions on the part of the remaining attendees. The final key to this blind ad call response was that the person answering the call committed the attendee to the appointment. Some engaged in this practice have even gone so far as to call the night before the presentation (when the time lapse[4] between the incoming call and the appointment exceeds twenty-four hours) and reconfirm attendance at the sales presentation.

Now let's consider an ad call response which provides the caller with considerably more information, as in this scenario used in conjunction with a Customer Service Representative ad shown on p. 216.

---

[4] (Tip: The longer the time lapse between when the incoming call was received and the actual presentation, the greater the attrition. Fewer people will actually show up for the appointment!)

"Hello can I help you?"
"Yeah, I'm calling about the ad in the paper."
"Okay, and what is your name?"
"My name is Cathy."
"Hi, Cathy. My name is (Your name) and I'm with the Human Resources Department here at (Company name). I need to ask you a few quick questions to see if you meet our basic qualifications. Do you have a car? Do you enjoy working directly with the public? Do you have friends and family in this area that would keep you anchored here? Are you looking for a full-time job, or a part-time job?

"Okay, you do meet our basic qualifications. The whole reason we have the ad in the newspaper is because of our recent expansion in your area, and we are looking to fill several positions. We've been in business since (?), and we have (#) offices worldwide. We deal with the manufacture, marketing and servicing of several different lines of products ranging from carpet steam cleaners to air filtration units, but our main focus is on a product called the 'Example: Rain dance.' Have you ever heard of it before?

"It's a small appliance designed by doctor's and allergists that uses 2 ½ quarts of cold tap water to filter the air that your family breathes. It also deodorizes, aromatizes, sanitizes and cleans. It's amazing to see! We work on prearranged appointments, so there's no cold calling or door knocking. You simply take your appointment and go over to their home or office. Set up the equipment and explain to them how and why it works. You do not have to sell any of our 'Rain dance' units in order to receive our base salary of ($?) per week. However if any of our clients would like to purchase the equipment it would be your responsibility to fill out a purchase order of which you would receive a percentage of the profit. In this way you can exceed the base salary. Does this sound like something you would enjoy doing? Okay great!

"We do have benefits, which cover such things as medical, dental and optical, but this would not take effect until your standard ninety day probationary period has ended. The next step would be to schedule you for one of our initial interviews. We are scheduling interviews for (day).

"Would you like me to see if we still have room for another person? Hold on, while I see what's still available okay? (*Book appointment.*)

"This interview will consist of a short personal interview and a group presentation. Because we only have a limited amount of seating I would like to know, can you commit to this appointment? Fantastic, then, Cathy, we'll look forward to seeing you on (day).

"Because this is a business interview we ask that you do dress in business attire and bring a pen and paper just in case you want to jot anything down. Bye."

Notice in this example the respondent provides the caller with enough information to make a decision as to whether or not they would enjoy the act of setting up and presenting a product directly. This is a major issue and cause for attrition when employing blind ad techniques. For this reason, a greater rejection rate may be observed at this time. However, the hold-up rate of attendees increases because those who have agreed have a greater understanding of what the position involves.

A commission is mentioned, which is enticing to accomplished sales persons, but a salary is comforting as well. The Company appears to be large because of the description of several product lines and the assertion of the geographic coverage of distributorship. The product (a water trap vacuum system) is explained enough to pique curiosity, but without evoking any stereotypical response. It is endorsed by the fact that doctors and allergists have designed it.

Notice especially the reassuring of the caller that there is no "cold calling" or door knocking involved. This dispels common objections to this line of work. The same basic principals explained for the first example apply, but based on this script it is easy to see how this deviates from a completely blind process.

As a distributor you may be worrying about the benefits package, but my advice is not to run out and purchase insurance for all your potential candidates. Remember, the high attrition rate means you may not need a lot of coverage. Wait and see who makes it for 90 days, then you can purchase insurance if you're offering it.

Regardless of what method you choose, the next phase of the process is the actual presentation, or the ultimate presentation. Yes, a sales presentation must be performed employing the same direct sales techniques as were previously discussed, but these must be tailored toward recruiting, and consideration should be given to energy transfer.

A recruitment-driven presentation incorporates a focus on the "team" effort, company assistance, coaching, and potential for future sales through the accomplishment of the immediate sale (convincing your prospects to work for you) even if this sale is only psychological. The attendee may reason that the products/services are so good that he would purchase, and therefore concludes that others will feel similarly, given a resembling stimulus.

After the presentation, a determination must be made as to who will ultimately be participating, and will therefore be in need of training. One method for performing this is by administering an aptitude test that the participants take at the beginning or end of the interview. This test can be authored by the distributor or acquired elsewhere. The interviewees are told if they are able to pass the test, they will be contacted for employment; another version has them call you for the results. This allows you to effectively separate those who are genuinely interested from those who simply stayed throughout the presentation out of some obligation or politeness, and to dismiss those you determine to be unacceptable.

Where recruiting and "simply selling" differ is that a typical sales presentation does not involve the erection of the prospects' self-confidence or desire for accomplishment (important to note is that some companies encourage the recruiting goals rather than sales, and consider sales merely a byproduct of a great recruiting demo). A sale-oriented demo merely requires the prospects to decide whether or not they feel enough emotional attachment and desire to a product or service to complete the transaction with a financial instrument.

When the purchase has been decided upon, whether favorably or unfavorably, there is usually no further communication necessary (unless a repeat customer is the consideration) or these communications naturally begin to deteriorate until they no longer exist at all. This is because there is seldom any need for further communications, with the exception of the perpetuation of leads, or in the case of after-sale service.

When recruiting, however, the initial sale is merely the beginning of a project that ultimately is purposed to last indefinitely. Barring death or unforeseen circumstances, your continued communication and assistance will be necessary as long as the individual is progressing under your umbrella. This means that a much greater commitment is required when selling with the intent of recruiting as opposed to selling with the intent of generating a sale. In this case the *Sale* refers to the transfer of financial resources in exchange for a product or service.

When performing for groups, the amount of energy required to be transferred between the speaker/salesperson and the audience is increased by the number of audience participants. Also, questions may be modified to elicit an affirmation from the group as a whole, rather than from individuals. This is recommended because of the discord among answers provided by the prospects/audience.

When group selling, it is important to win the majority over and to try to add individual experiences which the audience members can relate to.

Another idea is to use a thrust stage which extends outward into the audience. With very large groups, the intensity of audience enthusiasm aids the speaker requiring less energy from the speaker in order to reach the audience members. Instead, the audience begins to feed on the energy of the group itself. It is then interesting to note the direct relationship a great audience can have on a speaker. Rather than taking all the energy from the speaker, the audience may actually uplift and even fuel the speaker himself.

Consider the mob mentality. It has been demonstrated that large groups have committed actions, which they would not normally as individuals. These claim to have been caught up in the mentality (energy) of the group as a whole. This phenomenon is not always negative and should be recognized as a tool for the speaker/salesperson.

If you are able to harness the power of this energy/force, and perform a sales presentation worthy of the admiration of your potential recruits, you will without a doubt attain the certain success you are seeking, ultimately to the degree that you are able to master both the art of selling, and the science of it.

Group Sales & Motivational Energy Transfer

Universal Power

Speaker

GROUP

Leaders, motivational speakers and group salespersons must tap into the unlimited power of the universe to empower others.

Training

Now that we have the people, we have to train them. Training can be done in the field while performing demos just by having your recruits watch and participate. It is at your discretion whether or not to compensate them for this participation, but it is recommended that you give them something so that they can participate in the emotional high that accompanies the made sale.

I have always advocated training within 24 hours of the recruit learning of their acceptance for a position. The drop-out rate will increase dramatically if too much time passes from their having seen the demonstration to beginning the training, much like buying temperature does after the in-home demonstration.

The training should be informative, motivational, and exciting. It should not be too exhausting, and if it is too advanced, the recruit may quit before they begin, asserting that it is too difficult. Remember to teach only the key elements. In direct vacuum sales I would say the product comparison (Vac knock) is the all-important part of new recruit training.

If you are a trainer, you should note that excitement is far more valuable than knowledge. Over my many years of training one observation that has continually astounded me is the degree to which an excited new recruit can accomplish the sale. Teach them every fact and figure and leave them feeling blah and it will seem as if your product became really difficult to sell over night. I would say that the sale with new recruits is made by 100% of the enthusiasm produced by 80% of the excitement and 20% of the facts.

Make sure you divide up the administrative duties over your training occasions if they are in-class. For example, if you are conducting three-day training, you might have them make a list of friends and family on the first night. On the second you may wish to cover booking scripts, how to fill out appointment slips, an introduction to the Marketing Department (the administrative hub of the office), and get them on the phones booking appointments for their initial weekend[5] (blastoff). The third day, you would cover paperwork such as The Independent Dealer Agreement ("We don't withhold taxes, you're self-employed" and other legal protections for the company), filling out emergency contact forms listing five references (in case they go missing in action [MIA] and you want to track them down to get your consigned equipment back), making a copy of their driver's license, reading the Compensation Agreement (Outlines what you have agreed to pay them for duties performed. For example, $2000.00 for performing 12 qualified demos per week with an average of six qualified leads per demo being turned in to the Marketing Department.) etc.

"You know you get more flies with honey…" (u.a.).

You may find that making a contest of each element of training is successful. For example, "Whoever can write down the most names of friends and family tonight will win five bucks cash!" Or, "Whoever books the most appointments (over four) tonight will win (insert promo gift here)." Or a contest for promotion based on the number of demos

---

[5] (**Important note**: If they have no demos for the initial weekend then there is no need to give them equipment and they can easily become a casualty of attrition before getting started making all the work performed up to this point an exercise in futility. Demos are critical!).

performed on their initial weekend also works well. Of course a contest based on sales made through their initial weekend demos is a must.

I recommend having them practice cleaning equipment if we're talking about vacuum sales, and demonstrating an understanding of how things are put back in the box in the event of a no-sale. There's nothing worse that a new dealer that has scratched equipment because of improperly storing the equipment in the box (usually the distributor ends up replacing the damaged part). You're probably thinking that the Distributor can charge the new recruit for the damage, but these small amounts can become difficult to collect, especially if the dealer becomes a victim of the company's attrition before he earns a check. Improper storage of equipment can cause damage to the boxes as well, and customers might request another machine should they purchase because the equipment appears to be used.

Finally, I recommend evening training sessions for two reasons. First, if the new recruit has trouble attending evening training sessions, he is likely to be just as preoccupied when the time comes to begin performing demos (which happen mainly in the evenings). Second, you can combine your full-time applicants with your part-time applicants and run both successful ad hiring and in-home recruiting campaigns simultaneously.

If your training sessions are held during the day, you will likely have to break for lunch. This is another potentially dangerous opportunity for increased attrition. New recruit goes home for lunch and gets distracted. He does not return for training. Keep your training exciting, fun, and motivating. Your only goal each night is to have your recruits return. Over time they will learn everything they need to succeed. As mom always said, "Rome wasn't built in a day" (u.a.).

Chapter 13

STDs—Attrition Doesn't Lie!

- **UD-NWT**—Up-line Distributors Never Work The Trenches
- **PNI**—Protective Negative Influence
- **QIM**—Questionable Identity Modeling
- **NBD**—Narcissistic Behavioral Disposition
- **SNIOP**—Swayed by the Negative Influence of Other People
- **BDNSG**—Bad Deals Never Seem Good
- **TPRH**—Talented People Rot at Home
- **IHP&PHM**—I Hate Phones & Phones Hate Me
- **RBTS**—Rookies Brag Too Soon
- **IPE**—I Prejudge Everyone
- **BITS**—Back In The Saddle
- **NBD**—Narcissistic Behavioral Disposition
- **PMA**—Positive Mental Attitude; a good defense against STDs

What are STDs and what effect can they have on you as a salesperson, and on your sales organization or distribution network? STDs are Sales Transmitted Diseases. Perhaps you were thinking of something different, but these diseases are real and they can have a profound impact on your sales-oriented business.

Once, while on one of my gypsy-like sales adventures, I met a highly regarded and successful veteran salesman whose ability to close deals seemed natural and without effort. I began to talk with him at length about what causes attrition and he related to me these STDs, and how he had come to learn them. I'd now like to share his lessons with you:

"Be very careful how you live. Do not live like people who aren't wise. Live like people who are wise. Make the most of every opportunity…" (Eph 5:15 & 16, *Bible New International Reader's Version*, 1996)

The veteran salesman warned that if one is going to build a big business now-a-days, they must be aware of these STDs. They are real and they have been influencing business since way back. Let me tell you about the first STD I ever came down with. This one I inherited from my family. Being poor as a child, I never had the luxury of knowing what quality products really cost. I guess it was my own fault though, because I never really had a desire to learn, knowing that we could never have afforded most of these products anyway.

So the first STD I want to warn you about is common among new people, and even some that we do demos for. I call it BDNSG Syndrome. That stands for **Bad Deals Never Seem Good** Syndrome. What does that really mean? It means that if the prospects or your new dealer already have a perceived idea of the cost of your product, and they cannot associate enough new value to the product through the sales presentation to override their current beliefs, than when they find out the actual price they will probably feel like it isn't that good of a deal. Prospects tend to say; "It costs too much," or "We can't afford it!"

Rookies with this disease are harder to detect because they usually drop out of training and quit before they even get started. This is usually to the shock of the trainer and the up-line distributor because the new recruit exhibited no signs of lack of motivation prior to learning the actual price. However, these new people will sometimes continue on, even though in their hearts they deny the value meets the price. As their blastoff weekend (the initial demos for friends & family) nears, they have no, or very few, demos lined up. This is because they have already decided that no one in their circle of family and friends has enough extra money to *waste* on an item which is over-priced, in the recruit's mind.

These new recruits tend to display symptoms often misunderstood by their up-line distributor and trainer. The up-line distributor and trainer usually interpret the problem as the new sub-distributor having an unqualified circle of leads (not reaching his/her target market). Thus, as a purely reactionary response, the up-line distributor and his trainer tend to lose confidence in the new sub-distributor/sales representative and focus on the others. This new sub-distributor is then pronounced dead on arrival.

There is hope though! This new sub-distributor can be saved with a little preventive communication and a strong value-building presentation initially performed by the person who is in authority over the orientation of the sub-distributor. Never underestimate the power of true value.

Another STD responsible for a great deal of attrition is one that attacks when a lack of leads threatens the ambition of a sub-distributor. Another way of looking at it would be to consider the following illustration: a man and his wife plan a road trip. They have financial resources saved for the occasion. They have food. They have a map. The only thing they do not have is a target. They do not know where they want to go. A friend drops over to wish them a safe trip and inquires as to how long they will be gone. The man is perplexed because he cannot answer the question as he does not know where they are going. This illustration is silly but it makes clear one critical element to success. It is difficult to hit a target that you cannot see! It is difficult to arrive at a destination if you have not first determined where you will go. You may end up somewhere if you simply move forward, but is likely that where you will end up is not where you want to be. This is called TPRH Syndrome. That stands for **Talented People Rot at Home** Syndrome.

Basically it means that even the greatest salesperson in the world is wasted if he has no opportunities to use his skills. As I have learned over the years, if you don't use it, you lose it! These individuals often go home, realize what's beginning to happen to them and lose confidence. But their self-confidence is unfortunately a large part of what makes them a talented salesperson. They have already started down the dark path. The up-line distributor and the trainer usually assume that this person is not going to make it. They view the sub-distributor as just another victim of attrition. Then they often abandon this person to cure themselves of whatever it is that ails them. Later they say things like, "Hey, do you remember Joe? He could have been great huh!" or, "Do you remember Mary? She was a real winner. I just wish she could have gotten off to a good start!"

The good news is that if you're really on top of your business you can save this individual. It takes a lot of patience and you have to have a genuine interest in seeing this person succeed. If you're just in it for the quick buck, this person's not for you. You have to start off with honesty. Let them know you care, but that they have a little hill to climb. Most importantly, though, is that they don't have to climb this hump alone. You are going to be right by their side, climbing it with them (literally by their side, not just in thoughts, words or prayers).

"So what do I do now?" He or she might ask. This is the perfect opportunity to explain a new lead acquisition program and to tell them that you will give them any extra sales presentations you might have on the 'books' until they get rolling.

Contest these new lead acquisition programs. *Go out with this person personally* and help them. If you won't go out & knock a few doors if needs be, can you really expect them to? A great leader demonstrates the he cares about his followers. In turn, they will surely come to appreciate and feel gratitude for the kind acts shown them. These are often repaid with loyalty, admiration, and respect. The loyalty and respect you'll get for helping your people be successful is the greatest prize you could receive. These mentored sales representatives/sub-distributors also become the best recruiters when it becomes their turn to do so. This is because, due to your helping them when they needed it, they will see to it that no future sub-distributor generation that desires to do well will be neglected. When these individuals have matured into healthy distributors they tend to exhibit the same kind of "I'll help you get through the hard times" attitude. Recruits appreciate this because it calms their fears and makes them feel like they're not alone.

There is a common antidote for STDs. It is simple, but highly effective when used as a treatment, as long as the patient's mentality doesn't reject it. It is a concentrated dosage of PMA or **Positive Mental Attitude**. I was able to fight off TPRH Syndrome by going to the office everyday and finding ways to uplift my spirit. As a sales representative, your PMA is like your spiritual immune system. If it is strong it helps you fight off STDs. I caused my up-line distributor and trainer to regain faith in me by never exhibiting any signs of giving up. In fact, I continued to learn everyday even though I wasn't doing demos.

It wasn't long before I learned that I wasn't the only one prone to these STDs. My up-line distributor had caught a bad bug also. I now call it UD-NWT Syndrome, which stands for **Up-line Distributors-Never Work the Trenches** Syndrome. This is what happens after an up-line distributor suffers from narcissistic behavioral disposition, which will be discussed a little later. Basically, it is when up-line distributors have difficulty sympathizing with new recruits because they cannot remember that they got to where they are through experience and time, rather than simply inheriting it through some genetic miracle. Although I depended on the rest of the sales organization for PMA refills, I now realized that, in point of fact, we were all interdependent.

Another terrible STD is IHP&PHM Syndrome (**I Hate Phones & Phones Hate Me**). I regret to inform you that if you are having your sub-distributors book all their own appointments, some of them will get this disease and never recover from it. PMA is most certainly the best self-cure. If you illustrate to your people that it is not the phones they are afraid of, but merely the thought that picking it up and trying will lead to some painful experience or rejection, this STD can be cured effectively. The phone is a useful tool! If you had just witnessed a family member or friend get into a serious accident, isn't a phone one of the first things you would wish you had? Would you be afraid to make the call to 911? Of course not, because you are confident your call will meet with certain success! That is why sub-distributors must be trained well before attempting to do phone work and why your target market and demographics research are vital when choosing a location.

Signs that a sub-distributor has IHP&PHM include the fact that they tend to have few if any appointments, little or no phone time scheduled, a lack of appointments or claims that they do their bookings from home (i.e., without your supervision), so that you won't be able to observe their failure or their lack of commitment If you have an office outside of your home, it is recommended that you install multiple phone lines and monitor the phone activities, so you can provide assistance to those who may need it. Especially before they 'burn' their leads; the most common symptom of this disease.

As soon as you observe this behavior, you have to get this sub-distributor involved in some one-on-one training and do some calling together, pointing out possible pitfalls. You make a call for him, then he tries one for himself. I remember going through this disease myself. I felt like the fighter Rocky. It was me (alone) versus the phone."

Just then a voice in my head said, "Queue 'Eye of the Tiger.'" That really inspired me to do something about my phone-fearing STD! It became an obsession at one point; a personal challenge if you will. I eventually began to have some success, but not until I had first used up over a hundred hard-earned leads. My up-line distributor was teaching me that information and knowledge are very valuable. I wouldn't realize this fully until years later when I observed countless distributorships go bankrupt because of a lack of both information and knowledge.

I warned you of some pretty nasty STDs, but this next one has got to be the most destructive influence in recruiting and networking I have ever seen. It is called quite simply PNI (**Protective Negative Influence**). I don't even know how I caught this STD, but I did. PNI is a disease which strikes you when your PMA is at its all-time low. Family and friends give it to you when they do not wish to see anything hurt you. They feel that it is their responsibility to help you get out of whatever is causing the pain. They will often link this to whatever you are spending your time doing. So if you are trying to sell, they decide that your new job is what is causing the pain and they say things like, "Why don't you get a real job? You're not a salesman! You should go back to school or something! Maybe I can get you a job somewhere! I think that distributor of yours has got you brainwashed." Sometimes they'll even try a bribe, "If you'll go to college, maybe we can get you a new car!"

Friends sound different when they're trying to give you PNI. They say things like, "I don't know why you got your hopes up!" or, "You should get a job like what I'm doing!" They sometimes give you PNI for a different reason.

Sometimes they'll try when your PMA is strong. This is because they are jealous. You appear to be having too much fun, and they can't understand why you should. Fighting off PNI can be very difficult. If you stacked all those who have failed to fight off PNI one atop another, it would stretch far into space beyond the distance you can imagine. It can cause friendships to fall apart and family members to distance themselves from you. But if you can win, if you can beat PNI, you have an obligation to be successful. This way you can prove why you had to do what you did, with financial freedom and success. If you fail, everyone will say, "I told you so..."

Once, I was out in the field selling vacuums door to door. Got my first sale, and as you can imagine I was walking about ten feet off the ground. Little did I know what sinister forces lay in the shadows, waiting for the accomplished salesperson.

I sold three more partly on skill, and mostly with momentum. It was about two days later that there was a call from one of my customers. I had no associations that this call could cause me pain, so I grabbed the phone, prepared to provide great service!

"We thought it over," began the voice on the other end. And then it ended with, "we changed our minds, and we want to cancel." My heart sank a bit. Then I made arrangements to go out to their house and pick up the vacuum. While I was picking it up, my heart sank again. But at least I had three other deals, I said to myself.

When I got back to the office, everyone knew I was a little down so they tried to cheer me up, "Hey, look on the bright side. You still have all those other sales!"

"Yeah, you're right," I replied.

My up-line distributor avoided talking about the other sales and tried to push me to keep selling. In retrospect, I know he had caught an STD of his own. I call it PUDPL (**Protective Up-line Distributors Pretend Longer**). This is a disease which causes distributors to pretend things are in order to protect themselves or others. In this case, my up-line distributor was pretending that two of my remaining three sale credit applications had not been turned down by the finance company because of bad credit. He thought that if he told me the truth, it would hurt me so much I might not recover from it. So he planned not to tell me until he absolutely had to. Perhaps I could get some more good sales before that time came and then I might not feel as bad. But little did he know, my mental medical sales condition had already worsened. I had moved on to my next STD: RBTS (**Rookies Brag Too Soon**). I had flaunted money I didn't have. Made promises about things I soon would realize I couldn't keep. I would soon feel embarrassed, like I was a flop; a fraud! This STD just brings you down.

It makes your PMA very weak. But you usually won't die from it. You have to be careful you don't get PNI while you're in this weakened state.

The good news is that if you can just hold out for a bit, time cures RBTS and teaches you a valuable lesson. That lesson is simply not to count your eggs until they've hatched.

Over time I learned not to get over excited about my sales, and to focus whatever excitement I did have into continuing momentum. In this way, I trained myself not to get too anxious should a deal fall through, or if I was experiencing a low time. Once again PMA is a great cure-all. Ask yourself questions like, "If I sell a bunch in the next couple days how will I feel?" Make daily affirmations like, "If history repeats itself, I am sure to sell again real soon. The reason people have purchased from me in the past is because I already possess great sales skills. If I have impressed others, still others will continue to be impressed, and when they are impressed they will buy my goods." These kinds of daily affirmation will boost your PMA even during the rough times.

> Look! A sewer went out to sow; and as he was sowing, some [seeds] fell alongside the road, and the birds came and ate them up. Others fell upon the rocky places, where they did not have much soil, and at once they sprang up because they did not have depth of soil. But when the sun rose they were scorched, and because of not having root, they withered. Others, too, fell among the thorns, and the thorns came up and choked them.

> Still others fell upon the fine soil and they began to yield fruit, this one a hundred fold, that one sixty, the other thirty. Let him who has ears listen. (Mathew 13: 3-9, *New World Translation Bible*, 2006).
>
> You then listen to the illustration of the man who sowed. Where anyone hears the word... but does not get the sense of it, the... [negative ones] ...come and snatch it away from where it has been sown in his heart. This is the one sown along side the road. As for the one sown along the rocky places, this is the one hearing [your words], and at once accepting it with joy. Yet he has no root in himself but continues for a time, and after tribulation or persecution has arisen on account of... [your words] ... he is at once stumbled. As for the ones sown among the thorns, this is the one hearing your words, but the anxiety of this system of things, and the deceptive power of riches chokes... [your words]... and he becomes unfruitful. But as for the one sown upon the fine soil, this is the one hearing your words and getting the sense of it. Who really does bear fruit and produces, this one a hundredfold, that one sixty fold, the other thirty. (Mathew 13:18-23, *New World Translation Bible*, 2006)

This is how the word of mouth advertising is when you're recruiting. You must ask for the recruit many times for one to blossom. Some catch STDs like those mentioned above, but don't be discouraged.

Another STD common among distributors is IPE (**I Prejudge Everyone**). This disease can affect rookies too. So mind yourself. You see they prejudge everything. They prejudge leads, appointments, sales, and of course recruits, but it effects recruiting the most. It is after all such a difficult task to know who to spend your time training and who not to. But the cure for IPE is a simple one.

> "...While men were sleeping, his enemy came and sowed weeds in among the wheat and left. When the blade sprouted and produced fruit, then the weeds appeared also..." (Mathew 13:25 & 26, *New World Translation Bible*, 2006).

The moral of the story is that you never know whether a recruit or potential recruit will be the one who joins you on your journey to success. Therefore, if you decide to be in the people business, you will have to work hard. No matter how financially well you may be, you cannot afford to allow IPE to run rampant. A wise man once said, "Either you run your business, or your business runs you" (u.a.).

Make it your Standard Operating Procedure to never prejudge. Simply accept them as they bear fruit. When I was recruiting people I would prejudge them often because when I invited them to attend an open house at the office to discuss the opportunity, they would rarely honor the appointment. Most of these didn't even have the courtesy to call. I just assumed they were not interested, until one time I was curious about a fellow who seemed very genuine about joining my sales team. I called him back and it turned out he had been experiencing some personal difficulties and had forgotten all about our appointment. When he realized he had made a mistake, he was too proud to call me because he feared my disappointment. He figured I would probably no longer be interested in him since my first experience might indicate that he was not punctual or courteous.

However, on the contrary, I was still very much interested in helping him come into our business and grow. We managed a great friendship from this relationship and I resolved several issues. First, never prejudge, and second, recognize the wisdom in this simple formula: 100% of everyone you bring to open house shows up.

"Persistence and determination alone are omnipotent. The slogan 'press on' has solved and always will solve the problems of the human race" (Coolidge, n.d.).

I was no longer a salesman. I had somehow transcended this title and become a talent scout, but I admit my new recruiting style needed some tweaking.

That's when I first realized the importance of attire. How you look really does matter! So I got dressed for success! There was another critical error I was making in my recruiting attempts. I was powerless to call my potential recruits because I had failed to obtain their phone number! I wouldn't let that happen again. So dressed to kill, cleanly shaven, shoes shined, and head held high I headed out into an all new world. That was when the sales business was over, and the people business began! Everywhere I went I gave out cards, and I took numbers. I worked my magic at the mall, in the parking lot, while fueling up, while having drinks.

I followed up the night before open houses with each one of my potential recruits:

"Is this Mary?"

"This is."

"Do you remember talking with me about the job in show business? You're not going to believe this but I had a chance to talk to my boss about you, and guess what? I got you an interview!

"There are going to be several people there learning about the job opportunities. Are you available on Monday night at 6 pm?" (The night designated for open house at our office.)

"Yeah sure I can make it!"

"Okay, I'll pick you up. I'd have you just come over, but unfortunately you can only get into this interview with an escort."

The rest, as they say, is history. I really began to love the people business, and somehow the passion for helping others find information, strategies, and direct selling systems swelled inside me.

> "Nobody should seek his own good, but the good of others" (1 Corinthians 10:24, *New International Version Bible*, 1973).

People still quit, sometimes, though, and at one point, my PMA couldn't have been weaker. PMA is something that you lose when you least appreciate it, because you are too busy taking it for granted.

> For what glory is it, if, when ye be buffeted for your faults, ye shall take it patiently? But if, when ye do well, and suffer for it, ye take it patiently, this is acceptable with God.(1 Peter 2:20, *King James Version Bible*, 1987)

So I took a small break from selling while I tried to figure out the difference between good intentions and really making a difference. That's when I caught my next STD (BITS), which stands for **Back In The Saddle** Syndrome. This STD works on your self-confidence. It causes you to question your proven abilities and usually starts when you begin asking yourself dumb questions: I wonder if I can still do this. I wonder if I just got lucky before. What if I lost my "powers"? *Et cetera*.

Then, you unconsciously put off doing that first demo. You're wondering if your reputation for closing (every sale) will be questioned. Will those around you question your abilities? Will they then use this to support their own excuses for failure? The best cure for BITS, believe it or not, is doing demos. As soon as that first sale comes your way, you're cured!

> There are those who make things happen. There are those who watch or follow others who make things happen, and finally there are those who wonder what the heck happened. (Walsh, 2000, *Personal Communication*)

This saying is the basis of what my experience has to teach. Make sure you are someone who makes things happen and be confident when asking your due for this work we love so much called sales. You deserve every penny of your due and your age is not a good enough reason to accept anything less than what you truly deserve!

Here's another conundrum. The question is, should you make your best salesperson your trainer? At first glance the answer seems obvious. Of course! Who else would you want to train your sales people? However, the answer is not as simple as you might first think. Back in my day, I was requested to train others, mostly because I had a better than average closing ability (closing ability: the average one sells as compared to the average one shows), and because I had been recognized as someone who could motivate others to do the same.

While I was being promoted up through the sales organization I encountered another STD: QIM, which stands for **Questionable Identity Modeling**. As salespeople, we are often left to create an identity for a position or title because we are frequently promoted to a title which has no model or example for what is expected because distributors often fail to provide adequate job descriptions when promoting. QIM attacks when you are asked to switch roles frequently within an office or defined position.

For example, as a salesperson it is your responsibility to obtain leads, qualify leads (Make sure the leads are financially able to buy your product/ the right income bracket), contact such leads and book appointments, perform demonstrations, and sell your products. As a trainer your duties might be to choose and run newspaper ads, or perform at open house. They might involve the need to motivate others, or to participate in training in the field, and so on. There are many different positions within a direct vacuum sales distributorship and each of these positions is interdependent. QIM occurs when one person is asked to switch roles repeatedly in order to compensate for a lack of properly trained people for all of these positions, causing an identity crisis to be formed. "What am I to do? Who am I?" I have found that it is only the very flexible who can perform well under these conditions, so I implore you to define your people's positions and roles within the direct sale distributorship well, so as to dispel the existence of QIM.

At one point I had the opportunity to catch a segment of an infomercial by a renowned motivator named Anthony Robbins. I was impressed and quickly purchased one of his audiocassettes entitled *"Awaken the Giant Within"*(Robbins, 1991). This was timely because I was just beginning to realize (from a psychological standpoint) what an affect one individual's words could have on others.

Becoming puffed up with pride is the root of a very destructive STD known as NBD (**Narcissistic Behavioral Disposition**). You must guard your mental prowess against such a prehistoric and commonplace a sin as vanity. Vanity diminishes your capacity for growth. How does one grow, if one believes they have already arrived? NBD is felt by those around you and lingers long after its initial effects are noticed. Few, if any, of the people I have encountered find those infected with NBD very attractive. You want young over-achievers that always want more. You gotta want more! That's how you get more. You have to help your distributor up-line assign a great value to having you as part of the team. Make yourself a VIP: the people who stretch and strive to earn more money; because they're worth it!

> The kind of people I look for to fill top management spots are the eager beavers, the mavericks. These are the guys who try to do more than they're expected to do- they always reach. (Iacocca, u.d.)

Another STD to watch out for is D+B=N. This is when a salesperson begins having a relationship with a telemarketer hired to aid the sales people by booking potential selling appointments. This STD has demonstrated itself to me time after time. It has always proven itself a worthy formula. **Dealer + Booker=Nothing**! You get "As the Vacuum Turns" going on in your office; it's a real soap opera! When a sub-distributor begins this, at first glance romantic, journey with the only hopes of increased fornication and friendship, the casual relationship usually in time becomes a source of bitter feelings for at least one of the working parties (the same can be said of relationships between sales representatives). One is often forced to quit at the expense of the other. If this doesn't happen right away, they usually begin to SNIOP others. (Remember, this stands for **Swayed by the Negative Influence of Other People**.) They get into groups of dealers and infect them with negative talk/gossip. The proper balance between telemarketers and salespeople is what it takes for an office to function successfully (unless the sales representative has been trained to book their own appointments or enlist the aid of their prospects; optimal scenario).

There are at work in this scenario two conflicting schools of thought. The first is that by co-existing with your dealers in both work environments as well as casually, you eliminate the possibilities for outside negative influences and increase camaraderie. Therein lay a danger though. The flip side to this school of thought is that dealers can become complacent and display a lack of respect to the office authority figures, and when the need for discipline arises, the dealer has a difficult time distinguishing between corrective criticism and friendly advice. The dealer will often procrastinate from making changes believing their distributor/friend will overlook their shortcomings because of their relationship. At this point, if the distributor is genuinely close to the dealer, correcting them becomes somewhat of a laborious activity because the distributor is trying to analyze the situation and act upon the words which he believes will best bring about the results required for that dealer's success. Similarly, you may observe the distributor attempting to sever emotional/relationship ties between the dealer and himself. The results of this action are often the loss of the dealer. Not right away, but in time the dealer usually begins to fade away because they have already left behind many of the friends/associates with whom they formerly associated because they no longer shared common goals/achievements. They must then regain acceptance by their former group of associates and this requires time together and commonly accepted routines.

You then see less and less of this dealer/sales representative. You care less and less as a distributor because you feel you have nothing to lose. This particular dealer has not generated any sales recently, which is usually the result of them not working.

There are two diseases at work here. The dealer has CDMS (**Complacent Dysfunctional Masking** Syndrome). This is an STD where the dealer appears to still posses the hunger for achievement, but lacks the self-motivation to implement the necessary changes which would create the desired result. When in the past this dealer portrayed the desire for success and achievement, the distributor's expectations were usually perfunctory because there was no history to compare their behavior against. Thus, distributors seldom seem disappointed by the results of would-be new comers. In retrospect, I would say there is most certainly a lesson here. The distributor will often exhibit signs of C&E Disappointment. This is stands for **Comparison & Expectation Disappointment**. Distributors could do well to realize the old adage that 'patience is a virtue' (u.a.).

Dealers/sales representatives are indeed much like growing children. In the beginning, a baby can somehow communicate many expressions simply by crying. It is only because of love, patience, and a sincere desire to understand what appears to be causing the displeasure that many parents are able to understand so much, from the mere cry of a child. Soon the child is able to communicate using words.

Many challenges may have to be overcome, such as the 'terrible twos.' Eventually, as the child grows, they reach the teenage years, in which they may display several attitude shifts and fundamental belief changes. Likewise, as their dealers/sales reps mature within the business, there are many challenges which the dealer and distributor may have to overcome together. At times, this relationship will be tested and proven. Other times, the lines of communication will appear weathered. However, as the dealer continues on the journey to enlightenment, there will be many Kodak moments; the dazzling memories of the legacy we will one day call the past.

What can help the distributor in this type of situation? First and foremost is the understanding of exactly what point on the highway of success the dealer may be. What types of challenges might be influencing the situation and exactly what options might one draw upon to optimize performance and enhance results? By comprehending the history of a survivor, a distributor may learn some of the more common behavioral patterns and, in time, readily recognize them by their symptoms and their effect on the business overall.

Another real issue for apprentice salespeople is knowing the difference between witnessing success and achieving it! I've seen this one attack a lot of people. I call it FB, FS & O disease. This stands for **Fueled Belief, False**

Support & Overconfidence disease. In short, it describes what so many dealers and distributors have failed to realize. When observing the success of others, it is very easy to become motivated and enthused. This is usually followed up by feelings of intense belief that the ultimate goal can and will be achieved. However, the status of one's ability to achieve success has not been altered other than by your mental interpretations of what is possible. Therefore, you may not posses any new skills or knowledge which can aid you in achieving your goals.

You may dispel the validity of your new beliefs. You may soon find yourself a victim of your own overconfidence. Remember, success observed, while enjoyable, does not translate into success gained! It is often more difficult to observe dealer/distributor behavior with the express purpose of learning some new knowledge and then implementing it, than it is to simply admire it. However, if no new knowledge or action is taken, a difference in your business will seldom be seen. In fact FB, FS & O disease often leads to a decline in your sales volumes. Why? Because the efforts you have made to succeed in your business to date, although not providing you with your ultimate desires, have proven to create some results, and or learning experiences.

Therefore, any changes made which affect the infrastructure, which has provided the results to date, could actually prove damaging to current sales volumes.

Especially if, in implementing new changes, the dealer/distributor has not gained any new knowledge from which to support the new elements of the modified infrastructure. That is to say, there is always a process at work. Even those who claim they have not taken the time to create a process have participated in one. This is because all action requires a process. For this reason corrections can be effective. Change the process which preceded an achievement and you will often change the result.

Many students of selling believe the best way to learn is simply by watching someone else's success. While this may be true in redundant types of applications, sales, albeit routine, necessitates an element of spontaneity and creativity which may differ dramatically from one occasion to the next.

Although the desire to self-correct is admirable, it is hardly attainable if one does not possess the experience and wisdom to properly diagnose what may or may not be preventing a person from selling. Thus, if you have a role model or coach to help you, it would be prudent to request that they watch your manner of sales presentation and then render a diagnosis. They are likely to catch any mistakes you may be making with little effort, and be able to give you a thorough explanation of why a possible behavior or pattern of communication is not conducive to the achieving of your ultimate goal, the sale.

There is, however, one note of caution. If the salesperson cannot perform the sales presentation in a manner indicative of how he has been performing it because of nervousness and anxiety created by the presence of a peer or coach, the diagnosing process may be contaminated. This means that if you are trying to help a salesperson you may have to accompany them on several sales presentations to allow them to fall into a comfort level which will permit them to regress into the sales presentation they have become accustomed to performing.

If you really want to help, you will need to take care when offering your corrective criticism. A good rule of thumb is to compliment the individual on some area before offering your criticism. Most people have a very low tolerance for criticism so you have to mix in several compliments to be really effective. You may even wish to break up a diagnosis into several sessions.

Don't let all this information cloud and complicate the first principal of selling: *show your product* and *have fun*!

No matter how much you learn, the knowledge is only as valuable as the level of success one might accomplish for having learned it. Plus, experiencing each of the master's lessons, which have earned me the right to pass on these gems is an experience few have endured and emerged victorious over. This is the wisdom of great selling, and it is the key to unlocking the fortunes of every purse.

Such was the wisdom from the old man. He had disappeared, but he had left behind his tattered bible. Picking it up, I saw worn slips of paper which I assumed were bookmarks. Curiously, I opened the bible, though I knew it probably wasn't my place to do so. A dozen folded slips fell precariously to the floor. Picking them up, I noticed each one had the same prayer written on it. "Please Lord, help me to attain and use the wisdom of sales to make the world a better place, Amen".

Each slip was dated and had a different person's name on it. The dates spanned some three hundred and twenty years and the inside cover of the bible indicated that it may have been handed down, father to son, for more than five generations. I thought it best to keep that old bible, in case I might see the old man again and return it.

I never saw the old man again but his words have revisited me as often as I have witnessed the truth of his experience in selling in my own dealings. In the end, I would tell you this. Learn what you can while you can. Then live it. Just keep your umbrella handy.

I suggest turning it upside down!

I don't know what became of the old man, but I always keep the bible he left close by. I added my own prayer a few years back so the family tradition would not be broken. See it for yourself at the conclusion of this book.

Chapter 14

Everyone's a Salesperson

➢ **Service Sale**—The sale of a particular service instead of a tangible product.

Throughout my career as a teacher and trainer of salespeople, I have heard many individuals talk about how they just couldn't see themselves as a salesperson. I have even heard some in other professions claim that they did not like salespeople. This chapter is about setting the record straight and giving salespeople the respect they deserve. If it's a jungle out there, then salespeople are at the very top of the food chain!

Every single man, woman, and child on the earth today is either directly involved in some manner of sales, or is dependent upon someone who is. One of the easiest ways to discover how we are all directly or indirectly involved in sales is to consider the very definition of selling. As we learned in chapter one, selling is the transference of one's thoughts and feelings to another. Yet I would say it's even simpler than that, because sometimes we have to sell ourselves an idea. We talk through a problem or challenge and sell ourselves the solution we think is best.

When a child convinces his parents to allow him to stay out later than usual, a sale has been made. When an employee convinces his employer to grant him a raise, a sale has been made. Every time you've been in a relationship, a sale has been made. Even when you decide what to wear, a sale has been made.

Sales in our thoughts, our feelings, and energy are all around us. Sales permeate everything we do and infiltrates even our dreams. Sales are motivating and intense, yet calm and gentle. When is selling truly magnificent? When the person being sold believes that they have not been sold, but that in fact they have initiated their own decision.

Sales and their influence are what make-up our environment. If we can all agree that we are all customers of our society, can we not just as easily come to the conclusion that we are all also selling something? Perhaps there are some who would rather not view themselves this way, because they would like to think that they are somehow above sales. But this thinking only demonstrates an ignorance of the depth to which sales has defined them and their lives. The acceptance of being a salesperson is not degrading. Don't deny yourself! Love who you are, and what you do. Respect yourself, and the revelation that in all the inhabited earth, selling is not some stubborn stain that refuses to go away, but rather the very fabric of our society. Without it we have nothing!

Rich and poor, educated and ignorant, black or white, anxious or calm, every person on this planet needs sales. If you're reading this book you have probably developed a love of sales yourself as much as you love being a customer or shopping. One does not exist without the other, does it?

Sales and selling are something like the truth. Winston Churchill said about the truth, "Malice may attack it. Ignorance may deride it, but in the end there it is" (n.d.).

Below is a list of some occupations which, you may be surprised, are directly involved in sales or are dependent upon them. Perhaps you are involved with one of these professions, or perhaps you are somehow connected to one. If your profession is not mentioned here, don't be discouraged because you are still involved. In fact, your life will inevitably become a part of history and thus a grain of sand in the ultimate and most intimate sale of life. Will you accomplish that sale? How it turns out is entirely up to you!

As you read through this list, see if you can see how directly related to sales each of these professions are:

1. Lawyer (Relatively expensive legal liaison/ **service provider.**)
2. Doctor (Health care **service sales**.)
3. Purchasing Agent (Negotiating **service sales**.)
4. Construction Worker (**Service sales.**)
5. Engineer (Structural design, integrity **consultant/service** provider.)
6. Bus Driver (**Service Sale** of bus operation and transportation.)
7. Cook (**Service Sale** of food preparation.)
8. Waitress (**Service provider**) *These even get a commission!
9. Mechanic (**Service Sale** of repairing items.)
10. Accountant (**Service Sale** of bookkeeping and financial advice.)
11. Teacher (**Service Sale** of education.)
12. Computer Programmer (**Service Sale** of computer knowledge.)
13. Janitor (**Service Sale** of cleaning.)
14. Lab Technician (**Service Sale** of science.)
15. Architect (**Service Sale** of planning & building.)
16. Electrician (**Service Sale** of wiring & electricity.)
17. Politician (**Service Sale** of Leadership.)
18. Gemologist (**Service Sale** of precious stones and jewelry.)
19. Pilot (**Service Sale** of operating an aircraft.)
20. Security Guard (**Service Sale** of protection.)
21. Policeman (**Service Sale** Protection, serving the public trust, protecting the innocent.)
22. Dealer at a Casino (**Service Sale** of aiding in gambling entertainment.)
23. Flight Attendant (**Service Sale** of monitor, waitress/waiter, emergency consultant.)
24. Priest (**Service Sale** of bible knowledge, God, history and morals.)
25. Soldier (**Service Sale** of protection through the art of making war.)
26. Lock Smith (**Service Sale** of the knowledge of locks.)
27. Tow Truck Operator (**Service Sale** of moving vehicles.)
28. Exotic Dancer **Service Sale** of sexual fantasy.)
29. Librarian (**Service Sale** of locating reference materials.)
30. Social Worker (**Service Sale** of community assistance.)
31. Private Investigator (**Service Sale** of uncovering facts.)
32. Plumber (**Service Sale** of plumbing knowledge.)
33. Alarm System Monitor (**Service Sale** of protection.)
34. Telephone Operator (**Service Sale** of assisting with telecommunications.)
35. Inspector (**Service Sale** of observing whether or not products meet requirements.)

36. Truck Driver (**Service Sale** of truck operation.)
37. Hotel Manager (**Service Sale** of accommodations and management.)
38. Fork Lift Operator (**Service Sale** of fork lift operation.)
39. Insurance Underwriter (**Service Sale** of insurance payment.)
40. Carpet Installer (**Service Sale** of carpet installation.)
41. Scientist (**Service Sale** of scientific investigation.)
42. Consultant (**Service Sale** of knowledge in a particular area or field.)
43. Comedian (**Service Sale** of entertainment through jest.)
44. Demolition Expert (**Service Sale** of the knowledge of explosives.)
45. Welder (**Service Sale** of the knowledge of welding.)
46. Waste Disposal Worker (**Service Sale** of refuse removal.)
47. Parking Lot Attendant (**Service Sale** of temporary vehicle storage.)
48. Taxi Cab Driver (**Service Sale** of transportation.)
49. Elevator Repairman (**Service Sale** of knowledge of elevator mechanics.)
50. Corporate Executive (**Service Sale** of managing & organizing others.)

As you can see, practically every vocation is sales related. A lot of people tend to forget that selling a service is every bit as challenging as selling a tangible product. Perhaps even more so, because the potential customer will never actually see, touch, taste, hear, feel or smell the product. Basically, everybody is selling something. The better you are at producing volume sales in your field, the greater your financial reward for such labor.

From this illustration, it is easy to understand why education is so important. The various careers usually have a precedent for their value. Thus it is easy to observe the difference between the financially wealthy and the financially strapped. By increasing your sales abilities, you increase your probability for success in the world. Some might argue that they're not in sales, nor are they dependent upon them, but these have been blinded by the ultimate sale. They have been "sold" on the idea of their independence from sales. Now that's irony!

Let's examine why sales and salespeople are so important to our western society. A woman named Shirley claims to be an internal clerk at a large corporation. She claims that she cannot see why she ought to respect and admire the salespeople in her aircraft corporation. She claims that her position has nothing to do with sales, and therefore she has no concern for the outcome of their sales presentations.

She was recently laid-off and is bitter about the loss of her job. She is looking for work, but has turned down every job opportunity in sales that has been offered to her. She claims that she has applied for thousands of jobs and attended literally hundreds of interviews, but that these companies always choose someone else. She refuses to learn anything about sales because she does not consider sales a prestigious or glamorous field. She considers the knowledge of sales a waste of her time.

Let's trace how Shirley was directly influenced by sales, why she lost her job, and how her lack of sales knowledge is ultimately robbing her of the future she wishes for. Perhaps Shirley should consider this illustration.

You see, Shirley lost her job, which she claimed was not related in any way to sales, because her corporation's sales volumes dropped after the September eleventh terrorist attacks in the US. When the sales force could not generate enough revenues to compensate for the staffing payroll requirements and still be profitable, the company was left with only one alternative: downsizing. This is why Shirley was laid-off. Perhaps there was nothing Shirley could have done to change this, but by acknowledging the importance of sales in relation to her position, she may have been able to anticipate the need for downsizing long before she actually lost her job. It is critical for all employees in a company to realize that no one is above the job-loss threshold when the "bottom line" rears its ugly head. For this very reason, companies around the world have undertaken the "Total Quality Management" initiative. By improving products and working environment, and encouraging strategic and creative thinking, even the lowest level laborer can do his part to aid the sales teams.

What does this mean? By doing a better job for your employer, you can directly assert an amount of pressure toward keeping sales momentums moving forward. You may think that the little bit of pressure or force that you exert does little, and under this school of thought this is true, but consider the pyramids in Egypt. They were not constructed by one person alone, but by teamwork. You as an individual will probably not shape the entire company, but your efforts, acting in unison with many others, can move mountains!

"When spider webs unite, they can tie up a lion" (u.a.).

Think of your company as a large, steel cable. The cable supports the company's prosperity. If the cable snaps, inevitably lay-offs, downsizing, company closure or bankruptcy will be the result. When you look closely at the profile of a cable segment you will see that it is made up of a multitude of smaller cables. These consist of a multitude of even smaller wires. By themselves, these wires could not possibly manage to support anything of real weight. Considering that the hopes and dreams of every employee rest on the company's success, the burden is great. Yet when the strength of these individuals is combined, the company has no trouble moving forward.

The caution to be monitored is complacency. When one individual becomes complacent, their effect on the integrity of the company is not all that great. However, if management style or environment is somehow fueling these feelings in employees, than the integrity of the cable is at risk.

Steel Cable Diagram

How did Shirley ultimately rob herself of the future she sought? By never learning anything about sales, she failed to learn even how to sell herself. It is for this reason that when creating her resume and attending her interviews, Shirley was at best ill-prepared. Sales training can benefit everyone. Of course it is of immense concern to all those in the field, but no less important to anyone seeking to tip the scales of life in his favor. For those who wish a greater sense of liberation from the affects of our sales-ruled environment, an education in sales is absolutely necessary. Sales skills will most certainly be required for any attempt to rise above such a global environment because sales skills are employed by all of us every day. The degree to which we are successful at using them is the degree to which we are able to motivate others to assist us in any initiative.

The Science of Selling for Everyday Life

The important thing in selling for everyday life is to stop telling and start selling. Frequently, when people are told to do things, they often rebel. Yet, whenever they are sold on the idea, they willingly participate in an initiative. Want to be a better manager, mother, or teacher? Start selling instead of telling, and the people you lead will do the tasks you assign with smiles and admiration. Have you ever explained something to someone and become frustrated because they didn't seem to understand you, and then later someone else explains the exact same thing to the person and they not only understand the reasoning, but also seem to admire the person who taught them. This is because they were sold, not told!

Think about when you were in school. Do you remember certain teachers better than others? Weren't these the ones who had the greatest impact on your life? These teachers sold their curriculums. A teacher with good selling skills can make even the most boring material interesting and fun. Tests will indicate an above average comprehension of any material that has been sold, rather than told.

Can you think of some sales you'd like to be successful with? How about selling your children on the reasons they should not take drugs, or why manners are important. It seems many of the people I meet today could use a boost in their self-esteem. This is accomplished through the act of selling yourself, showing an image of value and self-worth. Perhaps you have a cause you like to support. Sell your colleagues on raising money for charities. Teach your friends how to use sales skills to generate increased revenues. Sell your spouse on the reasons he or she ought to quit smoking. Sell yourself on the reasons for healthy dieting and exercise. Sell a friend on the negative effects of a gambling addiction. Sell your neighbors on organizing a neighborhood watch. Sell your community on slowing down in school zones. Sell your family on recycling, and less energy consumption. Sell our children good values. Sell, Sell, Sell!

Where does it end? That is the beauty of sales skills. They are effective in almost every interaction of humanity. Sell people on feeding the impoverished. Sell the public on housing the homeless. Sell the public on protecting endangered species of animals.

Consider even the government. The electoral process is the biggest popularity contest on the planet. The person best able to sell themselves to the public is declared the victor. A key point: the product you're selling doesn't have to be perfect. There are as many poor-quality products in this world, if not more, than there are high-quality products. The art of selling is the art of making whatever position or product you are supporting appear as if it is the best one.

World leaders, actresses and actors, talk show hosts, executives, teachers, managers, and mothers are all involved in the sales process every day. We can either participate by chance, or by choice, but either way we are all involved. How many sales this very day have you been involved in? Were you the customer or the salesperson?

When we begin to see the world as the largest trading playground in the universe, we can see that every event must be considered the object of a sale.

ABCDEFGHIJKL

Increased Sales through Education

Greeting Potential Customers.
Developing their desire.
Building Value.
Providing valuable information.
Satisfying their needs and Smiling.
Overcoming objections without pressure or aggressive behaviors.

Chapter 15

The Greatest Marketing Support Campaign of All Time

- **CEO**—Chief Executive Officer
- **Marketing Support**—An individual or team of individuals whose job it is to motivate, teach, and care for the needs of the sales force.

A very long time ago, a kind and generous CEO named Joel ran the most powerful company in the world, and he realized the need for marketing support. In chapter one, selling is the transference of one's thoughts and feelings to another. Yet I would say it's even simpler than that, because sometimes we have to sell ourselves an idea. We talk through a problem or challenge and sell ourselves the solution we think is best.

Joel believed that the secret to the ultimate success was in helping others succeed.

Not long after he had begun building his company, Joel consulted with his President, who agreed that helping others succeed was, indeed, the secret to success. Around this time, one of their corporate executives, Luc, became narcissistic and decided to quit and open up a company which would compete in the same marketplace. He even managed to convince several of their executives to join him. Despite this obvious political distraction, Joel and his company President forged ahead with the growth of the company. Together they began to train their sales force. It was very small in the beginning, consisting only of a husband and wife team. They worked hard but, sadly, were seduced by the competition who promised better working conditions. It wasn't long before they begged for their old jobs back, but Joel the CEO refused to allow them to return. Joel and his company President continued to build their sales team, and several times Luc came along and enticed them to join his company instead.

In time a new sales force began to develop, but many of the people that the kind and generous CEO and President had trained in the art of selling defected and joined the competition.

Luc was a greedy man whose selfishness often robbed his employees of a decent life outside work. Many of his employees quit working for him when they finally saw what a liar he was. Luc often promised raises and better working conditions, but he never delivered. He also told lies to his employees to discredit Joel and often made slanderous remarks about him to the press. Luc consistently told anyone who would listen that Joel's company's working conditions were no better than his own, and that his safety measures were too strict. At Luc's company, there were no safety protocols at all, and his workers could work whatever hours they pleased. There were investigations into Luc's company, of course, which showed that many of his employees had been severely hurt and even killed on the job, but Luc had his corporate staff bury these reports.

Despite the unfair and hurtful practices of their competitors, Joel and the company President perservered. Their sales force finally began to grow through network marketing and direct sales. Joel and his President eventually saw that it was difficult to teach such a growing sales force since the two of them could not be everywhere at the same time. Joel was, after all, a hands-on type of leader, but was always extremely busy. They needed more help.

Joel asked his best salesman to begin the task of producing marketing support materials for the sales staff and promoted him to Vice President of the company. Joel gave the new VP a list of the company's ten core values and explained that these were the most important things for his staff to adhere to in order to enjoy the greatest level of success. The VP understood Joel's wishes and was very proud and honored to have received this opportunity and to have had the privilege of talking directly with the CEO.

The Vice-President promptly called a meeting in the company auditorium, where all the employees had been asked to meet. He was so excited that he wanted to share his inspiration with them directly. But when he opened the door to the auditorium, the VP saw that the sales staff had been drinking and throwing a party at the company's expense. The VP became very frustrated, and nearly gave up completely on the sales staff. He thought that they did not deserve to have such a kind and generous CEO.

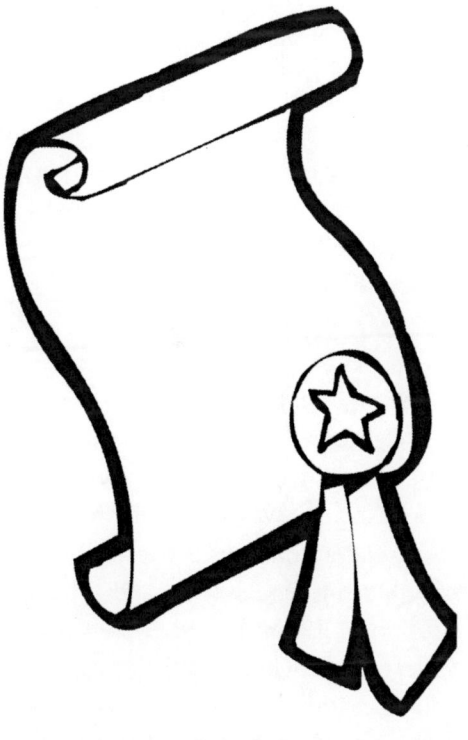

Soon after, the CEO asked his newly appointed VP how things were going, and the VP had to admit that he had lost the list of the ten core values. The CEO was patient with the VP, however, and kindly gave him another copy. The VP was so impressed by the undeserved kindness of Joel the CEO that he vowed to be loyal to the company forever.

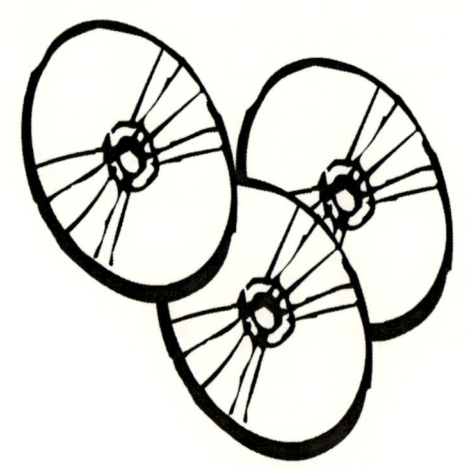

The VP eventually realized that he was a natural leader. He performed many motivational seminars for the sales force, and he produced six inspiring CDs during his forty-year career, which were later commissioned as the first part of a much larger collection. To this day, many of the company's employees revere his name and make mention of his helpful techniques. Eventually, though, all good things must end, and it was time for the VP to retire. To succeed him, he selected an apprenticing salesman named Hosh, who had demonstrated excellence in the field and who was willing to take up the worthy cause of teaching and helping others. Hosh only made one motivational CD during his time, but he filled it with all that he had learned and told how inspired he was by Joel, the kind CEO, whom he believed was the best mentor anyone could ever have.

Life at the company progressed and it was quite some time until the next great salesman would be revealed. His name was Sam, and he began learning with the salespeople as early as age three. Sam came from a family of eight, including his parents. He had three brothers and two sisters, and he is said to have worked long hours, sometimes even sleeping at the company. He was always the first to open the doors of the company in the morning and always the last to leave at night.

During his 22 years with the company, Sam produced two Marketing Support CDs and also helped to complete a further CD created by the two salespeople who would eventually take over for him. Their names were Nathan and Gad and after completing their first CD with Sam's help, they went on to create two more which continued to praise the verity and value of the company's ten core values.

After a while, Jerry came on board. He worked with the Marketing Support department for some forty years. He became known as a researcher and a historian, as well as a leader in the Marketing Support department. Jerry produced four audio CDs that were accepted by the CEO and the President. His courage and endurance were matched only by his love for his people. Jerry became discouraged several times in his career, though, and required the CEO's assurance, but even in the face of adversity, he did not forsake calling on Joel for help. Jerry had several friends who were also great salesmen in their own right, and they helped Jerry stay focused.

The CEO and the President were committed to the Marketing Support system they had dreamt about years earlier. They knew that this pioneering work had to be completed for the safety and security of all the workers.

The next to work in the Marketing Support department was a guy everyone called "EZ" for short. He was a scholar, an expert copyist, and law teacher. "EZ" had a real zeal for teaching and training the sales force. "EZ" was also credited for having organized the previous audio CDs produced by the Marketing Support department. He saw the demand and need for these materials and began making copies.

"EZ" had political connections which allowed him to expand his research and produce high quality work. As a result, many sales people have benefited from his work, even to this day.

The next salesperson to come along was a former Governor. He only produced one audio CD to aid in the teaching of the sales force, but on it he talked a great deal about the warm qualities of the CEO. He was a salesman, who displayed courage, decisiveness, integrity, and loyalty to the company. The Marketing Support audio CD series now consisted of seventeen audio CDs, which were used to teach every new employee at the company. These were all in harmony with the CEO's original ten core values.

The entire company viewed the Marketing Support audio CD series as a complete success. However, Joel the CEO and the company President weren't satisfied yet. They both wanted to see the series continued in the same manner it had in the past. They knew the marketplace would be even more competitive in the future, and the need for these CDs would be even greater.

Believe it or not, the pioneer of the Marketing Support department (now retired) produced the next CD in the Marketing Support series. This was his sixth and final audio CD.

The next CD in the series was mostly motivational music by an outstanding salesman named David. When the audio series was completed, it consisted of sixty-six audio CDs, participated in by some twenty-nine different motivators, lecturers, and sales teachers. David's sales skills were mentioned some one thousand one hundred and thirty-eight times in all. Something tells me that he was really, really good! Only two other great salesmen were mentioned more times in the training series.

David's life was very interesting. He had worked as a livestock farmer, a musician, a poet, a soldier, a statesman, and a political leader, before joining the Marketing Support cause. He, too, believed in the CEO's vision for the future. David came from a family of twelve, including his parents. He had seven brothers and two sisters. He grew up in the birthplace of the company President. David was even credited for having saved the company from a hostile take-over, initiated by an executive giant in the employ of the competition. David served as VP of the company for seven and a half years, and even successfully moved the company headquarters when the CEO requested it.

David's son, Sol, took over where his father left off. Sol had three brothers, but Joel was never as impressed with them as he was with Sol. At one point, the CEO wanted to reward Sol for his efforts and he offered him wealth, fame, and success. Sol turned down all of these, and simply requested the wisdom of all the sales knowledge the CEO could grant him. He reasoned that with this knowledge, he could easily attain wealth, fame, and success.

The CEO was so impressed with Sol's request that he not only taught him all the wisdom of selling that was ever known, but even went on and granted him great wealth, fame, and success. To this day, Sol is talked about as being one of the wisest of the sales gurus to have ever lived. Sol aided in the expansion of the company and built many new company buildings. He also initiated exports of the company's products and Marketing Support materials through a fleet of ships, and the money poured in. Stock values soared during Sol's involvement, but he was very humble and always gave the credit to the CEO.

Sol was an amazing student of Joel's and was thought by many to be a genius. He was the VP of the company for some forty years, but eventually, in Sol's old age, the competition was able to sway him away from the company by exploiting the virtues of many of its female employees. Sol became quite the stud in his later days. He got involved in relationship entanglements which probably accounted for his seven hundred marriages and three hundred affairs.

Of course the kind and generous CEO would never have approved of such poor moral conduct and that is why Sol was eventually fired. The good news is that Sol produced two audio CDs in the Marketing Support effort early on in his career while he was still prospering with the company.

This remarkable chain went on for many many years and many generations and over the next four hundred and forty years the company continued to grow, and vast numbers of CDs were added to the marketing support series, all completed by very celebrated sales gurus throughout the existence of the company.

The next person to be elected VP was named Dan. Dan had a real ability to clearly see and interpret the CEO's visions for the future, and he wrote them all down. At one time in his career, he was thrown to the lawyers in a legal battle that ultimately led to criminal charges. However, the court ruled that Dan was to be exonerated when Joel dispatched his expert legal staff to Dan's aid. Dan's motivational seminars were slightly complex and confusing because he used a lot of illustrations, many of which the employees had some difficulty interpreting. This did not stop him from being inspired by the company's core values, however.

After Dan, there were twelve exceptional salespeople to produce a CD in the ever-growing Marketing Support series. One of these was involved in a terrible boating accident in which he was thought to have died, but was later miraculously saved. Coincidentally, he joined Greenpeace and was an avid Save the Whales activist. Before his accident, however, he did manage to finish an audio CD first.

All of these people put so much of their lives into this company, and during their time, they each created audio CDs which they hoped (and they succeeded!) would inspire others in the company's sales force.

These CDs were absolutely fabulous! Many company employees would listen to them over and over again. By practicing the teachings within the marketing support series, millions of people's lives were changed for the better and they were all so grateful to Joel, the kind and generous CEO, and his company President. There were now thirty-nine CDs in the marketing support series, and it had become so popular that people outside of the company began buying the series and teaching it to their children.

In time, however, the CEO saw that the company's employee morale was very low and he wasted no time in dispatching the one person he could trust to help set things right again. He turned to his son, Jeho, who was the company President at that time. Jeho had been so involved in the corporate day-to-day operations, however, that he could not remember what it was like to be a salesperson for the company. So he asked his father to allow him to take a very low position in the company. So he started out at the bottom rung of the company among his fellow employees and he did not reemerge as a sales guru until he was about thirty years old. Jeho was only involved in the Marketing Support work for some three and a half years, but he was able to make a powerful statement. He was regarded as possessing even more wisdom and genius than Sol.

While he did not produce any Marketing CDs, he did do a lot of public speaking. Jeho was an amazing person who was credited for saving many lives. In his spare time, he devoted himself to helping the sick and feeding the hungry all around the world. He was an amazing salesman and an even better motivational speaker. Jeho spoke so eloquently that it was almost impossible to get front row seats at one of his seminars. Amazingly, he performed at no charge to the public. He really transcended the boundaries between the employees and the general public.

He eventually hand-picked twelve people with little or no sales experience and demonstrated how the science of selling and Marketing Support could empower people.

Their names were Simon, Andy, Philip, Matt, Tom, Jim, Pete, John, James, Thad, another Simon, and another who was later convicted of corporate espionage. Two of these were Jeho's cousins, and not very well educated. Four of them worked for a seafood restaurant, and one was a member of the IRS. James and John, it seems, were very ambitious and quarreled about who would obtain the better title at the corporate office in the future. Peter, James, and John were the closest to the President. They seemed to be enchanted by all the sales knowledge that he possessed, and they were very eager to learn.

One of the twelve, namely Tom, was said to be very skeptical of the President's marketing strategies, but President Jeho took Tom by the hand, and helped him when his faith in the brave leader's sales validity was in question. Jeho became known for his amazing teaching abilities, and many simply called him professor, or teacher.

Jeho became so popular that the competitive companies attempted to entrap him in political entanglements. The headhunting CEO of their largest competitor even sought to entice the young motivator to come work for his company, but the young motivator was loyal to his father and the traditions he had grown up with and benefitted from.

Other so-called motivational speakers became very anxious and jealous when their own revenues began to slump, and they felt they had lost their grip on the people. Greed and jealousy can cause people to do things they might not otherwise do, and one of Jeho's closest assistants and apprentices, perhaps in league with the headhunting CEO, betrayed him, which led ultimately to Jeho's assassination. His assistant was convicted of espionage and conspiracy to commit murder.

Most would witness the public assassination and murder of President Jeho as a major setback and a possible reason to shut down the company, but what actually happened was quite the opposite. Fueled by the inspiration of their President, now martyr and coach, the faithful students of Jeho opened the best marketing school in the world. They began teaching (tuition free) everything they had learned to others. They honored their teacher by opening up schools across the country. These schools have continued to grow to this day.

In all, twenty-seven more CDs were produced and President Jeho became known throughout the world as a great leader and political influence, both while he was alive and after his death. The marketing support materials he and the company pioneered have surpassed any in history.

> According to the 1988 edition of Guinness Book of World Records, an estimated 2,500,000,000 copies were printed between 1815 and 1975. No other material in history has come close to such circulation figures. You can purchase a copy of the original marketing support training materials in more than 1800 different languages today. [i]

It is accessible to 98% of the population of our planet. Want to hear some of the reviews? "The New Encyclopedia Britannica calls the training material 'probably the most influential in human history'" (*The New Encyclopedia Britannica*, 1987, Vol. 2, p. 194). The 19th century German poet Heinrich Heine confessed speaking of the training material, "I owe my enlightenment quite simply to the reading of a book" (Goldman, 1948, p. 219). During the same century, antislavery activist William H. Seward proclaimed, "The whole hope of human progress is suspended on the ever-growing influence [of the training materials]" (Seward, as cited by Haley, 1965).

Abraham Lincoln, the 16th President of the United States of America, called the training collection "the best gift God has ever given to man" (Lincoln as cited by Haley, 1965).

"The existence of [this] book for the people is the greatest benefit which the human race has ever experienced" (Kant as cited by Haley, 1965).

"It is not without great personal sacrifice that these training materials have survived," said William Tyndale, a 16th century Englishman who was educated at Oxford University and became a respected instructor at Cambridge University.[ii] Tyndale was the person chiefly responsible for producing the English translation of the training materials and competitive companies were no less aggressive in his time. He was forced to live as a fugitive for many years just so you could have the opportunity to read these fabulous training materials.[iii]

Millions of people around the world agree there is little doubt; if you can apply the training materials in your life, you will experience a rare success granted to humanity. Part of what makes the marketing support training materials so amazing is that some forty-plus individuals in all had a hand in their production, and the ten core values, later expanded, carry a beautiful theme throughout. Politicians, farmers, fishermen, civil servants, priests, at least one general, and a physician were all involved. Believe it or not, it was produced over a period of 1,600 years.

The Marketing Support Series began over 3000 years ago and it has not stopped gaining momentum or support to this day. The CEO, Joel, and his President, Jeho, are alive in the minds of millions around the world. President Jeho, later referred to as *teacher*, was being questioned one day by one of his students about the marketing support materials.

"What is this training series to be called, teacher?"

"The Bible, Peter, and haven't I repeatedly asked you to call me Jesus?"

In this illustration, it was necessary to make some modifications to maintain the story line. Moses was the first participant in the writing of the Bible mentioned in the story. The ten core values are commonly known as the Ten Commandments (Exodus 19:1-25; 20:1-21; 24:12-18; 31:18) and Moses was the first participant in the writing of the Bible mentioned in the story. Other writers included Joshua; Sam was short for Samuel; Jerry was Jeremiah; "EZ" was used for Ezra.

David, preventing a "hostile takeover," slew a giant Philistine soldier named Goliath with a slingshot (1 Samuel 17:1-54). Sol, short for Wise King Solomon; did however, really have seven hundred wives and three hundred concubines.

Daniel was thrown to the lions, not the lawyers, but some might argue that this roughly amounts to the same thing. God saved him by sealing the mouths of the hungry lions, not by commissioning his expert legal team (Daniel 6:1-28).

Jonah is the writer of the Bible who was in a boating accident (Book of Jonah). He was commissioned to warn the Ninevites of God's anger, but took a ride on a ship bound for Tarshish instead. A tremendous storm rose up and the mariners feared a shipwreck. They singled out Jonah as the cause, and he told them to cast him overboard because he too believed the storm was his fault. The mariners, though reluctant, threw him overboard and the storm promptly abated.

While Jonah was in the water, it is believed that he was swallowed by a large fish. Some suggest a whale. He was later vomited out onto dry land, unharmed. He did not join Greenpeace and protest whaling, although he might have, had there been such a movement at the time.

President Jeho was substituted for the lengthier Jehoshua and is the person you may commonly refer to as Jesus. Regarding Jehoshua as a name, the 1997 book *Oxford Dictionary of the Bible* by W.R.F. Browning says:

> A common personal name for Jewish males in the centuries BCE; it is the Latin form of the Greek translation of the Hebrew Joshua or Jehoshua, and means 'He whose salvation is Yahweh." [Jehovah]

Jesus's life is a truly remarkable story and can be read about in most of the later twenty-seven books of the Bible also called the Christian Greek Scriptures or the New Testament. The 66 audio CDs were actually books of the bible. Joel, the kind and generous CEO of the company was representing the only true sovereign ruler of the world, Jehovah God, sometimes referred to as Yahweh. The competitive Executive/CEO (Luc, short for Lucifer) who tempted Jesus was none other than Satan, the devil (Luke 4:2-13).

Tom was used short for Thomas sometimes now referred to as "doubting Thomas" because he refused to believe that Jesus had returned from the dead. He was so skeptical of these supernatural events that he requested he be permitted to touch the wounds he had witnessed previously inflicted on Jesus (John: 20:24-29).

The student of Jesus who was said to be convicted of corporate espionage was the disciple who betrayed Jesus, Judas Iscariot (Mat. 26:45-49).

This illustration shows how powerful our beliefs, visions, and dreams really are. Who would have known that one initiative to help mankind would have such a profound and lasting effect? Perhaps your sales knowledge, desire to lead others, and your vision for the future, can help others in such a magnificent and loving way.

I wish you all the success that this world has to offer. I hope that this book will truly benefit you with your goals for the future, and encourage you to practice the guidelines illustrated in the greatest marketing support achievement ever written: the Holy Bible. It is certain when you have succeeded in following the admonishments therein, you will have a great reward, both in heaven and on earth.

"May the love and favor of our grand creator shine upon you, and all your hopes and dreams be accomplished, Amen."

The End

---

[i] *The Bible: God's word, or man's?* 1989, p.7
[ii] International Bible Students Association, 1989, *The Bible—God's Word or Man's?* p.9.
[iii] Taken from Way of Life Literature's Fundamental Baptist Information Service, 2001.

Chapter Overview

Chapter 1: Decide to Dream Again

- Making the commitment to the sales profession is a conscious decision.
- Book goals.
- Learn from the success and failures of others before you invest.
- Setting goals.
- Being prepared.
- Salespeople are not born; they're trained.
- Knowledge is life's greatest currency.
- Believe in what you do.
- Education in salesmanship can begin from childhood.
- Mastering the science of selling can impact your whole life.
- Keep the good and throw out the bad (previous sales experience).

Chapter 2: The Sales Savior's Six Secrets for Being the Best Salesperson

- Defining the Sales Savior's Six Secrets for Being the Best Salesperson.
- Getting and procreating leads.
- Reaching your target market.
- Quantity yes; but quality first (leads).
- Contacting leads.
- Set-up rates understood, calculated and tracked.
- Smiling while on the phone.
- Appointments understood.
- Hold-up rates understood, calculated and tracked.
- The PWEC principle.
- Presentations & Sales.
- Defining the sale.
- Net/Gross percentages understood, calculated and tracked.
- Why sales are lost.
- Why closing percentages spike and level.

Chapter 3: The Lost Art Scrolls

- The 'Ten Coincidental Personality Dispositions'.
- Using the "your own style" approach to selling.
- Tracking your objections.
- The recipe for the ultimate sales personality.

Chapter 4: Hexagonal Leadership Qualities

- ✧ The recipe for the ultimate leader.
- ✧ Passion; motivation; courage; faith; optimism; inspiration and perseverance.
- ✧ Searching for the man that opened the door.
- ✧ The golden frog

Chapter 5: The Need-Greed Factor

- ✧ Identifying your product in the need or greed category.
- ✧ Defining our needs.
- ✧ Diagnosing customer needs.
- ✧ Selling the intangibles; emotions, services, health.
- ✧ Creating desire.
- ✧ Want to buy a toothbrush?

Chapter 6: Salespeople are Full of BS

- ✧ The BS Protocol.
- ✧ Dissecting the professional sales presentation for the BS protocol.
- ✧ Customers need a reason to buy.
- ✧ Being above average.
- ✧ Understanding the importance of syntax

Chapter 7: Little Details; Big Difference

- ✧ Understanding and exercising control.
- ✧ Using commitment questions to pre-close.
- ✧ Overcoming challenges during the presentation.
- ✧ Understanding the psychology of sales scripting.
- ✧ Consistency and momentum, powerful allies.
- ✧ Changing perspective from made sales to lost sales for improving.
- ✧ Rhythm and tonality a subtle difference.
- ✧ Breaking the ice and asking for leads.
- ✧ Contacting the warm market.
- ✧ Premium gift incentives a must.
- ✧ Word whiskers a bad habit.

Chapter 8: Great Salespeople Build Value

- ✧ Defining value.
- ✧ How to build value.
- ✧ BBD's.
- ✧ Price reduction vs. value building.
- ✧ A visual representation of building value (thermometer).
- ✧ Sincere and insincere objections (knowing the difference).

Chapter 9: Enthusiasm and Salesmanship are Greatness

- ✧ How do you spell enthusiastic (acronym).
- ✧ Keeping the pace (tracking and predicting sales).
- ✧ The affect of the net/gross sales percentage on sales representatives.

Chapter 10: Asking for the Order and Closing the Sale

- Waiting for customers to make the first move (a long wait).
- The two basic questions so you can draw first blood.
- The choice close.
- Assuming the sale and the yes, yes method.
- The "if & would" technique.
- Third party closing.

Chapter 11: Overcoming Objections

- Why people object to a purchase.
- The 7-up approach to closing and answering objections.
- Diversionary reasoning (the power to persuade).
- The 50¢ pay cut close (we can't afford it).
- The mortgage Close (we can't afford it).
- The reduction to the ridiculous close (it costs too much).
- The prescription close (we need to think about it).
- The switching close (we need to think about it).
- The kid and scooter close (we never buy on the spur of the moment).
- The live forever close (I'm too old to buy anything).
- The honeymoon close (husband doesn't support wife in purchase).
- The puppy dog close (customer is on the fence).
- If and would close (the every occasion close).
- Critical and strategic thinking.
- The greatest salesman that ever lived.
- Tailoring closing techniques to suit your business.
- Asking for the order again.

Chapter 12: Recruiting In-Home, Casual Recruiting, and Ad Hiring

- Expansion; a natural progression.
- Duplicatability.
- People; the most valuable possessions.
- Think before you leap into Distributorship.
- Defining the customer at the Distributorship levels.
- Up-line behavior consistent with logic and growth?
- The psychology for sabotage.
- Upward mobility.
- Recruiting as a lead source.
- Contacting potential recruits.
- Utilizing ad hiring (a dissection).
- Having the lead program first.
- Energy transfer when speaking to groups.
- Training apprentice sales representatives.

Chapter 13: STD's-Attrition Doesn't Lie

- Defining sales transmitted diseases.
- Bad deals never seem good syndrome (BDNSG).
- Talented dealers rot @ home syndrome (TDRH).
- The healing power of a positive mental attitude (PMA).
- Up-line distributors never work the trenches syndrome (UD-NWT).
- I hate the phone and the phone hates me syndrome (IHP & PHM).
- Protective negative influence (PNI).
- Protective up-line distributors pretend longer (PUDPL).
- Rookies brag too soon (RBTS).
- I prejudge everyone (IPE).
- Back in the saddle syndrome (BITS).
- Narcissistic behavioral disposition (NBD).
- Complacent dysfunctional masking syndrome (CDMS).
- Comparison & expectation disappointment.
- False support & overconfidence Disease.

Chapter 14: Everyone's A Salesperson

- Sales encompass every human interaction.
- All company resources revolve around the sale, not in spite of them.
- The science of selling for every day life.
- Marketing support the key to company growth.

Chapter 15: The Greatest Marketing Support Campaign of All Time

- A kind and generous CEO opens a company.
- A competitor corrupts the first salespeople.
- The kind and generous CEO appoints a President.
- The greatest marketing support campaign of all time is initiated.
- The kind CEO produces the company's ten core values.
- A President with a temper (the ten core values are lost).
- A compact disc (CD) collection begins as the marketing support department's first tool.
- The CD collection grows despite adversity.
- David defeats a corporate giant.
- A wise President reigns.
- The Presidential scandal that motivated the CEO to appoint a new President.
- Corporate lawyers are hungry for Dan's blood.
- An author of the ever growing CD collection joins Green Peace.
- The greatest salesman in the world becomes President.
- President Jeho initiates a motivational speaking campaign and becomes involved in enormous charity efforts.
- President Jeho resists tempting offers by the competition.
- The company grows beyond predictions.
- 12 amazing managers become President Jeho's inner circle.

- ✧ A President betrayed and assassinated.
- ✧ The 12 Managers vow to carry on marketing support campaign and CD collection.
- ✧ The marketing support materials survive repeated attacks.
- ✧ 44 CD's produced over 3000 years comprise the final works.
- ✧ People all over the world base their lives on the marketing support CD's.
- ✧ The true story revealed.

References

Armstrong, N. (1969). Nasa: Apollo 11 lunar surface journals. Retrieved December 12, 2007 from http://history.nasa.gov/alsj/a11/a11.step.html

Arnold, S. (n.d.). Quote. Retrieved June 14, 2007 from http://thinkexist.com/quotes/stanley_arnold/

Bacon, F. (n.d.). Quote. Retrieved June 12, 2007 from http://www.googlesyndicatedsearch.com/u/IlWesleyan?q=%93For+knowledge%2C+too%2C+is+itself+a+power%94+&sa=Search

Balzac, H. (n.d.). Quote. Retrieved June 12, 2007 from http://quotationsbook.com/quote/22455/

Balzac, H. (n.d.). Quote. Retrieved June 13, 2007 from http://www.brainyquote.com/quotes/authors/h/honore_de_balzac.html

Barrie, J.M. (n.d.). Quote. Retrieved June 13, 2007 from http://www.worldofquotes.com/topic/Beauty

Barrymore, D. (n.d.). Quote. Retrieved June 14, 2007 from http://thinkexist.com/quotation/i_pray_to_be_like_the_ocean-with_soft_currents/203713.html

Bertrand, R. (1917). Mysticism and logic and other essays. London : G. Allen & Unwin.

Bonaparte, N. (n.d.). Quote. Retrieved June 18, 2007 from http://www.quotationspage.com/quote/2191.html

Bovee, C. (n.d.). Quote. Retrieved June 14, 2007 from http://www.brainyquote.com/search_results.html?domains=www.brainyquote.com&q=The+small+courtesies+sweeten+life%3B+the+greater+ennoble+it&sa=Search&sitesearch=www.brainyquote.com&client=pub-9038795104372754&forid=1&channel=6423399426&ie=ISO-8859-1&oe=ISO-8859-1&safe=active&cof=GALT%3A%23008000%3BGL%3A1%3BDIV%3A%23F0C808%3BVLC%3A663399%3BAH%3Acenter%3BBGC%3AFFFFFF%3BLBGC%3A0000FF %3B A L C %3A0000FF%3BLC%3A0000FF%3BT%3A000000%3BGFNT%3A0000FF%3BGIMP%3A0000FF%3BLH%3A50%3BLW%3A760%3BL%3Ahttp%3A%2F%2Fwww.brainyquote.com%2Fimages%2Fbrainy_logo_search.jpg%3BS%3Ahttp%3A%2F%2Fwww.brainyquote.com%2F%3BFORID%3A11&hl=en

Brown, L. (n.d.). Quote. Retrieved June 14, 2007 from http://www.quotegarden.com/yearbook.html

Browning, W.R.F. (1996). Oxford dictionary of the bible. Oxford University Press, USA.

Bryan, W.J. (n.d.). Quote. Retrieved June 14, 2007 from http://www.quoteworld.org/quotes/2011

Camus, A. (n.d.). Quote. Retrieved June 13, 2007 from http://www.quotationspage.com/quote/24906.html

Carlyle, T. (n.d.). Quote. Retrieved June 13, 2007 from http://quotationsbook.com/search/quotes/?term=the+man+who+cannot+laugh+is+not+fit+for+treason

Chesterfield, P. (n.d.). Quote. Retrieved June 13, 2007 from http://www.quotelady.com/subjects/present.html

Cicero, M.T. (n.d.). Quote. Retrieved June 11, 2007 from http://thinkexist.com/quotation/i_am_not_ashamed_to_confess_i_am_ignorant_of_what/156257.html

Confucius. (n.d.). Quote. Retrieved June 11, 2007 from http://www.quoteworld.org/quotes/3109

Confucius. (n.d.). Quote. Retrieved June 11, 2007 from http://www.quoteworld.org/quotes/3124

Coolidge, C. (n.d.) Quote. Retrieved June 15, 2007 from
http://www.quotedb.com/quotes/3162

Cunningham, D., Rexair Inc. (1991). Selling yourself. Troy, MI: Infonet Video Series.

Curtis, D. (n.d.). Quote. Retrieved June 10, 2007 from
http://thinkexist.com/quotes/Donald_curtis/

De Puisieux, M.M. (n.d.). Quote. Retrieved June 11, 2007 from http://www.giga-usa.com/quotes/authors/marie_madeliene_puisieux_a001.htm

Devos, R.M. (n.d.). Quote. Retrieved June 11, 2007 from
http://quotes.zaadz.com/Richard_M_Devos

Dictionary.com. Definitions. Retrieved June 13, 2007 from
http://dictionary.reference.com

Dodd, B., Rexair Inc. (1991). Being the total person. Troy, MI: Infonet Video Series.

Emerson, R.W. (n.d.). Quote. Retrieved June 11, 2007 from http://www.quotationspage.com/quote/29687.html

Emerson, R.W. (n.d.). Quote. Retrieved June 14, 2007 from http://www.wisdomquotes.com/cat_life.html

Emerson, R.W. (n.d.) Quote. Retrieved June 16, 2007 from http://www.whatquote.com/quotes/Ralph-Waldo-Emerson/822-The-Only-way-to-have.htm

Emerson, R.W. (n.d.) Quote. Retrieved June 16, 2007 from http://thinkexist.com/quotes/with/keyword/employment/

Eves, F. (2007). Quote. Retrieved June 9, 2007 from
http://liveyourbestdreams.com/

Farlex. (1988-2005). Quote. Retrieved June 10, 2007 from http://acronyms.thefreedictionary.com/Prior+Planning+Prevents+Poor+Performance

Ford, H. (1947). Quote. Retrieved June 11, 2007 from http://www.brainyquote.com/quotes/authors/h/henry_ford.html

Givens, C.J. (n.d.). Quote. Retrieved June 14, 2007 from http://www.motivational-inspirational-corner.com/getquote.html?categoryid=124

Goethe, J.W. (n.d.). Quote. Retrieved June 14, 2007 from http://www.worldofquotes.com/topic/will/index.html

Goldman, S. (1948). The book of books: An introduction. New York, NY: Harper & Brothers.

Haley, H. (1965). Quote. Retrieved June 16, 2007 from http://www.bible-history.com/quotes/henry_h_haley_1.html

Hill, N. (n.d.) Quote. Retrieved June 10, 2007 from http://www.quotationsbook.com/search/quotes/?term=Nature+wraps+up+in+the+impulse+of+strong+desire

Hill, N. (n.d.) Quote. Retrieved June 15, 2007 from http://thinkexist.com/quotation/it_is_literally_that_you_can_succeed_best/256330.html

Hill, N., Stone, W. & Mandino, O. (1960). Success through a positive mental attitude. New York, NY: Pocket Books.

Hunt, L. (n.d.). Quote. Retrieved June 15, 2007 from http://www.geocities.com/wisdomforthesoul/categories/courage.html

Iacocca, L. (n.d.). Quote. Retrieved June 14, 2007 from http://www.quotationspage.com/quote/38461.html

Iacocca, L. (n.d.). Quote. Retrieved June 15, 2007 from http://www.brainyquote.com/quotes/authors/l/lee_iacocca.html

International Bible Students Association. (1989). The Bible—God's Word or Man's? Brooklyn, NY: International Bible Students Association.

Juvenal. (n.d.). Quote. Retrieved June 12, 2007 from http://www.quoteworld.org/categories/hope/1/?sort=quote

Keller, H. (n.d.). Quote. Retrieved June 17, 2007 from http://www.quotationspage.com/quote/30190.html

Kuypers, J. (2002). What's important now. Burlington, ON: Present Living and Learning Inc.

Lafayette, M. (n.d.). Quote. Retrieved June 15, 2007 from http://www.quoteland.com/search.asp

Lamb, T., Rexair Inc. (1991). How do you spell enthusiastic? Troy, MI: Infonet Video Series.

Lamb, T., Rexair Inc. (1992). Dream. Troy, MI: Recorded Sales Conference.

Landers, A. (n.d.). Quote. Retrieved June 14, 2007 from http://www.quoteworld.org/quotes/8010

Lincoln, A. (n.d.). Quote. Retrieved June 13, 2007 from http://quotationsbook.com/search/quotes/?term=Let+us+have+faith+that+right+makes+might%2C+and+in+that

Lippmann, W. (n.d.). Quote. Retrieved June 14, 2007 from http://www.worldofquotes.com/topic/Leadership/1/index.html

Longfellow, H.W. (n.d.). Quote. Retrieved June 12, 2007 from http://oldpoetry.com/opoem/show/4413-Henry-Wadsworth-Longfellow-A-Psalm-of-Life

Lovelace, R. (n.d.) Quote. Retrieved June 10, 2007 from http://thinkexist.com/quotation/stone-walls-do-not-a-prison-make-nor-iron-bars-a/532194.html

Lytton, B. (n.d.). Quote. Retrieved June 11, 2007 from http://www.giga-usa.com/quotes/authors/edward_george_lytton_a001.htm

Machiavelli, N. (n.d.). Quote. Retrieved June 14, 2007 from http://www.quotegarden.com/appearance.html

Mandino, O. (1968). The greatest salesman in the world. Hollywood, FL: Frederick Fell Inc.

McKain, R.J., (n.d.). Quote. Retrieved June 14, 2007 from http://www.motivational-inspirational-corner.com/getquote.html?categoryid=124

McTiernan, J. (1990). The hunt for red october. Hollywood, CA: Paramount Home Entertainment.

Meyers, B., Rexair Inc. (1991). Overcoming objections. Troy, MI: Infonet Video Series.

Michaels, L. & Thompson, B., (Segal, P.). (1995). Tommy boy. New York, NY: Broadway Video Inc.

Miller, A. (1948). Death of a salesman. New York, NY: Viking Penguin.

Nietzsche, F. (n.d.). Quote. Retrieved June 10, 2007 from http://brainyquote.com/quotes/authors/f/friedrich_nietzsche.html

Peterik, J. & Sullivan, F., (1982). Survivor. Westchester, NY: Atlantic Records.

Plato. (n.d.). Quote. Retrieved June 12, 2007 from http://en.proverbia.net/citasautor.asp?autor=15744

Reeve, C. (n.d.). Quote. Retrieved June 22, 2007 from http://www.quotationspage.com/quote/34109.html

Robbins, A. & McClendon, J. (1997). Unlimted power: A black choice. New York, NY: Fireside.

Robbins, A. (1991). Awaken the giant within: How to take immediate control of your mental, emotional, physical and financial destiny! New York, NY: Free Press.

Roosevelt, F.D. (n.d.). Quote. Retrieved June 10, 2007 from http://www.whitehouse.gov/history/presidents/fr32.html

Roosevelt, T. (1899). Speech before the Hamilton Club. Chicago, IL. Retrieved June 21, 2007 from http://www.quoteland.com/search.asp

Sanders, J.V., Rexair Inc. (1991). Being above average. Troy, MI: Infonet Video Series.

Schwartz, R. (n.d.). Quote. Retrieved June 10, 2007 from http://thinkexist.com/quotes/robert_l._schwartz/

Shakespeare, W. & Hattaway, M., (1993). King henry vi part iii. New York, NY: Press Syndicate of the University of Cambridge.

Shakespeare, W. (n.d.). Quote. Retrieved June 18, 2007 from http://www.enotes.com/shakespeare-quotes/question

Shakespeare, W. (n.d.). Quote. Retrieved June 19, 2007 from http://quotes.zaadz.com/41479/sir_i_am_a_true_laborer_i_ea/by_william_shakespeare?printable=1

Syrus, P. (n.d.). Quote. Retrieved June 15, 2007 from http://quotationsbook.com/quote/1317/

Trollope, A. (n.d.). Quote. Retrieved June 14, 2007 from http://www.getmotivation.com/favorites3.htm

Vidovich, P., Rexair Inc. (1991). The vacuum comparison. Troy, MI: Infonet Video Series.

Wilson, C., Rexair Inc. (1991). The harmonica airflow demo. Troy, MI: Infonet Video Series.

Wright, L. (n.d.). Quote. Retrieved June 14, 2007 from http://www.quotationspage.com/quote/1959.html

Young, O.D. (n.d.). Quote. Retrieved June 14, 2007 from http://www.brainyquote.com/quotes/quotes/o/owendyoun189976.html